THE FORMULA FOR LUCK

FOREWORD BY **SALIM ISMAIL**

of OpenExO, Singularity University, and XPrize;
bestselling author of *Exponential Organizations*

THE FORMULA FOR LUCK

LEAVE NOTHING TO CHANCE

TEN POWERFUL PRINCIPLES FOR BUILDING A LUCK MINDSET

STUART LACEY

Published by Advantage, Charleston, South Carolina.
Member of Advantage Media Group.

ADVANTAGE is a registered trademark, and the Advantage colophon is a trademark of Advantage Media Group, Inc.

Printed in the United States of America.

10 9 8 7 6 5 4 3 2 1

ISBN: 978-1-642251-33-3
LCCN: 2020925663

Cover design by David Taylor.
Layout design by Megan Elger.

This publication is designed to provide accurate and authoritative information in regard to the subject matter covered. It is sold with the understanding that the publisher is not engaged in rendering legal, accounting, or other professional services. If legal advice or other expert assistance is required, the services of a competent professional person should be sought.

Advantage Media Group is proud to be a part of the Tree Neutral® program. Tree Neutral offsets the number of trees consumed in the production and printing of this book by taking proactive steps such as planting trees in direct proportion to the number of trees used to print books. To learn more about Tree Neutral, please visit **www.treeneutral.com**.

Advantage Media Group is a publisher of business, self-improvement, and professional development books and online learning. We help entrepreneurs, business leaders, and professionals share their Stories, Passion, and Knowledge to help others Learn & Grow. Do you have a manuscript or book idea that you would like us to consider for publishing? Please visit **advantagefamily.com** or call **1.866.775.1696**.

The mountains we climb are those only of our mind

and our path upward made possible only by the Tribe we chose to accompany us.

Our packs filled by their kindness,

our footsteps made sure by their support,

our energy replenished by their encouragement, and

our path made clear by their guidance.

Progress reveals that our mountains are not what at first they seemed to be.

It was not about the summit, nor the climb—

it was always about the Tribe.

CONTENTS

FOREWORD ix

INTRODUCTION 1
Why Me?

CHAPTER 1 11
Are You Lucky?

CHAPTER 2 35
Thoughts and Actions

CHAPTER 3 43
Your Own Worst Enemy

CHAPTER 4 53
How to Use the Next Ten Chapters

CHAPTER 5 61
The First Principle: Curiosity

CHAPTER 6 79
The Second Principle: Passion

CHAPTER 7 97
The Third Principle: Connectivity

CHAPTER 8 123
The Fourth Principle: Positivity

CHAPTER 9 141
The Fifth Principle: Empathy

CHAPTER 10 .161
The Sixth Principle: Adaptability

CHAPTER 11. 181
The Seventh Principle: Situational Awareness

CHAPTER 12 199
The Eighth Principle: Serendipity

CHAPTER 13 221
The Ninth Principle: Choice

CHAPTER 14 243
The Tenth Principle: Fail Forward

CHAPTER 15 263
The Formula for Luck

CHAPTER 16 291
The Luck Mindset

CONCLUSION 305

EPILOGUE .311
The Future of Luck

ACKNOWLEDGMENTS 331

FOREWORD

For two thousand years, we've subscribed to the familiar formula attributed to the Roman philosopher Seneca: "Luck is what happens when preparation meets opportunity." But, as Stuart Lacey details for us here, it is so much more than that. Or rather, there's a heck of a lot that demands explanation in that otherwise straightforward and simple-sounding phrase!

My path and Stuart's crossed for the first time in 2013 at Singularity University. We struck up a conversation about the links between his vision for the company he founded called Trunomi and my observations about a Massive Transformational Purpose, a common trait among companies that achieve ten times the output compared to their traditional counterparts and a topic on which I was writing my book *Exponential Organizations*. Initially, we bonded over our interest in big-impact processes and ideas, and since then we have shared stages as keynote speakers and collaborated on large-scale impact projects through which we built mutual admiration for our shared values and passions. This collaboration has continued into the domain of luck, which it turns out has been a topic of deep interest to both of us for many years.

My own quest has been more of a metaphysical one. Along with a colleague, John Hagel, I have been examining the foundational basis for luck as a general concept applicable to people, institutions, organizations, and even countries and cities. We believe luck can be both defined and measured.

As it applies to you or me, many examinations and explorations of luck are a litany of anecdotal stories and new age positive thinking. While aspirational, previous literature has been sadly lacking in any prescriptive methodology. In this long-overdue work, Stuart fabulously ties together his experiences, decades of wide-ranging topical research, and the stories and insights of great leaders and minds—all to create a tightly argued case for personal luck being, as he puts it, more "up to us" than we are traditionally inclined to recognize.

This is an insightful and cutting edge work that closes the book for good on the notion that luck strikes as a result of forces beyond our control. Stuart convinces us that luck is—more than anything else—a mindset, and as a mindset, it is capable of being generated and multiplied by clearly articulable habits and actions.

Not only does Stuart offer us an innovative and detailed approach to becoming lucky and a formula by which we can begin to track and assess our personal progress, he also covers strategies for bringing luck into our business practices and shares tips, tricks, and other tactics for boosting the ability to invite luck into our larger communities on a regular basis.

Stuart's great feat is to have drilled into what actually constitutes *preparation* and *opportunity* and to have translated those complex components into ten simple, easy-to-practice principles. *The Formula for Luck* harnesses the power of real-life case studies—stories from today's "luckiest" leaders and entrepreneurs—to create the compelling case that luck can be learned. Not since Stephen Covey wrote *The 7 Habits of Highly Effective People* has another author so powerfully simplified and codified an easy-to-learn operating system that empowers anyone to dramatically increase the quality and quantity of their outcomes—in this case, to live a lucky life that leaves almost nothing to chance.

Whether you're a corporate executive, company manager, or anyone who has ever felt unlucky, *The Formula for Luck* will teach you new skills. The structure, content, and approach are so compelling that Stuart has already developed a curriculum for sharing and deepening its insights for executives and senior managers, and for their teams.

In a sense, it is both a relief and a challenge to discover that we can train ourselves to be luckier. Thankfully, Stuart has anticipated the challenge by producing an easy-to-understand, simple-to-use, and inspiring book that offers hope to anyone who has ever imagined that circumstances were out of their control and gives them the chance to change their lives and all those around them for the better.

Salim Ismail
Cofounder and Chairman, OpenExO and Exo Works
Founding Executive Director, Singularity University
Board of Directors member, XPRIZE
Bestselling author, *Exponential Organizations* and *Exponential Transformation*

$f(x) = \ell^{-x} + 1\,\varepsilon$

$a = b$

$cx\vartheta + x_7$

$y = \sqrt[2]{3+1}$

$H_2\ SO_6$

$y^3 + Z^2 + xyz = 2$

$\left(\dfrac{2}{5} \times 2x\right)$

a^2

$x^2 + y^3 + Z^2 + xyz = 2$

$\sqrt[6]{3+1}$

b^2

$f(x) = 2^{-3} + 1\,\varepsilon = 0.00$

$c.005$

$\dfrac{b}{\text{9ind}} = \dfrac{c}{\sin}$

a^2

H^3

$\dfrac{a}{\text{iv}}$

$= 2^{-1}$

$H_2\ SO_4$

$2^2 + 1\,\varepsilon = 0.005$

$C1$

SO_4

$6^2 + C^2 = 26\,C$

$cx\vartheta + x_7$

$xyz = 2$

$y = c^2$

$y = \sqrt[2]{3+1}$

$\left(\dfrac{2}{3} \times 2x\right)$

$\dfrac{c}{\text{9h}}\ f(dx) = 26 + C^2$

$Z^2 + x^2$

$y = \sqrt[2]{3+1}$

WHY ME?

As adults, many of us ask *why me* from time to time, especially when things go badly or result from circumstances beyond our control. Why has the universe, or fate, chosen to pick on *me*? Why has it singled me out ... for failure or for an unwelcome challenge or to teach a costly lesson at the worst possible moment?

As adults, we can usually step back from asking *why me* and look at the logical progression of cause and effect. We often come to see that our problems are not caused by some supernatural force but by real circumstances, some of which may have been beyond our control, others of which may have been the result of actions we took or didn't take.

For children, however, for whom so much is often beyond their control, the question *why me* might occur with greater frequency.

That was most definitely my experience in childhood.

Imagine moving from surroundings you are only beginning to explore and understand to a whole new place that's not across town or even across the country but across an ocean, a third of the way around the world. At age seven, that's exactly what happened to me. My parents migrated from South Africa to Canada.

Not long afterward, I discovered how mean children could be.

As a January baby who had also skipped a grade when in South Africa, I was the youngest in my new classroom. I was also the smallest boy in my class, with a foreign accent to boot. My well-intentioned parents tried to assure me that my transition to a new school would go smoothly, but the steps they took had the opposite effect. They urged me to be a model student, and so I raised my hand for everything, not realizing how much more of a target that made me. And at a time when everybody was wearing jeans and T-shirts to school, they dressed me in corduroys and collared shirts.

But even if I'd been the class clown or dressed like everyone else, there'd have been no getting past my foreign accent. In the eyes of my peers, I "talked funny." I was the classic "other" that psychologists talk about, and that made it easy for my peers to marginalize and bully me.

On many afternoons, I had to walk home through a community park. Going around the park was not really an option, but even if it were, my bullies would have followed. I received the same beating each day at three thirty in Lawson Park.

Why me?

I didn't understand why my luck had turned out as it had, but I really wanted to make sense of my experience. My gift was intellect, and I was paying the same price "nerds" have paid for generations. I would never be in with the in crowd, and so I focused instead on developing a strong mind.

I became a strategic thinker at an age when most kids don't have to do so. To sharpen my mind in high school, I joined the debate team and the drama club. I didn't get any girls and was still harassed mercilessly right through secondary school. I was certainly no direct threat to anyone, but I had let myself become an easy target and had done nothing to change my situation.

Why me gradually transformed into *This is me,* along with a quiet determination to apply my intellect to understanding human nature in general—and specifically to consistently beating odds that seemed stacked against me. I now look back on that experience as my very first attempt to "create" my own luck.

From that time forward, I essentially became my own guinea pig and worked on learning, iterating, and refining my own behaviors and thoughts. I created my own laboratory for life, and the habits I subsequently developed have since led me to be able to live a life beyond my wildest dreams. This book is the product of that research and experience. I learned to be lucky, and I'm happy now to share the products of my experience and my research with you.

· · ·

My research into my own seemingly "bad" luck convinced me that the age-old quote attributed to the Roman philosopher Seneca— "Luck is what happens when preparation meets opportunity"—was not the whole story. There was something else that contributed to manifesting good fortune. Sure, solid preparation (like training to run a marathon) is a clear improvement over a lack thereof, and yes, opportunity (like entering or qualifying to run in a race) is the most obvious contributing factor. But somewhere between those two, I believed, was yet another element—or perhaps another kind of preparation. Certainly, there were also a million different things that could interfere to derail the "preparation + opportunity" scenario. I was convinced that a significant amount of luck relied on one's mindset toward, and flexibility in relation to, all those elements that remain outside our direct control. So, I looked for that "something else" and, piece by piece, put it together. As I assembled its constituent parts into a formula, I became certain that applying that formula—in our personal lives, in the business world, wherever— nearly *guaranteed* success.

> I was convinced that a significant amount of luck relied on one's mindset toward, and flexibility in relation to, all those elements that remain outside our direct control.

Of course, I didn't just think this through. I set out to prove it so.

I had learned some things from my formative experiences. Seven years of Olympic sailing campaigns culminating in 1988 taught me the ten-thousand-hours rule: try at something long enough, and you can succeed. But finishing fourth in the Olympic trials was also a lesson: ten thousand hours alone is insufficient.

Racing on the McGill University alpine skiing team taught me that genetics were to be respected: my five-foot-eight frame and 145 pounds made me competitive in slalom, but I simply was not big enough to compete in the high-speed thrill event I loved most: the giant slalom. Ten thousand hours of practice got me a long way, but not to the ultimate inner satisfaction of proving that I could accomplish anything I wanted.

After college, I joined my first company in Toronto, Canada. My inspirational CEO, Michael, and lifelong friend and mentor, Neil, were instrumental in challenging me and giving me all the rope

I desired. Rather than hanging myself with it, I pulled myself up and, with their support, earned an incredible opportunity to build a new venture in balmy Southern Florida. That venture was supremely successful, and I had that first sweet taste of success that I had craved since being the kid who was bullied every day on his way home from school. My venture was a success, and I was cash rich.

I lived on a beach road and learned to surf. I had the adoration of beautiful women and drove a gorgeous convertible. I felt like I was living my dream.

Then, in skiing terms—I got out over my tips.

We sold the company, and I was arrogant enough then to think that I could go it alone. The result: I overextended myself and completely squandered the proceeds. Less than one year later, at age twenty-five, I had almost zero financial net worth.

For a year I bounced along, trying to find direction. I was consumed with figuring out what had worked and what hadn't. I reflected on all the times in my life when I was at my best and looked at them alongside those when I was at my worst. What emerged was a clear set of attitudes and behaviors that I had practiced when at my best and had neglected—even worse, quite consciously ignored—when at my worst.

Reflecting on my own successes and failures, I generated a set of principles that I wrote out by hand. That list became a sort of hypothesis upon which the next twenty years of my life, and ultimately this book, would be built. Starting that year and then every January thereafter (on my birthday), I would review the year that had just passed and then write a plan for the year ahead, the baseline and compass for which were these very principles.

My first accounting of my life against these principles was in 1998. I was inspired by the resulting vision as much as by the deep sense of humility they engendered, so I made a decision that—much as it might have looked otherwise to others—made total sense to me.

I wanted a fresh start for my new life. I loved the beach, hated paying taxes, but wanted to be close enough to fly only a few hours to see my family. So I sold my last asset—my TV—and purchased a one-way plane ticket to Bermuda.

· · ·

They say that when you are at the bottom, everywhere else is up. I had decided that the best thing for me was to start over. On some level, I sensed that doing so would force me to focus and to think outside the box.

As opportunities crossed my path, I would make a concerted effort to pursue those which most invited me to live according to my new principles. Each of those opportunities eventually unlocked yet another, and a better life emerged with each transition. I saw these opportunities as solutions, and my principles as the components of a formula leading to them.

While practicing using my new principles, I first worked for others who could help me develop new skills and networks. Whenever I bumped into a wall, or a business partner I could not convincingly see a future with, I either pushed through or moved on. It took a total of five years, but by 2003 my life again had changed momentously. The woman of my dreams agreed to marry me. I was building the first company that I would own 100 percent and operate with a vision that I controlled.

By December 2009, a series of mergers and acquisitions resulted in my business becoming part of a larger conglomerate—seven group-owned companies working in twenty-three different markets.

My wife, Lisa, and I had a four-year-old son, Ethan, and a six-month-old baby, Max, and were living in a home less than one hundred feet from the pink-sand beach on Grape Bay in Bermuda. I'd gained the respect of my peers and community to the point that I'd been invited to join the prestigious Young Presidents' Organization (YPO). By this time in my life, I was regularly applying seven or eight of my still-growing list of principles on a daily basis.

And then, something amazing happened.

Thanks to an open and curious mind, extensive reading, and the network I had built of inspirational and well-connected people, I was struck one May evening in 2012 by a realization: the largest asset class in the world is our personal data. This produced in me the deep, profound conviction that the world's largest companies (think Facebook, Apple, Amazon, Google) should not break trust with us by building empires off of our personal data without our knowledge or permission. Rather we should control its use and benefit from its value. Later on, this concept would become known globally as the self-sovereignty of data.

Taking the advice of Salim Ismail (which he wrote about so eloquently in his book *Exponential Organizations*), I decided to define and pursue a clear purpose—what Salim calls a *Massive Transformational Purpose*. I believed I'd had an idea big enough, brave enough, and important enough that it might just change the lives of a billion people. I would return the rights, ownership, privacy, identity, and ultimately the value of personal data to individuals.

So, in 2013, after a year of "stealth mode" research, I once again, and to the surprise of many, *sold everything I had* (this time it was a hell of a lot more than a TV) and pursued my plan for global impact. I founded a high-tech start-up called Trunomi to build the world's first platform to solve for the self-sovereignty of personal data. Two years later I delivered a groundbreaking TEDx Talk, "The Future of Your Personal Data," that explored both the risks and the potential benefits technology holds for actually securing—and profiting from—our digital footprints instead of helplessly relinquishing control of them. If you'd like to get to know me a bit better or if you love TED Talks, I invite you to take a break one evening this week and spend seventeen minutes with me learning something fascinating about "The Future of Your Personal Data."[1]

Born in Bermuda, nurtured in Silicon Valley, and then matured in London, Trunomi, at this writing, is four rounds of venture capital into its existence, has been recognized with forty-one major global awards, has been issued six patents (and has nine pending), and, in 2018, led me to be named by Barclays as its FinTech (financial technology) Entrepreneur of the Year and by *CV Magazine* as the Most Influential FinTech CEO of the Year. Trunomi is now a true force for good and its technologies are able to deliver incredible value to large corporations and their customers on a global scale.

It all happened for one reason: I put together and worked on developing my capacity to live by what had now become ten simple yet powerful principles that I'd turned into a personal operating system to generate high-performance outcomes. Anything—I mean that quite literally—had become possible.

Even now there are days that I walk down the beach with my family, past smiling tourists who have paid thousands to visit Bermuda for only a few days, and we pinch ourselves and are equally overcome with gratitude. I remind our two boys how it is not by chance or "mere" good luck that we live in this beautiful place and

---

1   Stuart Lacey, "The Future of Your Personal Data - Privacy vs Monetization," December 20, 2015, TEDxBermuda, 17:51, https://www.youtube.com/watch?v=Jlo-V0beaBw.

that we must all be mindful, respectful, and appreciative of how profoundly important the principles that I had lived by, which have now become the Formula for Luck, were to that success.

My two boys' futures lie in their hands, just as your own future lies in yours.

. . .

In this book, I offer you the Formula for Luck as the means of unlocking your potential for success. The experiences, interviews, and research collected in this book will show you that the ten principles are accessible to everyone, just waiting for us to apply them.

I was able to pick myself up, create not one but a series of successes, and with each new success have an impact even more profound than the one prior. The thing is, that's not my story alone; it's quite the same for many of the world's most successful people. The difference is that many of them, like many of the rest of us, tend to think of that story as one that was not up to them in crucial ways and at the most important moments. In other words, many of them tell a story of their dependence on influences well outside their control. How frequently do you hear or read successful people saying, "I can't believe how lucky I was!" even when they've worked hard toward making their goals and wishes manifest?

When I began researching luck, I was stunned by how little we've learned about it across fifty centuries of recorded history. We still think of it as attached to supernatural forces, the luck that's supposedly "caught" by the horseshoe hanging above the doorway—tips up, of course, lest all that good fortune come tumbling out.

I want to change that way of thinking for good. It's my plan to do so in this book, by showing you that there are skills we can develop—sometimes quite basic habits of thinking and acting—that are absolutely essential to success and to increasing exponentially our capacity for entertaining greater and greater amounts of luck. Think of it like this: if you know to get off the golf course when you hear thunder, you're already practicing a version of the sort of thing I'm talking about.

> There are skills we can develop—sometimes quite basic habits of thinking and acting—that are absolutely essential to success and to increasing exponentially our capacity for entertaining greater and greater amounts of luck.

The formula that I've developed will guide you through ten different components that, when practiced individually or altogether, will produce measurable results, making noticeable and positive differences in your daily life.

If you believe luck is mystical and inexplicable, like the vast majority of people do, then brace yourself. You're about to know more about luck—and how to create it—than most people.

CHAPTER 1

ARE YOU LUCKY?

Does the idea of a *formula* for luck seem like an impossibility verging on the ridiculous? Are you wondering how anyone could subject to analysis something as unpredictable and mysterious as Lady Luck's grace and all the benefits it brings? I hope the introduction to this book has already encouraged your curiosity about how it is not only possible to let go of some long-standing cultural superstitions about what luck is and how it works but also to approach luck systematically in a way guaranteed to produce results.

Over the course of five thousand years of recorded history (and before, if the records passed to us on cave walls are any indication), we humans have favored incantations, awe, and superstition in our efforts to attain luck. We've long believed luck is enigmatic—bestowed at random upon some and denied, just as scattershot, to others—and decided that it must therefore be beyond analysis.

In fact, it is anything but.

I devised the Formula for Luck by taking a logical approach to understanding what luck is and how we manifest it in our lives. In doing so, I've pored over the studies and insights of both historical and contemporary thinkers, theorists, and business leaders who've attempted similar analyses of how humans can attain the highest levels of success. I've also discovered some elements missing from all those accounts, elements that I believe expand on the knowledge of others in ways that have yet to be codified and put into practice.

We've long believed luck is enigmatic—bestowed at random upon some and denied, just as scattershot, to others—and decided that it must therefore be beyond analysis.

In other words, I've done all the research for you and, in so doing, have landed on an approach to luck that I think significantly improves upon all those others.

Let's begin with what most other theorists believe luck *isn't*.

Luck is not random. It isn't unpredictable or mysterious. It is also not a lady. Or found in a four-leaf clover. You can't produce it by blowing on dice or finding a penny and picking it up. If you don the same jersey you wore to your favorite team's last win, it'll have precisely the same external influence on the outcome of today's match as when you wore it last: zero.

You know what else? "Bad luck" is not a thing. Break all the mirrors you like. Walk under a ladder with a black cat under each arm on Friday the 13th (or Tuesday the 13th in Spain, Portugal, and Greece).

The beliefs we humans have propagated, cultivated, and (often fiercely) held on to relative to luck are ubiquitous and seemingly inescapable. Need proof? Just a moment ago, as I composed the last paragraph, I started an internet search by typing, *things that cause bad …*

Care to guess what the autofill function brought up? Which word completes the *most popular search* beginning with that phrase? That's right! And *luck* was followed by *breath, gas mileage, credit, karma, dreams, gas,* and *vision.* We're actually more interested in *avoiding bad luck*—which, it bears repeating, *is not a thing*—than we are in oral hygiene, our fuel budget, or our credit score.

Our curiosity about luck only makes more surprising how little we care to learn about it. Down through history, we humans have been content to think there is good and bad luck and view ourselves as having either more of the first or of the second.

HOW LUCKY ARE YOU?

When it comes down to it, our beliefs about luck are more nuanced than the simple measures "good" and "bad" would suggest. We tend to believe there are degrees of luck—a continuum ranging from "not lucky" to "heck yeah" lucky. We also tend to believe that wherever we are along this luck continuum, we're stuck there, and there's very little we can actively do to improve our fortunes.

In fact, there are *ten* things: the *Ten Principles of Luck.*

You'll find them in the middle of this book, between my arguments in favor of trying them out and additional research showing you ways to go even further than the Ten Principles toward enhancing your luck. Most of this book, in other words, is filled with practical insights and things you can begin doing right now that *will increase* your luck—in some cases exponentially. You can start with any one of the Principles and combine them in any way you wish depending on your needs.

To help you prepare for those ten chapters, I want to introduce you to a concept that I call the Luck Ladder.

Always Lucky

Usually Lucky

Often Lucky

Sometimes Lucky

Occasionally Lucky

Blue-Moon Lucky

Never Lucky

Think of the Luck Ladder as a way of visualizing progress along that continuum we mentioned earlier. There are seven steps on the Luck Ladder:

1. Never Lucky: I never win anything, so why bother even trying?

2. Blue-Moon Lucky: I won a TV once in a raffle. Oh yeah, and the Pinewood Derby back in Cub Scouts.

3. Occasionally Lucky: There's no rhyme or reason to any of it, so I just let life happen naturally.

4. Sometimes Lucky: It's an elusive concept, but it's real.

5. Often Lucky: I know luck when I see it, and I grab by the horns the opportunities it offers.

6. Usually Lucky: I am a veritable "bag of luck."

7. Always Lucky: Luck is a huge element in my strategy for living my best life!

Do you already have a sense of which one best describes you?

I've devised a simple self-assessment tool to help you determine your current position on the ladder and to help you to track your progress over time. The tool—the Luck Assessment—is a Q and A that takes only a minute to complete. It will give you an indicative score and some structure for thinking about how to approach the rest of this book. So turn the page and let's get started on the assessment.

THE LUCK ASSESSMENT

1= totally disagree   10=totally agree

1	*I am more motivated by any reward and recognition I might receive than I am by any impact I can make.* 1 2 3 4 5 6 7 8 9 10
2	*I ask myself why as often as I ask myself why not, as I am interested in seeing things from different perspectives.* 1 2 3 4 5 6 7 8 9 10
3	*At times I am affected by my negative thoughts, and it's not always easy to check them or overcome them.* 1 2 3 4 5 6 7 8 9 10
4	*I often prefer to go with the flow and just trust my gut and instincts that it will all work out.* 1 2 3 4 5 6 7 8 9 10
5	*I sometimes find myself saying words like* It's not fair, Why did that happen to me? *or* Why am I being punished? 1 2 3 4 5 6 7 8 9 10
6	*I describe myself as disciplined, and I am able to commit to regular investments in exercise and healthy eating.* 1 2 3 4 5 6 7 8 9 10
7	*I can easily judge who a person is based on what they say or how they appear/act in public.* 1 2 3 4 5 6 7 8 9 10
8	*If something does not work out the way I wanted it to, I can easily move on and put my mind to something else.* 1 2 3 4 5 6 7 8 9 10
9	*I generally look to tried and proven methods to solve issues that arise. If they don't work, it's unlikely anything else will.* 1 2 3 4 5 6 7 8 9 10
10	*I know the four main types of workplace violence and how best to identify, minimize, and, if needed, manage them.* 1 2 3 4 5 6 7 8 9 10

11	I find it hard to ask for help and usually trust only myself to get through whatever is facing me.
	1 2 3 4 5 6 7 8 9 10

12	I am often described by others as passionate, high energy, authentic, driven, motivating, and/or engaged.
	1 2 3 4 5 6 7 8 9 10

13	When coincidences occur, I pay little attention to them and tend to quickly move on to more meaningful things.
	1 2 3 4 5 6 7 8 9 10

14	When things don't go my way, I try to accept and make the best of it rather than push even harder to get my way.
	1 2 3 4 5 6 7 8 9 10

15	I sometimes procrastinate and am fine with not attempting something if the effort or risk involved is too great.
	1 2 3 4 5 6 7 8 9 10

16	I actively engineer new opportunities to meet new people in new places rather than stick with what is known and easy.
	1 2 3 4 5 6 7 8 9 10

17	I am uncomfortable with threats, large risks, or adversity, and I don't like the added pressure of having to react swiftly.
	1 2 3 4 5 6 7 8 9 10

18	When considering options and alternatives, I regularly put myself in others' shoes to gain perspective.
	1 2 3 4 5 6 7 8 9 10

19	When I develop a new relationship (personal or work), I focus first on what I can get or how I can benefit.
	1 2 3 4 5 6 7 8 9 10

20	I approach all challenges and obstacles with a positive, can-do, and optimistic attitude.
	1 2 3 4 5 6 7 8 9 10

NOW CALCULATE YOUR SCORE AS FOLLOWS:

PRINCIPLE   **SCORE**

$$\textbf{Curiosity} \quad = \frac{}{2} + \left(10 - \frac{}{9}\right) = \boxed{}$$
Question #

$$\textbf{Passion} \quad = \frac{}{12} + \left(10 - \frac{}{1}\right) = \boxed{}$$
Question #

$$\textbf{Connectivity} \quad = \frac{}{16} + \left(10 - \frac{}{19}\right) = \boxed{}$$
Question #

$$\textbf{Positivity} \quad = \frac{}{20} + \left(10 - \frac{}{3}\right) = \boxed{}$$
Question #

$$\textbf{Empathy} \quad = \frac{}{18} + \left(10 - \frac{}{7}\right) = \boxed{}$$
Question #

$$\textbf{Adaptability} \quad = \frac{}{14} + \left(10 - \frac{}{5}\right) = \boxed{}$$
Question #

$$\textbf{Situational Awareness} \quad = \frac{}{10} + \left(10 - \frac{}{17}\right) = \boxed{}$$
Question #

$$\textbf{Serendipity} \quad = \frac{}{4} + \left(10 - \frac{}{13}\right) = \boxed{}$$
Question #

$$\textbf{Choice} \quad = \frac{}{6} + \left(10 - \frac{}{11}\right) = \boxed{}$$
Question #

$$\textbf{Fail Forward} \quad = \frac{}{8} + \left(10 - \frac{}{15}\right) = \boxed{}$$
Question #

Total Score $= \boxed{}$

                                                            SUM

Be sure to record your score here so that you can reference it later on as you begin to apply the Principles. Now take that score, divide it by two, and place a mark on the corresponding Luck Ladder diagram below.

THE LUCK LADDER

91 + Points ⟶ **Always Lucky**

76-90 Points ⟶ **Usually Lucky**

61-75 Points ⟶ **Often Lucky**

46-60 Points ⟶ **Sometimes Lucky**

31-45 Points ⟶ **Occasionally Lucky**

16-30 Points ⟶ **Blue-Moon Lucky**

0-15 Points ⟶ **Never Lucky**

Here's what I've noticed so far from those who have communicated with me after bringing one or more of the Principles into their regular practice:

1. People who practice *two* of my Ten Principles advance at least one level on the Luck Ladder.

2. People who practice as many as *five* Principles advance two levels or more.

3. People who regularly practice all Ten Principles are *guaranteed* to reach one of the top two rungs on the ladder.

I'm very serious about gaining the fullest possible understanding of luck and how it works and about converting that knowledge into clear processes for increasing luck—processes that any of us can apply and benefit from.

That is why, throughout this book, I'll share all my research and conclusions about luck. Specifically, there will be a full-chapter deep dive on each of the Ten Principles in chapters 5–14. I have structured each of those chapters to make them easy to navigate, impactful, and highly relevant to you, the reader. In each chapter you will find stories from my personal experience, an exploration of others' views on the topic, and guest-star interviews with very successful people—many of them well-known to you and some amazing people you have never met—about how they cultivate luck in their own lives. You'll see how each Principle might apply to your personal and professional experiences, and you'll find exercises encouraging you to work through at least one application of each Principle while reading the chapter, along with links to where additional exercises can be found. Finally, in each of those ten chapters, you'll find a brief chapter summary as well as some takeaway recommendations (I call them *Stuart's Secrets*) for you to put to use immediately as you strengthen your everyday capacity for luck. Then chapter 15 wraps it all together into the Formula for Luck and provides clear use cases and examples of the formula in action.

That said, I encourage you to not skip ahead to those Ten Principles just yet! The few chapters that precede them are intended to set the stage, challenge some of your preconceptions, and put in place some building blocks that help make sure you will get the most out of what those ten chapters offer when you get to them.

While we are setting our intention here, I wish to reinforce one key tenet before you proceed. It is one thing to enjoy reading this book, and I have made every effort to share stories and takeaways and weave it all together so that it is a joy to read and easy to re-reference. However, what matters most is that you *take action by applying the Principles as part of your everyday practice.*

Let's talk a little more about why that's so important.

LUCK VERSUS CHANCE

Many of us see our personal growth and success as a fifty-fifty proposition, split between two primary factors, as this chart illustrates:

PERCEIVED PERSONAL GROWTH
AND SUCCESS INFLUENCES 1

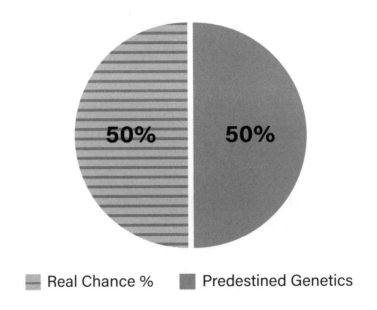

In other words, some people believe that how far they get in life is completely—and pretty much equally—dependent on chance and genetics. If that seems simplistic or small minded, think of that place where every mind *is* still small: the school playground! Nobody there has developed any real skill yet, but there are most definitely some kids who are better at some things (or bigger or faster) than others.

As we mature and our knowledge grows, we learn that practicing something consistently helps us to become proficient or even highly skilled doers. Our understanding of chance—a word we may have mistakenly believed to be synonymous with *luck*—shifts a bit, and a new slice of the pie emerges: talent development.

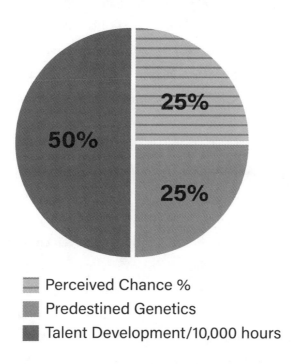

There might be no better example of talent development than Icelandic strongman, actor, and businessman Hafþór Júlíus Björnsson, who at six feet, nine inches tall and 425 pounds is literally and factually the strongest man in the world. He is known today more for his acting role as Gregor "The Mountain" Clegane in the hit series *Game of Thrones* than for what he spent the entirety of his life training for and competing in: the World's Strongest Man competition.

Among his many titles and competitive achievements, he is also the first person to win the Arnold Strongman Classic, Europe's Strongest Man, and World's Strongest Man titles in a single calendar year.

Björnsson was born in Reykjavík in November 1988 and started his athletic career playing basketball as a teenager, something he did until a recurrent ankle injury led him to consider a career as a strongman instead. Björnsson's journey to winning the World's Strongest Man competition started in 2008 when he met Magnús Ver Magnússon at their gym, Jakaból. Magnús recognized his talent, and from there, Björnsson trained for three years, eventually earning a wild card entry to the 2011 World's Strongest Man competition, in which he placed sixth. Björnsson subsequently committed his life to the competition and over the next six years won three bronze and three silver medals, finally securing the overall championship for the first time in 2018.

In his landmark best seller *Outliers,* Malcolm Gladwell posits that with ten thousand hours of progressive practice, we humans can master pretty much anything. Note well that word—*progressive*—and appreciate that often ten thousand hours isn't even enough to win or otherwise reach the ultimate success so many of us desire. Björnsson took this principal to its extreme. For the ten years between 2008 and 2018, he trained an estimated thirty thousand hours—approximately fifty to sixty hours of training every week, and ultimately three times the Gladwellian amount—before he finally achieved a first-place global standing. This investment of time and effort suggests that although it is *a* method (albeit a very grueling one) for reaching success in life, it is by no means the deciding factor or guarantee. Think about it like this: had Björnsson given up in 2017—the year before his big win and after failing to win the title seven attempts in a row—he would have still invested twenty-seven thousand hours of talent development and never won.

Ten thousand hours of practice can get us very far when we also have the genetics or natural ability already in place, but it is not a sufficient condition in and of itself for mastery or success.

There's one more element, one last slice of the pie—and that's our mindset.

ACTUAL PERSONAL GROWTH AND SUCCESS INFLUENCES

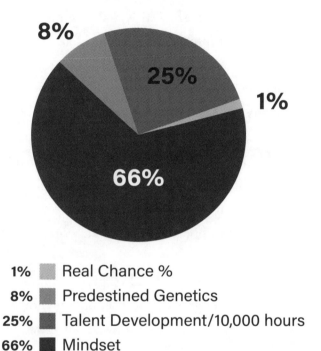

1% ▨ Real Chance %
8% ▨ Predestined Genetics
25% ▨ Talent Development/10,000 hours
66% ▨ Mindset

My hypothesis here is that how we think nearly obliterates chance to become a huge factor in our ability to succeed. Approximately two-thirds of all our outcomes can be attributed to our mindset. It's that thinking piece—I've named it the Luck Mindset—on which we'll focus throughout this book.

THE LUCK MINDSET

The Luck Mindset is essentially the next step in the evolution of Carol Dweck's 2006 work *Mindset: The New Psychology of Success.* In that book, Dweck explored the ways that our striving in life is based on an underlying sense of who we believe we are.

What Dweck's research showed was that some people operate with the belief that their intelligence, character, and creative abilities are essentially static and so don't really change in any substantive ways throughout life. These people believe, in other words, that their abilities and talents are *fixed*, that any success (or failure) they ultimately achieve is an affirmation of those inherent abilities.

Alternatively, Dweck noticed that people with a *growth* mindset believe that their abilities can be developed through effort. These people tend to thrive on challenges and see failure as a jumping-off point for evolution, an opportunity to stretch and improve upon their innate powers.

Whether we operate with a fixed or growth mindset indicates that self-perception has a significant impact on our choices, our relationships, and our actions—on all the ways we show ourselves to the world. Ultimately, our mindset shapes the things we do in our pursuit of happiness and meaning in life.

What Dweck observed is that people with a fixed mindset tend to see risk-taking or putting in effort as potential doorways for others to witness their inadequacies. These people don't put themselves out there because they are too fearful of the embarrassment and shame that might result. But those with a growth mindset—precisely because they believe that effort and deliberate practice will lead to improvement—possess a commitment to practice and improvement that requires that they take some risks and invest a lot of hard work.

If the fixed mindset leads to a vicious cycle in which fear ultimately turns to frustration and back, the growth mindset fosters a more victorious cycle in which openness to opportunity leads to accomplishment and greater development.

It's my aim in this book to further expand upon Dweck's insights by adding the Luck Mindset as a third classification. If you're already well practiced in having a growth mindset, this book is an invitation to go further and develop a new set of targets, goals, and aspirations aimed at leveraging your thoughts and beliefs into creating highly impactful actions and outcomes. And if you suspect you might be operating with a fixed mindset, this book can help you move in the direction of both growth and luck.

FFL PRINCIPLE	FIXED MINDSET	GROWTH MINDSET	LUCK MINDSET
	BELIEVES POTENTIAL IS DETERMINED AT BIRTH. GENETICS BASED.	BELIEVES POTENTIAL CAN BE DEVELOPED. EFFORT BASED.	BELIEVES POTENTIAL IS UNLIMITED. MINDSET BASED.
CURIOSITY	Ignores useful feedback and gets defensive. Judges others.	Accepts and learns from feedback and criticism. Judges self.	Seeks out feedback to improve process and outcomes. Non-judgmental, unconditionally accepts self.
PASSION	Desire to watch and look smart. Seeks ease and gratification. Focus on WHAT we do.	Desire to do and learn. Seeks knowledge and Progress. Focus on HOW we do it.	Desire to create and teach. Seeks meaning and impact. Focus on WHY we do it.
CONNECTIVITY	Process based: Focuses on what they can get / take. Stays in close-knit trusted groups.	Principles based: Focuses on what they can learn / earn. Builds large networks, collaborates well.	Values based: Focuses on what they can give / impact. Acts as influencer and super-connector.
POSITIVITY	Pessimist: Why bother, it's not going to change anything.	Realist: Growth and learning require effort, and effort is a means to an end.	Optimist: Effort is a valuable end in itself. The more effort involved, the more impactful the result.
EMPATHY	Jealous of others. Follows established leaders and well-known paths.	Plays well with others. Attempts new paths and leads others on their journey.	Acts in service of others' success and builds new pathways.

ADAPTABILITY	Gives up easily when faced with obstacles. Hides and evades and is Fragile.	Perseveres in the face of setbacks. Sticks at tasks for long periods and is Robust.	Adapts rapidly in the face of adversity. Adjusts, builds resilience and is Anti-Fragile
SITUATIONAL AWARENESS	Internal Approach: Often caught unawares. Reactions often inconsistent.	External Approach: Commits to action and follows proven methods. Responsive to threats and dangers.	Systemic Approach: Takes pre-emptive action to mitigate anticipated obstacles. Highly adaptable.
SERENDIPITY	Avoids challenges. Attempts only what they know they can achieve. Little goal setting.	Embraces challenges. Attempts harder challenges when reward justifies the effort. Sets SMART goals.	Seeks out challenges. Attempts challenges even when path to achievement is unclear. Sets stretch goals.
CHOICE	Reactive: Ignores opportunities / often procrastinates. Believes asking for help is a sign of weakness.	Active: Takes responsibility for their learning. Believes accepting help is key to learning and improvement.	Proactive: Creates opportunities for their own learning. Seeks out help because to do so is a sign of strength.
FAIL FORWARD	Believes that when they fail, it shows they are a failure. Lies about failures or covers them up.	Believes it's ok to fail and try harder next time. Recognizes and owns up to failures.	Believes in using failure to iterate, learn, and improve. Promotes and uses failure as tool for development.

Here's how to think of the three mindsets in relation to one another: someone with a fixed mindset is likely to associate effort with failure and only do things that come easily to them. Dweck's studies of four-year-olds, for example, showed that after completing a puzzle and being given the choice either to complete the same puzzle again or try a much harder one, those with a fixed mindset chose to repeat the same puzzle while those with a growth mindset were prepared to try the new, more difficult option. If, in this instance, the growth mindset is characterized by openness to new challenges, it's my argument that the Luck Mindset goes even further by seeking new challenges as a path to mastery.

Let's review a couple more examples. Someone with a fixed mindset often turns down help and support, whereas someone with a growth mindset accepts help and support; they take the opportunities that are presented to them. A person with a Luck Mindset, however, actively pursues help and support and sees it as a necessity for constant improvement. When dealing with challenges, a person with a fixed mindset attempts only what they know they can achieve, whereas a person with a growth mindset embraces challenges and attempts harder ones when the reward justifies the effort. A person with a Luck Mindset actively seeks out new challenges and opportunities, attempting them even when the path to achievement is unclear.

> Someone with a Luck Mindset is not just comfortable with opportunities for learning and development; instead, they actively create, pursue, and jump on those opportunities, thoroughly convinced of their value.

The Luck Mindset is an

evolution of the growth mindset insofar as it's a ramping up of desire for, and action toward, self-development with a key focus on generating positive outcomes that materially will change the course of your life for good. Someone with a Luck Mindset is not just comfortable with opportunities for learning and development; instead, they actively create, pursue, and jump on those opportunities, thoroughly convinced of their value. They evaluate in real time the world and systems around them, rapidly identifying key opportunities and adjusting their trajectories (to avoid loss and maximize gain), and they have the wherewithal to take timely action before an opportunity has passed.

LEAVING (ALMOST) NOTHING TO CHANCE

Luck manifests for people who make smart choices.

We know, for example, that walking into a casino with the intention of gambling greatly increases the chance that, when we walk out, our wallet or purse will be lighter.

Still, there's a sense we sometimes get—inexplicable, yet magnetic—that whispers, "Just maybe … who knows?" And we throw ourselves on the mercy of chance.

One conclusion of this book is that luck is really very simple: *luck results, in large part, from knowledge.* When you hear thunder, do you make a run for the nearest swimming pool or open field? Certainly not! You know better, and you manifest luck—by staying inside.

In a sense, making smart choices is a bit like following nature's lead. Those who study natural systems know that algorithms— another word for *formulas* or *recipes*—are at work everywhere. There are individual variations, of course, but there is also something that remains the same, something that, in the long run, continues to evolve to become as efficient and effective as possible.

From fruits and vegetables to seashells to beehives, nature gets very good at something, then *keeps improving* on it by applying what it has learned. A deer foraging in a field has not the slightest inkling of "luck" any more than does a dolphin playing in the waves or a bird soaring in the sky. But these creatures do learn from and respond to, or sometimes even transform, one another and their environments. They develop a kind of "knowledge" that allows them to reduce the impacts of chance and change.

Both luck and chance are exclusively human constructs, the names we've given to all the factors that we've come to believe are entirely outside of our control. In part, we're correct to see that there are some things we simply can't influence. On the other hand, we have a tendency to overlook so very much of what actually *is* within our power. We do not pay enough attention to those aspects of "chance" that we can reduce nearly to zero.

The primary conclusion of this book, and the one on which the Ten Principles are focused, is that increasing our capacity for luck comes down to two primary elements that are very much within our power: how we think and how we act.

CHAPTER 2

THOUGHTS AND ACTIONS

It would have been quite easy for young Stuart Lacey to decide, "These bullies are right. I'm not cool. I'm not talented. I'm short, and I'm a nerd. I'll never amount to anything. What's the point?"

Despite dressing me inappropriately for the times, and despite their insistence that I be a model student, my parents bestowed upon me a gift beyond intellect, and one that further leveraged that capacity: a belief in myself. They believed in me, and that helped *me* believe in me, which ultimately propelled me forward.

It is astounding what one's own confidence can produce alongside one's thoughtful action. In fact, one of the insights I've taken from the fact of my confidence despite being bullied and failing hard early on in my career is that luck (and the success that follows upon it) relies on more than either genetics or talent on the one hand, opportunity and practice on the other.

Had I been more introspective after my first taste of success, I'd have likely maintained that success. Instead, I chased after what

I thought was "the good life"—24/7 surfing, women, a convertible sports car, etc. In short, I became my own worst enemy, something many of us do without even realizing it, and I was not happy. The things I chose to do were not conducive to cultivating, let alone maintaining, luck.

In rebuilding my life, I learned that success and happiness are not mutually exclusive. If anything, they *lean on* one another, which makes the Ten Principles a set of tools for attaining both.

No matter where you are in life—on top, at the bottom, or anywhere in between—*how you think and what you do (or don't do)* can help you make the most of what you have. The Principles for creating luck will help you break out of any rut you're in—or help you avoid falling into one if you're having a good run.

I've come to think of the implementation of the Principles as involving a shift from one way of thinking to another. Now, that doesn't mean that we necessarily give up the one for the other (imagine if you forfeited analytical thinking for instinctual responses in your every encounter!), but for many of us, it may mean developing more "instinctual" responses if we're always dependent on analyzing every detail before we make a decision or act.

> No matter where you are in life—on top, at the bottom, or anywhere in between—*how you think and what you do (or don't do)* can help you make the most of what you have.

To help you get started thinking about these shifts, I've listed them below. You'll see many of them again as you read through the chapters focused on each of the Ten Principles. For now, think of this first set as a matter of transforming how we think—our capacity to cultivate positive as well as flexible habits of mind:

Closed off	Open
Know-it-all	Lifelong learner
Ignores feedback	Seeks feedback
Introvert	Extrovert
Disengaged	Engaged
Unmotivated	Motivated
Back stage	Center stage
What we do	Why we do it
Build walls	Build bridges
Taking	Giving
Speaking	Active listening
Pessimist	Optimist
Half-empty	Half-full
No	Yes
Selfish	Selfless
Thinking	Feeling
Jealous of others	In service of others

Think of the second set as a matter of how we respond to our environment:

Routine	Random
Rigidity	Flexibility
Frozen	Rapidly adjusts
Fragile	Antifragile
Blinders on	Radar out
Unaware	Preemptive
Internal	Systemic
Analytical	Instinctual
Avoid	Embrace
Ignores feedback	Explore

And think of the third as a matter of cultivating optimal skill and capacity for action:

No control	Control
No choice	Choice
Reactive	Proactive
Procrastinate	Get on with it

Rest	Motion
Passive	Active
Impossible	Not yet done
Failure	Learning opportunity
Cover up	Promote

Together, the movement from left to right corresponds to our shifts, and thereby our progress toward achieving a Luck Mindset.

SCRATCHING THE SURFACE

In an article in *Fast Company* magazine from 2003, social scientist Daniel Pink introduced to the world one Richard Wiseman.[2] Pink interviewed Wiseman about his research into what, up until then, had been considered a decidedly unscientific subject: luck.

"Luck isn't due to kismet, karma, or coincidence," Pink paraphrases Wiseman as saying. "Lucky folks, without even knowing it, *think and behave* in ways that create good fortune in their lives."

At the time, Wiseman's book *The Luck Factor* had just been released; to this day it is regarded as the only serious research on the subject. As a professor at the University of Hertfordshire in the UK, Wiseman had explored luck from a strongly investigative point of view, with a particular emphasis on his specialty: psychology and the public understanding of psychology. Wiseman also wove into the

---

2   Daniel H. Pink, "How to Make Your Own Luck," FastCompany.com, June 30, 2003, https://www.fastcompany.com/46732/how-make-your-own-luck.

book his avocation as a practicing magician, a skill which plays on our concepts of and sensibilities around luck and chance.

Wiseman's book resulted from a decade spent tracking four hundred people with the goal of understanding how they thought about their own good or bad luck. And though its findings did not rise even to Wiseman's own definition of groundbreaking, *The Luck Factor* did offer these four main takeaways. Lucky people

1. are skilled at noticing and acting on opportunities,

2. listen to their hunches,

3. expect good fortune, and

4. turn bad fortune into good.

The Luck Factor tweaked my curiosity in a couple of areas. One was its contention that people who routinely find good fortune do so because, unlike everyone else, *they believe* in it—or more specifically, in their ability, through persistence, to create good outcomes in their lives. That fascinated me because it is essentially saying that luckiness is largely based on our *perception* of reality, our ways of thinking, or our mindset.

Wiseman teaches us that you can acknowledge that bad things happen—but you can also choose how to think about all the good results that spring from them. When you are able to do that, you can also conclude that there's no *totally bad* luck. This leads us to the notion that *perception* is *one key difference* between a lucky and unlucky person.

Take a car crash. One person will get out of their vehicle, survey the damage, and say, "Oh my God! My car's totaled! It's the worst thing that's ever happened!" They're inconsolable. But another gets out, surveys the bigger picture, and says, "Thank God. I wasn't injured. No one else was hurt. *How lucky am I?*"

Wiseman's book also encourages its readers to keep a Luck Diary. This really spoke to me, because I'd started my own luck diary in college, long before *The Luck Factor* was published, as a way of tracking my thoughts and actions, and their outcomes.

Wiseman's research into how we think about luck fed my fire for digging deeper and sharing more. I wanted not only to add to what Wiseman learned but also to synthesize that knowledge into specific practices each of us can pursue in order to increase our luck. You're holding the result of that twenty years of work and research in your hands.

NOT JUST HOW *YOU* THINK

Why stop with our *individual* thoughts and actions?

As you continue to read, remember: the Principles of Luck presented here apply as much to organizations as they do to individuals. In fact, to assist in this regard, you will find that in each of the ten central chapters, I include business examples, exercises, and key learnings that you can take back to your companies and share with your management teams and boards. These learnings are curated to present success factors for high-performance business outcomes and relate them to easy-to-understand use cases and examples.

The skills and mindsets that you practice individually can be amplified to apply to the teams around you, whether a family unit, a business unit, or both.

To better understand how the Principles might scale for groups, I studied successful organizational structures from all corners. During the time that I was in Silicon Valley, between 2013 and 2017, I visited the campuses of pioneering companies like Google, Facebook,

PayPal, Adobe, and Apple watching, learning, and speaking to their leadership and HR and innovation teams, all the while trying to understand the intersections of business culture and business policy when it came to influencing business success. Subsequent investigations took me to the MIT Media Lab in Boston and the campus at Singularity University under the stewardship of Peter Diamandis and Salim Ismail. I later visited the INSEAD campus in France and the IFC in Dubai to understand how larger entities like the EU and GCC operated and cooperated. I even started a company to link the stock markets in twenty-one different African nations and in so doing learned much about how and why countries do not always cooperate even when they could and possibly should. The sum of these learnings has helped me shape the lessons from this book into stories and thought-provoking examples that are applicable to companies from 25 to 2,500 employees.

> The skills and mindsets that you practice individually can be amplified to apply to the teams around you, whether a family unit, a business unit, or both.

Simply put, I can now unequivocally state that if your company applies the same practices that create luck in our personal lives, it will become capable of capitalizing on opportunities and securing success.

CHAPTER 3

YOUR OWN WORST ENEMY

A recent survey found that nearly 25 percent of Americans possess at least one good luck charm. Superstition still plays a role in our relationship with luck.[3] More of us than might be willing to admit as much can find ourselves convinced that luck is something that some ride high on and others are down on, and whichever end of the spectrum we occupy is due to forces beyond our control. So we hustle as best we can—sometimes clinging to talismans or other charms that we think might coax the forces of success in our direction. Lucky charms, amulets, the hand of Fatima—these and many other "traditional" symbols invoking luck illustrate the compelling power of the universal human belief that supernatural powers have a role to play in our fate.

In truth, I should admit that I have a lucky seashell, and I know

---

3   Hoang Nguyen, "Nearly a Quarter of Americans Carry a Lucky Charm," YouGov.com, July 11, 2018, https://today.yougov.com/topics/lifestyle/articles-reports/2018/07/11/nearly-quarter-americans-carry-lucky-charm.

some very successful people who have lucky shirts, lucky shoes, and the like. But my argument here is that while we may sometimes indulge our inclinations to hold on to superstitious beliefs, we absolutely *cannot in any way rely on them to help us achieve our goals*. It's one thing to have a lucky shirt or wear an amulet, wholly another to do everything within your real human power to set yourself up for success.

> It's one thing to have a lucky shirt or wear an amulet, wholly another to do everything within your real human power to set yourself up for success.

TRAPS OF OUR OWN SETTING

Superstition has been part of many cultures' beliefs and rituals for centuries and is very tightly linked to ideas about luck, almost always having to do with *avoiding bad luck*. In markets all over the world, from San Francisco to San Juan, Canberra to Kiev, just ask the keeper of any stand selling trinkets to show you their icons for influencing fortune. There are charms and amulets for invoking the favor or disfavor of divine forces for nearly everything you might want to affect.

But you don't have to travel anywhere to notice the influence of cultural superstition. Lost your car keys or wallet? Send up a prayer to Saint Anthony of Padua. Not sure which saint to call on? Wikipedia offers a full list of patron saints by occupation and activity, another list organized by "ailments, illness, and dangers," and a third that enumerates saints by place.

Invoking lucky charms or the divine may provide something that can *actually improve* our outcomes: the comfort that comes from belief. Still, the mere act of holding a rabbit's foot, blowing on dice, or invoking a particular aspect of the divine does not in and of itself hold much of a realistic probability of changing your outcome.

What believing in the influential power of charms shows us is not the power of those charms but the power of our thoughts. And our thoughts, along with what we do as a result of having them, directly impact our results.

Consider the career of Phil Esposito.

One of the best ice hockey players of all time, "Espo" was big, strong, and when he wanted to be, immovable. He would park himself in front of his opponent's goal to block the goaltender's vision and then pounce on loose pucks for conversion into easy goals.

> What believing in the influential power of charms shows us is not the power of those charms but the power of our thoughts.

But if this hugely talented player saw two crossed hockey sticks in the dressing room before the game, he would play terribly. His belief that this was an omen of bad luck affected his play so completely that his teammates would actually check the entire room for crossed sticks before he entered.

Esposito is a prime example of the ways we devise traps of our own setting. Though he was without peer in nearly every game he played, he allowed dread to play with him. Now, his superstition didn't prevent him having a Hall of Fame career. But one can't help wondering: Without this trap of his own setting, how much more might Espo have achieved?

TRAPS VERSUS OPPORTUNITIES

What about beliefs that originate from evidence rather than superstition? Many of our routines can reflect just that: we engage in them regularly because they've proven effective time and again. But some routines can actually place limits on our luckiness.

One routine many of us perpetuate needlessly is that of creating negative or self-defeating *meaning* around occurrences. That's one I can speak to from personal experience.

As a young man, I did seven years of Olympic sailing campaigns. It pretty much goes without saying that one of the worst finishing positions, if you're involved in a medal race, is fourth. Less known is the fact that teams who finish in third place are typically *happier* than those who finish second.[4] Why?

Bronze medalists are happier because they realize that, had they performed marginally worse, they'd have finished in that worst spot, fourth, and would have no medal at all. Meanwhile, most silver medalists beat themselves up: "Just a few seconds better, and we'd have had a gold!"

An outside observer might just want to scream, "*Good God! You got a silver medal!*"

The tendency to look at what might have happened rather than what actually did happen is what psychologists call *counterfactual thinking*. Essentially, we have the ability to imagine possible alternative scenarios—something contrary to what actually happened—when reflecting on the past. This is a fine skill to have, but too often, we impose greater negativity on ourselves by thinking that things should have been better than they were. Thoughts like "if only I had ..." are

---

4   Vivian Giang, "Why Bronze Medalists Are Often Happier Than Silver Medalists," *Business Insider*, August 6, 2012, accessed September 4, 2019, https://www. businessinsider.com/why-counterfactual-thinking-may-make-you-more-relieved-to-get-third-place-rather-than-second-2012-8.

quite common after we've failed at something we'd intended to achieve. The silver medalist might wallow in regret by focusing on factors that might have led to achieving the gold. Counterfactual thinking's negative effects are more common than its positive ones, though you can see that there are ways in which counterfactual thinking might be useful to us insofar as it can help us notice or learn something that could enhance the possibility of our success *the next time*.

As Richard Wiseman's work began to excavate, and as I intend to explore more thoroughly here, the differences between lucky and unlucky people are striking: Lucky people tend to imagine how the bad circumstances they encountered could have been *worse*. They approach even the most challenging experiences from a habit of thought that allows them to *feel better* about themselves and their lives and to look forward to new opportunities for *doing better* as well. This helps keep their expectations about the future high and increases the likelihood that they will continue to have a lucky life.

BETTER THAN THE LOTTERY

On any given day, you'll see people lined up at the local corner store with cash in one hand and a lottery ticket in the other, just waiting to give their hard-earned money to the state.

Lotteries are nothing more than voluntary taxes too often paid by people with the fewest fiscal means. When the jackpot is a big number, people often have the feeling that they can't, even shouldn't, resist taking a chance on winning.

It's one thing to take a chance once or twice a year on a ticket or two, thinking maybe lightning will strike (actually, your chances of getting struck by lightning are *better*); it's something else entirely to play week in and week out. That really is no different than taking your money and setting it ablaze. The math is *undeniable.* In a typical 6/49 game, each player chooses six distinct numbers from a range of one through forty-nine. If the six numbers on a ticket match the numbers drawn by the lottery, the ticket holder is a jackpot winner. The probability of this happening is 1 in 13,983,816.[5]

And the satisfaction is minimal. Most winners might end up enjoying themselves for a year, maybe even a few years. But eventually, a large number of lottery winners return to their prior lots in life—and many end up worse off than they were before they won.[6]

So why buy that ticket?

If you found your place on the Luck Ladder in chapter 1, you may already know the answer: we *all* have certain beliefs that might make us think we have anywhere from no luck to an embarrassment of it. And sometimes those beliefs don't quite reflect the reality of our situations. Sometimes, too, it's easier to believe that luck will help us out when in fact our own efforts at self-development have a much greater chance of doing so.

If you also completed the simplified Luck Assessment in chapter 1, then you got some help identifying a North Star and setting your starting point for actually improving aspects of your life.

Before you read on, I want to invite you to participate in a data-driven version of the Luck Assessment that can be found at www.formulaforluck.com. Here's the benefit to you:

1. The version of the Luck Assessment in chapter 1 is a twenty-item assessment, whereas the online version is far more

---

5   "Lottery Mathematics," Wikipedia Foundation, last modified November 8, 2020, 00:58, https://en.wikipedia.org/wiki/Lottery_mathematics.

6   Ryan Hart, "What Percentage of Lottery Winners Go Broke? (Plus 35 More Statistics)," RyanHart.org, updated December 3, 2018, https://www.ryanhart.org/lottery-winner-statistics/.

thorough with a full eighty items to help you get an even more accurate sense of your status.

2. Recording your answers with a time/date stamp from today allows you to use your current results as a baseline for future assessments.

3. Whenever you feel that you've made some progress up the Luck Ladder, and again once you reach the end of the book and have implemented more of the Principles, you can pop back online to reassess yourself. Measuring your progress over time will help you uncover additional ways to further your skills at generating luck.

4. Recording your baseline assessment online also allows our artificial intelligence (AI) and data analytics tools to analyze your results and make specific, personalized, and contextually relevant recommendations about how to get the most out of this book, how to prioritize which Principles to start on first, and where you might find the greatest benefits.

5. If you wish, you can also subscribe to any of our blogs, find additional chapter-specific materials and FAQs, or work directly with virtual coaches and other support services to enhance this book's value for you.

Even just copying your answers from chapter 1 into the web version of the Luck Assessment will immediately help customize and prioritize your experience gaining value from this book. When you're through, use the space on the following page to complete the learnings from the online assessment and make a note of the resulting recommendation.

_____

_____

_____

_____

_____

_____

_____

_____

_____

_____

_____

All CEOs and leaders know that success must be measurable. If you don't establish some kind of metric, like assigning SMART goals (those are specific, measurable, actionable, relevant, and time-based), it is very tough to evaluate performance and gain true traction on your path to success. To help you really focus your energy and get the most out of what's to come, set a SMART goal right now.

All CEOs and leaders know that success must be measurable.

An example might look like this:

Specific: Climb at least two steps on the Luck Ladder.
Measurable: Take my Luck Assessment score from 2.2 to at least a 4.
Actionable: Read a minimum of two of the Ten Principles chapters in the next two weeks, and apply the learnings in real-life scenarios.

Relevant: Pick two chapters on topics that most resonate with me right now, and read them.

Time-Based: Evaluate myself on the Luck Assessment today and then again at the end of two weeks.

Writing down our goals is crucial to success, so grab a pen and complete your own SMART goal now:

Specific: Climb at least _____ steps on the Luck Ladder.

Measurable: Take my Luck Assessment score from _____ to at least a _____.

Actionable: Read a minimum of _____ of the Ten Principles chapters in the next two weeks, and apply the learnings in real-life scenarios.

Relevant: The two chapters that most resonate with me right now and that I will jump to first are chapters _____ and _____.

Time-Based: Evaluate myself on the Luck Assessment today and then again by DD _____ MM _____ YY _____.

If you've jumped in and taken these steps, let me congratulate you for being curious enough to honestly assess yourself, and also for taking action. Those two Principles are already starting to work in your favor. I invite you to engage with what follows with an open mind. If you're more than ready to do that, welcome. And if you're still hesitant or skeptical, more inclined to think, "Go ahead, Stuart: prove to me that this will work," then let me just say this:

Challenge accepted.

$$(\frac{2}{3} \times 2x)a^2 = b^2$$

$$\varepsilon = c005 \quad E = mc^2$$

$$1 \, \varepsilon = c005 \quad \vartheta + x_7 = \left(\frac{2}{3} \times\right.$$

$$H_2 \, SO_4 \quad 2x \quad a^2 = b^2 + c^2 = \quad bc$$

$$\left(\frac{2}{3} \times 2x\right) \quad \frac{a}{9in} = \frac{b}{9m} \quad H^3 \quad SO_4$$

$$y^3 + z^2 + xyz = 2 \quad y = \sqrt[2]{3+1}$$

$$z^3 + 1 \, \varepsilon = c005 \quad SO_4$$

$$\left(\frac{2}{3}\right) = x_7 \quad y = \sqrt[2]{3+1}$$

$$a^2 \quad H^3 \quad \frac{a}{in} \quad 1 \, \varepsilon = c005 \quad 1 \, \varepsilon = c005$$

$$1 \, \varepsilon = 0.005$$

$$x_7 = \left(\frac{2}{3} \times 2x\right)a^2 = b^2 + c^2 = 2x$$

$$N^2 \times H^3 \quad \frac{a}{9ind} = \frac{b}{9ind}$$

$$f(3) = 2^{-3}$$

$$NH_3 \quad y$$

$$2x \left(\frac{2}{3} \times 2x\right) \quad SO_4$$

$$a = \frac{b}{9ind} \quad f(3) = 2^{-3} + 1 \, \varepsilon = c005$$

$$x = \left(\frac{2}{3} \times c^2x\right)$$

CHAPTER 4

HOW TO USE THE NEXT TEN CHAPTERS

As an old song goes, the goal is to accentuate the positives and eliminate the negatives.

With a firm understanding of what contributes to luck and what doesn't, we can take steps toward *maximizing* luck. You'll remember my hypothesis from chapter 1 that how we think makes up two-thirds of our overall Formula for Luck. Your mindset is directly related to your ability to take action so as to increase opportunities for luck. The Ten Principles that we'll review in the coming chapters can help you grow the good habits you may already have and replace some not-so-good habits with far better ones.

THE TEN PRINCIPLES

One Principle of Luck is described in each of the next ten chapters. They are *Curiosity, Passion, Connectivity, Positivity, Empathy,*

Adaptability, Situational Awareness, Serendipity, Choice, and *Fail Forward.*

You should feel welcome to read about and practice these Principles in any order you choose. I have organized them here according to a certain logic—the earlier ones explore some of the qualities that define who we are and how we think, the later ones are more situational insofar as they tend to characterize the ways that we respond to whatever happens, and the final two are the most action oriented of the lot. The chapters do reference and build on one another, but they can also be accessed independently of one another. The Principles of Luck don't have to be introduced or practiced in any particular order. And each chapter allows you opportunities to explore and expand your practice.

> Your mindset is directly related to your ability to take action so as to increase opportunities for luck.

BUILDING BLOCKS OF THE FORMULA FOR LUCK

In the next ten chapters, you'll see the following symbols to help make sense of how luck is created, increased, and compounded.

First, let's look at **Operators**. (Don't worry! You already know what I'm about to tell you, and the actual amount of math involved is minimal!)

We'll be using two Operators you know well from your earliest math classes and that need no explanation at all:

+   The plus sign will be used to denote addition.

✖   The times sign will be used to denote multiplication.

Next, let's look at **Functions**. Each Principle is accompanied by one of the following three symbols showing its Function:

∞   Principles of Luck with an *infinite Function* can't be overdone. The more you practice them, the better. They are in effect limitless. Think of our capacity to keep learning throughout our lives. While some of us might activate this capacity more at some points in our lives than others, for the most part we are able to learn and try new things, read another book, or listen more carefully in our next conversation.

⚲   Principles of Luck with a finite Function are critical to building luck, but they come with a limit to our ability to apply or access them. Take, for example, the natural limitations on Situational Awareness, the fact that you can keep an eye on only so many different factors at once. If you're in an airport, you may notice those pieces of luggage that have been left unattended or the person pacing or acting erratically, but you simply can't keep an eye on every piece of luggage or every person on the scene.

0 1 The Principles of Luck bearing the symbol of a *binary Function* are critical to your decision path. One path multiplies the entire formula by zero (thereby effectively eliminating the value of all the other Principles), whereas the other path multiplies the entire formula by one (thereby keeping all the other Principles in play). The Principles in this book that bear this Function are Choice and Fail Forward. Some examples you may have experienced as a young person: if you chose *not* to walk across the gymnasium to invite someone to dance with you, or if you chose *not* to try out for a role you really wanted in the school play, the likelihood of these outcomes being positive is effectively multiplied by zero. If, however, you made the choice to act, then you bring to bear the power of every other Principle in the formula, and your likelihood of a positive outcome is hugely increased. Equally, if you decide to then repeatedly attempt that choice and not stop at failure, you multiply your likelihood of a lucky outcome by each successive binary attempt.

Here are the Ten Principles with their corresponding Operators and Functions:

PRINCIPLE	OPERATOR	FUNCTION
CURIOSITY	Additive	Infinite
PASSION	Additive	Infinite
CONNECTIVITY	Additive	Infinite
POSITIVITY	Additive	Infinite
EMPATHY	Additive	Infinite
ADAPTABILITY	Multiplicative	Finite
SITUATIONAL AWARENESS	Multiplicative	Finite
SERENDIPITY	Multiplicative	Finite
CHOICE	Multiplicative	Binary
FAIL FORWARD	Multiplicative	Binary

I invite you to keep these Functions and Operators in mind as you consider each of the Principles, though it will not be until I've introduced all Ten Principles that they will come into play to create the full Formula for Luck. Similarly, as we progress through the Principles of Luck, we'll begin to explore synergies that exist among them, but these, too, will be addressed in greater detail after all the

Principles have been reviewed.

CHAPTER SECTIONS

The next ten chapters will define and explore the Principles of Luck in specific sections: *Exploration, Guest Star, In Practice,* and *In Business.*

Exploration sections look at existing research (my own and others') into each Principle's impact on luck.

Guest Star sections introduce someone who has directly applied the chapter's Principle of Luck in their own life. Guest Stars offer interesting and tangible advice for implementing the Principles in our lives.

In Practice sections present brief exercises for you to engage in as you are reading and learning about the Principles. I include at least one exercise in every chapter. If you wish to do more, a complete workbook full of exercises is available for download from www.formulaforluck.com.

In Business sections, as the name suggests, explore techniques for optimally applying the Principles of Luck in business settings.

Finally, each chapter ends with a *Chapter Summary* as well as a *Stuart's Secrets* list that includes resources you can use immediately—tips and tricks I've picked up over the years that have helped me attain luck beyond my wildest dreams.

If you're feeling ready, let's explore some Principles!

$a = b$

$y = \sqrt[2]{3+1}$ H_2

$y^2 + z^2 + xy z = 2$ $\left(\frac{2}{3} \times 2x\right)$

a^2

$x^2 + y^3 + z^2 + xyz =$

$\sqrt{3+1}$

$f(3) = 2^{-3} + 1$ $\mathcal{E} = 0.005$

$= 0.005$

b^2

$\dfrac{b}{sind} = \dfrac{c}{sin}$ a^2 H^3

H_2SO_4

$(3) = 2^{-3}$ C1 $2^2 + 1$ $\mathcal{E} = 0.005$

SO_4 $b^2 + C^2 = 26C$

$b^2 - C^2$ $cx9 + x_7$ $xyz = 2$

$y = \sqrt[2]{3+1}$ $\left(\frac{2}{3} \times 2x\right)$

$\dfrac{o}{sin}$ $f(dx) = 26 + C^2$

$\dfrac{a}{sin}$

$Z^2 + x^2 = 2x$

$y = \sqrt[2]{3+1}$

$\left(\frac{2}{3}\right) = x_7$

a^2 $cx a (2 \cdot a)$

$2x$ $a^2 = b^2$

CHAPTER 5

THE FIRST PRINCIPLE: CURIOSITY

Be a Lifelong Learner

Operator: **+ (additive)**

Function: **∞ (infinite)**

Luck Mindset Category: **Habit**

Shift: **Moving from being a know-it-all to being a lifelong learner, from being closed off to being open to all things, from ignoring feedback to seeking feedback**

On Twitter: **#lifelonglearner**

> *Curiosity did not kill the cat, ignorance did.*
>
> — Unknown

INTRODUCTION

Let's kick off our inquiry into Curiosity by recognizing someone who's done great work in this space: Richard Wiseman, professor of the public understanding of psychology at the University of Hertfordshire in the UK. Dr. Wiseman published *The Luck Factor* after having spent about a decade conducting thousands of interviews and hundreds of experiments to determine what makes some people lucky and others not.

Interestingly enough, Dr. Wiseman started his career as a magician in London. He received some critical acclaim in 2001 for his research into the world's funniest joke, testing forty thousand of them on 350,000 participants. (If you're curious, you can check out the winning joke at www.formulaforluck.com.)

Wiseman was also interested in curiosity. He built a database of four hundred people from all walks of life throughout the UK and balanced it between those who thought they were lucky and those who felt they were not. He then asked each participant whether they were open to new experiences or preferred routine.

His hypothesis: people who are more open and curious recognize opportunity and seize it, and tend to "feel" lucky. Wiseman further suspected that those who favored routine—i.e., were less open and curious—would tend to *miss* opportunities and therefore "feel" unlucky.

> People who are more open and curious recognize opportunity and seize it, and tend to "feel" lucky.

To confirm these suspicions, Wiseman needed to present his subjects with an opportunity and see how they responded. He devised a timed exercise in which each of four hundred subjects was asked to look through a newspaper, count the photographs, and report their findings.

Wiseman didn't tell them that the newspaper included two half-page advertisements. The first was on page 2 and read: "STOP COUNTING. THERE ARE 43 PHOTOGRAPHS IN THIS NEWSPAPER."

The second, about halfway through, sweetened the pot, saying: "STOP COUNTING. TELL THE EXPERIMENTER YOU HAVE SEEN THIS AND WIN £150!"[7]

Almost everyone who said they were lucky spotted opportunity—the full-page ads—and leveraged it to their immediate advantage, quickly finishing and leaving Wiseman's laboratory £150 richer. Those who self-described as unlucky either didn't notice the ads or were amply constrained by their closed-mindedness to a page right by them. Most of this group counted and reported the photographs correctly, but it took a much longer time, and none made £150 in the process.

This was foundational research on how curiosity and openness to new information impacts our perceived luckiness.

EXPLORATION: THINK LIKE DA VINCI

Each of us is born curious. Our early years are dominated by an unquenchable thirst for knowledge, with all of our senses focused on exploring and learning and experimenting in the world's largest and most diverse lab: the world itself.

Before we can even walk or speak, we experience pain and discomfort and hunger—and pleasure and joy and satisfaction—and

---

7   Richard Wiseman, "The Luck Factor," *The Skeptical Inquirer*, May/June 2003 issue, http://richardwiseman.com/resources/The_Luck_Factor.pdf

we learn from these experiences. Once we become mobile and vocal, watch out! "What is this, how does that work, and why?" In these respects, we are no different from any of the great minds of history.

Then, ironically, the more we learn in school, often the less curious we become.

"Don't let schooling interfere with your education," Mark Twain warned. Another of history's greatest thinkers—Leonard da Vinci—never did.

In *The Creators: A History of Heroes of the Imagination,* published in 1992 by Penguin Random House, author Daniel Boorstin contrasts da Vinci, the prototype Renaissance man, to some of his contemporaries:

> *Unlike Dante, he had no passion for a woman. Unlike Giotto, Dante, or Brunelleschi he seemed to have had no civic loyalty. Nor devotion to church or Christ. He willingly accepted commissions from the Medici, the Sforzas, the Borgias, or French kings—from the popes or their enemies. He lacked the sensual worldliness of a Bocaccio or a Chaucer, the recklessness of a Rabelais, the piety of a Dante, or the religious passion of a Michelangelo.*

Though he may have seemed to be lacking in all these ways, what da Vinci *had* was something that has accompanied luck through time—and that still drives it: Curiosity. By his own telling as quoted in Boorstin's book:

> *I roamed the countryside searching for answers to things I did not understand. Why shells existed on the tops of the mountains along with the imprints of coral and plants and seaweed usually found in the sea. Why the thunder lasts a longer time than that which causes it, and why immediately*

on its creation, the lightning becomes visible to the eye, while thunder requires some time to travel. How the various circles of water form around the spot which has been struck by a stone, and why a bird sustains itself in the air. These questions and other strange phenomena engaged my thought throughout my entire life.

Leonardo's loyalty, devotion, and passion were all directed to the quest for truth and beauty. It's notable that, even in his tireless exploration of the world, Leonardo wasn't satisfied just to look at something with a questioning eye; he needed to see it from different aspects.

Almost all of his drawings take up three perspectives, further demonstrating his thirst for knowledge and for intimacy with the details of things. As historians Clark and Bronowski observed about da Vinci: "[We're] worn out by [his] energy. He won't take yes for an answer. He can't leave anything alone."[8]

Yet he was also one of the first people to realize that from time to time we need to step back from intense scrutiny in order to fully free our power of judgment.

Whether it's the simple act of standing up after extended sitting at a desk, taking a walk and going over our thoughts, or just letting go of what we've been working on, these and other approaches allow us to get another perspective as well as rest our mind and refresh our bodies. Then, when we revisit the matter at hand, we bring new energy, new questions, and often new solutions to challenges that perhaps seemed intractable.

On his walks through the streets of Florence, da Vinci was known to occasionally stop at merchants who were selling caged

---

8   John H. Lienhard, "Clark and Bronowski," *Engines of Our Ingenuity*, no. 1880, accessed November 2020, https://uh.edu/engines/epi1880.htm.

birds, buy the birds, and immediately set them free. For him, the quest for knowledge was synonymous with discovering freedom.

GUEST STAR: JAMES DONNELLY

James was given two gifts at birth. He was lucky enough to be born in Canada, and he was born to two very loving parents. The rest is a story of curiosity and hunger. James grew up with modest means; he started his first company—lawn maintenance—at thirteen and never looked back. He was a CPA with Arthur Andersen by the age of twenty-three and left to start one of Canada's fastest-growing investment operations at twenty-five that made him a millionaire by age twenty-seven. After some business setbacks, James moved his family to Florida and started the Castle Group. Castle is now one of the largest privately held residential property management companies in the United States, with over two thousand employees.

James has been widely recognized for his entrepreneurial success; he has been a finalist for the Ernst and Young Entrepreneur of the Year Award and gained admission into the NSU Huizenga business school Entrepreneur Hall of Fame. However, he is most proud of how he and his wife, Cathy, have become community leaders and philanthropists in South Florida. Collectively, their philanthropic arm— CastleCares—created a program that has served over one million meals to underprivileged children in Southern Florida and donated millions of dollars and thousands of hours of community service.

James's curiosity led him to research the factors that allowed him to become so successful from such a humble start. The result of this research is a formula for success that he calls Lifeshaping^{SM}, the components of which are consistent with and complementary to the Formula for Luck.

I caught up with James in Jackson Hole, Wyoming, in early 2019. We were discussing the book he was working on when the following conversation ensued.

SL: What single superpower or skill set can you attribute to getting you on the success track that you have been on?

JD: Without a doubt, it's curiosity. What happened in my twenties, when I really started to rock it, is that I went to see Tony Robbins in 1989. I think there's no better guy that's figured out the science of human behavior. I took a lot away from that event, and the result was an incredible thirst for knowledge and curiosity. I need to know the facts. I need to know why people behave the way that they do and what motivates them.

SL: Were you a curious kid? Or is it something you think you developed over time or at that point in your life?

JD: I don't recall being a particularly curious kid, so I'm going to suggest it was learned. The big triggers for me as a kid were my father saying, "There's always someone better than you," and second, what I call *the gift of want* that my parents gave me. We had no money, and back in those days, in 1961, nothing came with the house—no lawn and no driveway. You had to go buy sod to put on your front lawn. And, sure enough, we couldn't afford sod. So we had the only gravel driveway on the street and potatoes planted in our front yard. I think that inspired my thirst for independent learning, and as a result I was driven to learn and discover everything I could about the world around me to succeed.

SL: How do you allocate time to learning, and how do you filter or triage what to learn and what to skip?

JD: Every day is one less day, and my life is so incredible, I want to have one more day. For sure, learning is a matter of relevancy to me. For instance, I'm becoming a pilot now, and I'm leaving nothing to chance. I'm learning the science of weather and the science of aerodynamics. I just know that if I'm going to fly, I'm going to know everything I can. The differentiator for me is not whether there is a test or not; rather it's my level of passion for the subject.

SL: If every yin has a yang, what is the opposite of curiosity— what is its kryptonite?

JD: Hubris. It comes from ego, which means "I know." If you know, then you're not taking advantage of all the other information available to make the right decision or do the right thing— all of which ultimately makes you lucky. So I think we limit our luck by letting our egos drive things. A lot of people who have big egos do big things, but that makes them overconfident, arrogant, and more prone to their blind spots and to failure.

SL: Given all you have learned, how would you mentor your younger self if you had had the chance?

> A lot of people who have big egos do big things, but that makes them overconfident, arrogant, and more prone to their blind spots and to failure.
> — *James Donnelly*

JD: I would teach myself the success cycle. This has driven luck for me. No matter what you want, you (a) come up with a plan, (b) implement the plan, (c) evaluate the plan, (d) adjust, and (e) reimplement. The foundations for implementation are living a life with purpose and maintaining positive energy. Set aside time for the sort of unplugged thinking that leads to creativity. Finally, modeling was big for me. Most of the time, someone's already done what you want to do. A friend of mine told me that the concept of R and D—typically understood as research and development—more accurately means "rip-off and duplicate." Go actively search out best practices and locate a successful leader who has had the same issue and mastered the solution—and then model your solution with those lessons in mind.

IN PRACTICE: IDENTIFY YOUR CURIOSITY

Leonardo da Vinci kept many notebooks, which—in addition to being written right to left and requiring a mirror to read—were famous for their drawings, as they had no lines in them. I encourage you to choose as your next notebook one that also has no lines so that you can draw and doodle freely on the blank pages.

To get a fuller appreciation for your own Curiosity and to begin thinking about its impact on your life and luck, try this brief exercise:

Think of ten questions that are important to you, questions you want to use as your guide for a beautiful life. Take your time identifying these questions (and be thankful I haven't asked you to try the longer version of this exercise, which involves coming up with one hundred questions!). Even with these ten, be like da Vinci and step away now and then. Collect your thoughts. Refine them. Reflect on them. There is no time limit.

Once you've got your ten questions, rank them from most important to least.

WRITE DOWN YOUR TEN QUESTIONS IN RANK ORDER.

1 _____

2 _____

3 _____

4 _____

5 _____

6 _____

7 _____

8 _____

9 _____

10 _____

Next, compare your ten questions against the following, widely considered the top ten questions of all time:

1. When am I most naturally myself?

2. What one thing could I stop doing or start doing that would most improve my quality of life?

3. What is my greatest talent?

4. How can I get paid for doing what I love?

5. Who are my most inspiring role models?

6. How may I best be of service to others?

7. What is my heart's deepest desire?

8. How am I perceived by my closest friend, my worst enemy, my boss, my children, my coworkers?

9. What are my blessings in life, and what legacy would I like to leave?

10. Why do I go to work every day?

As you compare and contrast your own top ten to these, practice openness and Curiosity. The similarities—and differences—are sure to invigorate you. Do one or more coincide with or possibly inform your list of questions? Do any make you want to update or edit your list?

As with any goals-setting exercise, committing to paper is the first step in reaching your goal. Equally, aligning the time you spend with the things you value the most is a major step in the direction of your desires.

IN BUSINESS: CURIOSITY AND CREATIVITY

"The creative process." It's a phrase we hear often. But what does it really mean, and how does it work?

Michael Gelb lays out the process beautifully in his book *Innovate Like Edison*, which he cowrote with the famous inventor's great-grandniece, Sarah Miller Caldicott.

The process includes five steps, each of which relies on applied Curiosity: preparation, generation, incubation, evaluation, and implementation. While these steps might be applied to any thought process, I encourage you to consider how you might bring them into your business as explicit parts of your processes and policies.

Preparation. It is said that a problem well formulated is half solved, meaning that the more time you spend refining your questions, the more efficient you'll be at finding the best answers. Einstein said that if he were given one hour to save the world, he would spend fifty-nine minutes framing the question and one minute trying to figure out a solution.

That's wildly different from the approach many of us take. Confronted with a problem or dire situation, we often cast about, trying various approaches—when, if we'd take a little more time in preparation, we would greatly increase the odds of getting the solution right the first time.

Edison's approach also challenges us to consider what problems might result from the ways we choose to solve the problem. As medications have their side effects, some of our business solutions may have repercussions that negate or lessen their overall value. In short, preparation is all about asking questions, sometimes all the questions we can think of.

Generation. This next step is the creative brainstorming phase, and it turns on two key factors. The first is a refusal to evaluate *every* proposed idea. In other words, while there are no wrong answers, there are *right questions*, and we should try to begin with the best questions possible. The second is being open to humorous, unexpected, and serendipitous solutions. We will explore Serendipity and its effects on luck in chapter 12, but for now consider how science can attribute many of its greatest discoveries to the unexpected products of open ideation—or what we more commonly call *brainstorming*. That being said, care is needed—after all, *Aha!* and *Ha ha!* are first cousins.

Incubation. As discussed earlier, stepping away is a key part of learning. Whether you sleep on it, drink some wine, read poetry, take a bath, watch a movie, or go for a walk, letting a thought process sit idle can be just as important as engaging it. When you reconvene, check your gut—you may have more incubation yet in store. And that's OK.

Evaluation. Once you've got what you think are one or more workable solutions, it's time to test them. That means asking questions that arise from playing three roles: angel's advocate, devil's advocate, and final arbiter. It is impossible to objectively play either of the first two roles if egos or bias enter the picture, so be on guard. As in step two (generation) the goal is asking the right questions. At no juncture is the goal to embarrass, deride, or celebrate at the expense of other roles or stakeholders.

Implementation. Only after evaluation do we get to the payoff. Implementation is the first time we depart from Curiosity, leave questions behind, and commit to following three new steps: setting a goal, making a plan, and measuring/monitoring progress.

How, in your business's practices, do team members engage in each of the five steps? And what might you do to enhance one or more of those steps for your teams?

SUMMARY

- Curiosity's Operator is additive **+**, as we can incrementally build upon it, and we can train and retrain ourselves to access greater resources, write new neural pathways (learn more about this in chapter 16), and always find new ways to add to our knowledge.

- Curiosity's Function is infinite **∞**, as our capacity to learn and search out new and differing views and perspectives is without limit. We cannot have unlimited PhDs, but we can have unlimited thirst for knowledge and a desire to understand not just how things work or what people might say, but why.

- Recognize that history's greatest minds and makers have applied lifelong Curiosity and the urge to question the status quo in leading remarkable, consequential—and yes, lucky—lives.

- Unlocking the tremendous value of Curiosity requires a dedication to the creative process like that exemplified in the work of artists and inventors like da Vinci and Edison. Perhaps Albert Einstein put it best when he said, "I have no special talent. I am only passionately curious."

- Curiosity requires that we consider things from various perspectives—whether that domain be politics, science, beliefs, or even passions—as doing so only adds to our capacity to appreciate and better understand what we might otherwise consider as truths. Had Pythagoras not argued in the sixth century BC that the world might be round instead of flat, it would not have inspired centuries of discoverers like Columbus to set sail for the New World.

- The opposite of Curiosity is hubris, and you can limit your luck by letting your ego drive things, making you overconfident, arrogant, and more prone to blind spots and failure.

- Guest Star James Donnelly reminds us of the importance of cultivating our imaginations with his recommendation to "set aside time for the sort of unplugged thinking that leads to creativity."

- This chapter's personal exercise focused on practicing Curiosity about your life choices, purpose, and goals by inviting you to draw up your own prioritized top-ten list of questions that will guide your life and comparing that to what are considered the top-ten questions of all time.

- This chapter's business-focused exercise (available in the *FFL Workbook* by download from www.formulaforluck. com) invites you to learn how to use the Edison Process to spur Curiosity by actively searching out best practices and modeling your own solutions on those of successful leaders who faced similar issues.

- Michael Gelb, in his book about Thomas Edison, shares five steps for applying Curiosity to any problem: preparation, generation, incubation, evaluation, and implementation.

  □ Preparation is all about formulating good questions. The better and more thoughtful the questions with which you begin, the more efficient your path to answers.

  □ Generation is about brainstorming, and good brainstorming requires openness to unanticipated pathways or alternatives.

- Incubation relies on stepping away from your ideas so that you can return to them with a clear head.

- Evaluation involves testing solutions with an open mind. By playing angel's advocate, devil's advocate, and final arbiter, you relinquish attachment to particular solutions in order to more objectively determine which is best.

- Implementation is about following through on the chosen idea by setting a clear goal, making a plan, and monitoring progress.

STUART'S SECRETS

- Foster Curiosity by asking your friends about their top five books. Make a list for yourself, prioritize titles, and start listening to them as audiobooks so that you can access them no matter where you are or what you're doing. (To save *more* time, listen at 1.25x speed.) Remember that it's OK to bail quickly when you start reading a book that doesn't resonate with you. You can always return to that book at another time.

- If you're curious, here are some of the books on the top of Guest Star James Donnelly's list: *Unlimited Power* by Tony Robbins, *The Happiness Advantage* by Shawn Achor, *Man's Search for Meaning* by Viktor Frankl, and anything from the Jim Collins series.

- Watch the TED channel on YouTube or Netflix. TED's catchphrase is "Ideas worth spreading." There are literally thousands of inspiring and mind-awakening topics to explore.

- Pop over to another of my websites, www.litleadership.com, and see lists of the top-ten books and TED Talks I love the most—all with links to buy/watch them.

- Carry a "book of bad ideas," a small notebook in which you write down *every* idea you have. Don't call it the "book of good ideas," or you'll limit yourself by immediately judging whether an idea is worthy. Jot down your ideas, whatever they are—and give yourself time to reflect on them later. Remember: Curiosity (like creativity) begins with an openness to everything. Find a notebook with blank pages to encourage you to draw, doodle, map, and otherwise explore.

- Use Blinkist to supercharge lifelong learning. This unique app summarizes the key takeaways from books that match your interests and areas of focus—because let's face it: you won't have time to read (or even listen to) them all.

CHAPTER 6

THE SECOND PRINCIPLE: PASSION

Love What You Do

Operator: **+ (additive)**

Function: **∞ (infinite)**

Luck Mindset Category: **Habit**

Shift: **Moving from being disengaged to being engaged, unmotivated to motivated; from introvert to extrovert, from backstage to center stage; from what we do to why we do it**

On Twitter: **#lovewhatyoudo**

> *There is no passion to be found playing small, in settling for a life that is less than the one you are capable of living.*
>
> —Nelson Mandela

INTRODUCTION

By 2025, millennials will make up 75 percent of the workforce.[9] In the past decade, a tremendous amount of research and effort has been put into answering this question: How do we prepare, recruit, retain, motivate, and engage millennial workers? One common emergent thread is that passion and meaning figure prominently in how millennials make decisions and commit and express their loyalty.

You're likely familiar with Maslow's hierarchy of needs (developed in 1943), in which our human needs are presented in a pyramidal structure, from the most basic at the bottom to the most rarefied at the top. Physiological needs (like food, shelter, sleep) ground the pyramid, followed by safety, belonging and love, esteem, and finally, self-actualization.

The challenges posed by millennial workers are that their desires tend to cluster at the very top two tiers of the pyramid—esteem (status, recognition, and respect) as well as self-actualization (becoming the most one can be). What this suggests is that in work environments, as elsewhere, millennials are more focused than other generational groups on issues of engagement. That might amount to opportunities for civic involvement, teamwork, and creativity—or aspects of work such as job flexibility, feedback and encouragement, regular promotions or job changes, or the chance to work on personal passion projects. This isn't to say that members of other generations don't also want these satisfactions; rather, millennials are not likely to pursue or stay in jobs that don't provide them.

When it comes to the work needs of millennials as a group, they're committed to feeling motivated and to seeking out learning

---

9   "Big Demands and High Expectations: The Deloitte Millennial Survey," Deloitte, January 2014, https://www2.deloitte.com/content/dam/Deloitte/global/Documents/About-Deloitte/gx-dttl-2014-millennial-survey-report.pdf.

opportunities as a means of feeling motivated. They want to love what they do, and that means activating and renewing passion for the projects on which they work.

EXPLORATION: THINK LIKE PINK

Best-selling author Dan Pink explored forty years of research to uncover some vital truths about passionate engagement; the product of his efforts is the 2009 book *Drive: The Surprising Truth about What Motivates Us.*

Pink tells us that much of what we know about motivation is mistaken, especially insofar as we tend to think about motivation in terms of carrots and sticks, or rewards and punishments.

Sure, we are motivated by extrinsic rewards like cash bonuses or raises, and yes, those sorts of rewards can be particularly useful, especially when we're assigned what Pink refers to as *algorithmic tasks*—the sort where the same activity is repeated over and over. But the true secret to high performance is not about the drive to seek reward and avoid punishment, nor is it about biological needs for connectedness. It's a third thing: our deep-seated desire to purposefully direct our own lives.

With that insight as a guide, Pink draws up a new approach to motivation built on satisfying three essential needs: one, the need for autonomy or self-determination; two, the urge to master something that matters; and three, a sense of

> But the true secret to high performance is not about the drive to seek reward and avoid punishment, nor is it about biological needs for connectedness. It's a third thing: our deep-seated desire to purposefully direct our own lives.

purpose or our yearning to be in service of something larger than ourselves. These three elements not only help develop motivation but also sustain our interest—even when it comes to activities that may have unsatisfying aspects.

These satisfactions are as sought after by adults in the workplace as they are by young children. It's possible to activate children's intrinsic motivators such that receiving a reward has little impact on their motivation. Contingent rewards—of the "do this, get that" variety—can even have a negative effect on motivation, as they require us to give up some of our autonomy. External rewards, in other words, can actually inhibit internal motivation.

This was proven in a study that tested the effects of the offer to pay people for donating blood. Instead of increasing the number of blood donors, the offer to pay decreased the usual numbers by nearly 50 percent.[10] Imagine the ways that this same tactic encumbers organizations; when they set goals based on "rewards," often that results in employees' narrowed focus, unethical behavior, increased risk-taking, decreased cooperation, and decreased intrinsic motivation.

The easy-enough solution not often enough implemented is to allow employees to uncover their own goals rather than push goals that are decreed by the company leadership. In other words, a leader's aim should be to free up employees' desires to be self-determined and connected. It turns out that drive is best liberated when we get into a state of what's called *flow*. In flow we find that challenges are just right—neither too easy nor too difficult. Because these challenges are just a notch above our current abilities, they cause us to stretch ourselves but not to the point of breaking. When we achieve at this

---

10 Magnus Johannesson, "Crowding Out in Blood Donation: Was Titmuss Right?" *Journal of the European Economic Association* 6, no. 4, February 2008, DOI: 10.1162/JEEA.2008.6.4.845: 845-863.

level, our minds are most satisfied. In flow, people live so deeply in the moment and feel so utterly in control that their sense of time and place can even melt away.

Their activity is its own reward.

GUEST STAR: JACQUELINE THROOP-ROBINSON

When she was just five weeks old, Jacqueline Throop-Robinson was adopted by good, hardworking people. Their work ethic made an indelible mark on her own approach to life. Their faith in the world combined with their unconditional love embedded a belief that anything was possible. That experience of her family, and her subsequent research on passion at work, led her to see a strong correlation between passion and luck. Passion comes from focusing on and understanding what matters most to us and then pursuing that which is most meaningful through actions that lead to a high sense of progress. When we do that, we attract opportunities we often think of as "lucky."

Jacqueline discovered her own passion early on in her first management position. She was young and leading large teams of experienced professionals. Without leadership training, she drew upon her upbringing, especially her mother's words "Just trust in people." She did, repeatedly, and discovered that she had a talent for helping people ignite and pursue their individual aspirations while also building high-performing teams through creative and

> Passion comes from focusing on and understanding what matters most to us and then pursuing that which is most meaningful through actions that lead to a high sense of progress.

productive collaboration. Her passion led her to found Break-through Learning, a leadership development consultancy, and then Spark Engagement, a global employee engagement analytics company (offering answers to the question *What is, and how do we create, passion in our work?*). Through these organizations, as much as through her writing, speaking, and coaching, Jacqueline connects people to meaning and motivates them to generate momentum and progress, even from missteps and mistakes.

Jacqueline's thirty-year career has focused on uplifting leaders and inspiring engagement at all levels of an organization. She's the best-selling author of *Fire Up Your Team: 50 Ways for Leaders to Connect, Collaborate, and Create with their Teams* (2013), and coauthor of *Success University for Women* (2015).

I caught up with Jacqueline in Bermuda in late 2019 to unpack some of her learnings about engagement and passion:

SL: There's a fantastic story of JFK touring the NASA facility in 1961. As he passes through one of the hangers, Kennedy stops and asks a janitor about his work, and the janitor replies, "It's amazing; I'm helping put a man on the moon." Tell me what you think makes a meaningful career or a meaningful job.

JTR: Any job is one in which you can find meaning if you are self-aware and know what drives meaning and progress for you. Changing jobs is rarely the answer. Some think, "I'm not passionate here so I have to leave," but often it's a lack of awareness about your engagement drivers. Once you are aware, you can look to activate them in your current environment. In my experience, 95 percent of people actually can find meaning and a sense of progress in their current work. If you don't invest in locating these engagement drivers, chances are, when you change jobs, you're not going to be any better off, especially over time.

SL: Are you saying that meaningfulness is a requirement of passion?

JTR: Meaning and progress beget passion. When you're in the midst of doing something and you feel like you're in an elevated state, like you've lost yourself in the activity, stop and ask, What is it about this activity that gives me this experience? We get focused on outcomes rather than looking for the source of meaning within our activities. One of my favorite clients had a passionately engaged mailroom clerk named Michael. His passion score was one of our highest ever. Michael knew that when he researched and found a better glue for his mailouts, he was making his job more efficient and saving money. He knew that when he designed his mail drop-off route to align with department needs, he was improving client responsiveness. He understood how his job connected to the mission of the company, and he knew he made a difference, which gave him a sense of progress. Our research shows that meaning alone, without progress, is not enough to create passion. In fact, it elicits other emotions.

> Different, often negative states of engagement arise when you don't have enough meaning or enough progress.
> — *Jacqueline Throop-Robinson*

SL: Tell me about that please.

JTR: If you have high meaning but don't experience progress, you'll feel frustration. Or if you have a high sense of progress but little meaning, you'll feel disconnected. If you have neither, then you'll feel stagnated. Different, often negative states of engagement arise when you don't have enough meaning or enough progress.

SL: If progress is so important to creating and sustaining passionate engagement, what are some of the secrets to progress?

JTR: It's critical to identify how your effort has resulted in a difference. Each day, we need to stop, reflect, and identify all the ways we achieved progress: a relationship deepened, a project closed, a task we put off finally got done, or we learned from a mistake.

It's also really important to learn how to manage a disappointment or an obstacle, as these can stop a sense of progress in its tracks! Often, people don't see a way around a roadblock, or they fixate on a disappointment rather than finding other ways forward. We need to believe that there's always another way; we might just not be seeing it yet!

Additionally, we set expectations that are often unrealistic, or we are so focused on a long-term outcome that we don't break down a big task into achievable chunks that can create momentum and provide a sense of forward movement. People can be so focused on the big vision that they miss opportunities to celebrate real, valuable achievements along the way.

SL: So celebration is also key?

JTR: Organizations notoriously do not celebrate enough. Celebration offers a double hit to passion—it reinforces what's meaningful and reinforces a sense of progress. It also enables resilience. One of the things people talk about all the time now is that they never take a breather. It's always "on to the next thing." Celebration forces you to pause, even briefly, to appreciate the accomplishment, and it helps rejuvenate you for the next challenge.

IN PRACTICE: MEANING X PROGRESS FORMULA

Jacqueline, who was our Guest Star in this chapter, kindly shared this exercise with me from the work she has done with her company Spark Engagement, and now I am passing it along to you. Answering the following questions will enable you to sustain and self-manage your passionate engagement at work.

Step 1: Name a job title/role that you have:

_____

Step 2: Ask yourself, *As they relate to this role, which statements from the list below resonate most with me?* Perhaps there are other sources of meaning or signals of progress that you would add to the list. Please do! You want these to resonate deeply with you.

TYPICAL TYPES OF SOURCES OF MEANING AND SIGNALS OF PROGRESS

Sources of Meaning	Signals of Progress
Help the business	Help people
Collaborate with others	Apply my creativity
Solve problems	Establish order
Create solutions	Increase revenue
Build my reputation	Receive feedback
Create efficiencies	Generate goodwill
Make positive changes	Execute ideas
Organize tasks	Receive recognition
Attain high standards	Hit milestones
Share knowledge	Develop self

Step 3: Please then **circle / highlight** your top three in each column. Finally, **rank those** in order of importance from one to three.

Step 4: Summarize your choices below to complete your Meaning x Progress Formula.

Sources of Meaning   **Signals of Progress**

| |
| |
| |

×

| |
| |
| |

= PASSION

Step 5: On a separate sheet of paper, list all of your job responsibilities, and dig deep for ways that your personal Sources of Meaning and Signals of Progress appear in each. Identifying your Passion drivers is half the battle. Once you know your drivers, you can take action to bring them to the forefront of your work. Soon you will find yourself in a sustainable state of passionate engagement!

IN BUSINESS: PASSION FOR SHARED VALUES

Jim Collins, in his famous book *Good to Great*, offers an analogy for thinking about how successful businesses employ people who love what they do and feel motivated and engaged. Collins likened putting together a business team to getting the right people onto the bus and into the right seats. While the adage has stuck, its business application is often not clear.

The right people are the ones who share your company's core values; they fit and thrive in your culture. To have the right people in the right seats means that each employee is operating within their area of greatest skill and passion within the organization, that the role and responsibility expected of each fits their unique abilities.

Typical problems within an organization arise when the right person is in the wrong seat, or the wrong person is in the right seat. For example, maybe you have a legacy employee in a modernized role. That might be a great person with whom you have a long-standing relationship—the "right" person—but their current role does not match their abilities. Hopefully, that person can move to another, more fitting seat. If not, they may have to leave the bus entirely. Similarly, you may have a person who's clearly capable of their role, excited by it, great in it, but they don't connect to the company's core values. You might want to believe that's a short-term or overcome-able obstacle, but in the long term, this person is likely adversely affecting your organization's culture and chipping away at everything you're trying to build. That's the "wrong" person in the right role or seat.

I was fortunate to spend a day with Gino Wickman, the founder of the Entrepreneurial Operating System (EOS), a powerful set of practices and tools that has been used by thousands of companies to help them develop successful business operating systems. I learned from Gino that we truly can't identify the right people without reflecting on our core values. Knowing what a company stands for is critical, which means having and stating a *meaningful* mission. With that mission in hand, it becomes easier to compare a person's unique abilities with the available seats on the bus.

A fantastic tool for trying to understand whether or not we've got the right people in the right seats goes by the acronym GWAB. The G stands for *getting it*, the W stands for *wanting it*, the A stands for *ability to do it*, and the B stands for *believing in it*.

Do They *Get It?*

If they get it, they will have what seems like a natural ability, an intuitive grasp, even a biochemical match with their role or seat on the bus. We know when people just *get it*. Some of that is just their wiring. "Getting it" is the piece that's nontrainable. If they don't have *it*, they most certainly should not have a seat on the bus.

Do They *Want It?*

This is the passion piece. As we learned earlier in this chapter, you can't really pay, motivate, or otherwise externally force people to want it. Do they wake up every day and genuinely want to move the company forward? If they don't, they probably have to leave.

Are They *Able to Do It?*

Does the person have the mental, emotional, and physical capacity, as well as the time and the knowledge, to do the job? This category is negotiable, since there are many trainable skills. What this usually comes down to is the person's willingness to be trained or to change some aspect of their personal lives in order to have the time to devote to the job. If they're nontrainable, get them off the bus.

If they are trainable, then remember this parable. A CEO was posed the following dilemma by the company's CFO: "Boss, we're spending a tremendous amount of money training our employees, and I'm really worried about what happens if we train all of them, and they leave." The CEO responded, "You know what? I'm even more worried about what happens if we train none of them, and they stay."

Do They *Believe in It?*

Do they believe in and care about the values, the mission, the "why"? This is different from "getting it" insofar as "believing in it" names a serious and unwavering commitment to the company's mission and goals. Almost always, believers are keepers, and companies should find ways for them to train and grow.

In sum, although Passion is a major part of what companies need from their employees, it's also not something that can be taught. Nor, as we've learned, is it something that can be ignited by external motivators like the promise of material rewards or the threat of various punishments. At best, Passion can be kindled or sustained by the specific practices that facilitate it. In other words, keeping people happy comes back to the idea of triggering people's intrinsic motivators. That's a matter of clarifying goals, providing opportunities for self-direction and meaningful choice, providing instructive and useful feedback and encouragement, and facilitating a flexible and collaborative workplace.

SUMMARY

- Passion's Operator is additive **✚**, as our ability to enjoy and benefit from it incrementally adds to our own lives and to those of others around us.

- Passion's Function is infinite **∞**, as our capacity to find meaning in what we choose to do and then to make meaningful progress toward our stated goals is not limited by anything other than our imagination and decision processes. The secret is in the choices we make—work partner, lifestyle, etc. The result of getting this right is engagement and joy.

- True Passion comes from intrinsic motivators, from activities that feed our deep-seated desire to direct our own lives in a purposeful way.

- According to Dan Pink, unlocking the tremendous value of Passion is about identifying activities that are rewarding in themselves. These activities satisfy the need for autonomy or self-determination, the urge to master something that matters, and our yearning to work in service of something larger than ourselves. Activating our own and others' Passion is driven by caring not just for what we do but also why and how we do it. According to Simon Sinek, companies that have a clear *why* give people a reason to identify with them on a deep level.

- Guest Star Jacqueline Throop-Robinson reminds us that we can find meaning and progress in any work so long as we are self-aware: "Changing jobs is rarely the answer. Some think, 'I'm not passionate here so I have to leave,' but often it's a lack of awareness about your engagement drivers. Once you are aware, you can look to activate them in your current environment."

- This chapter's personal exercise used the Spark Engagement "Meaning x Progress" worksheet to help you to identify Sources of Meaning and Signals of Progress that will help you sustain and self-manage your passionate engagement at work. This is a great tool to share with friends and family members as well.

- This chapter's business-centric exercise (available in the *FFL Workbook* by download from www.formulaforluck.com) gives you an opportunity to practice the GWAB method (gets it, wants it, able to do it, and believes in it) and focus your Curiosity on making sure you have the right team members in the right seats.

STUART'S SECRETS

- Passion is enhanced when it is in full alignment with your personal values and with others' values as well. Updating your personal values statement annually and sharing that with your partner, your team, and/or your family will give you many opportunities to look for alignment of interests and outcomes.

- An exercise called "Your Best Of" can be downloaded from my website. It helps identify commonalities from experiences in your life when you were in full "flow" and operating in your most engaged and passionate best. Use it to help identify which specific characteristics of various past life choices might offer you a roadmap to selecting from an array of future choices so that you have the highest probabilistic likelihood of reacquiring passion and flow.

- Jacqueline Throop-Robinson has a practice and business focusing entirely on engagement (Spark Engagement). If you wish an introduction to her, please do not hesitate to ask.

$E = mc^2$

$1 \, \varepsilon = c \, 005$ $9 + x_7 =$

SO_4 $2x$ $a^2 = b^2 + c^2 = 6c$

$(+ 2x)$ $\dfrac{a}{9m} = \dfrac{b}{9m}$ H^3 SO_4

$z^2 + xyz = 2$ $y = \sqrt[2]{3+1}$

$2^{-3} + 1 \, \varepsilon = c \, 005$ SO_4 $y = \sqrt[2]{3+1}$

$\left(\dfrac{2}{3}\right) = x_7$

a^2 H^3 $\dfrac{a}{m}$ $1 \, \varepsilon = c \, 005$ $1 \, \varepsilon = c \, 005$

$1 \, \varepsilon = 0.005$

$x_7 = \left(\dfrac{2}{3} \times 2x\right) a^2 = b^2 + c^2 = 2c$

$y = 2$ $N^2 \times H^3$ $\dfrac{a}{9\text{m}d} = \dfrac{b}{9\text{m}d}$

$f(3) = 2^{-3}$

NH_3 y

$x^2 - 2x \left(\dfrac{2}{3} \times 2x\right)$ SO_4

$\dfrac{a}{9\text{m}d} = \dfrac{b}{9\text{m}d}$ $f(3) = 2^{-3} + 1 \, \varepsilon = c \, 005$

$(a^3 = b^2)$ $x_7 = \left(\dfrac{2}{3} \times 2x\right) a^2 = b^2 + c$

$b^2 + c^2 = 6c$ $9 + x_7$

$\dfrac{a}{9\text{m}d} = \dfrac{b}{9}$

$\dfrac{b}{9}$ NH_3

CHAPTER 7

THE THIRD PRINCIPLE: CONNECTIVITY

Take Only What You Can Give

Operator: **✚ (additive)**

Function: **∞ (infinite)**

Luck Mindset Category: **Habit**

Shift: **Moving from building walls to building bridges, from taking to giving, from speaking to active listening**

On Twitter: **#takeonlywhatyoucangive**

The human connection is the key to personal and career success.

—Paul Meyer

INTRODUCTION

You already know my friend James Donnelly from our conversation about Curiosity in chapter 5. Whenever James and I travel anywhere together, he always reminds me to try something new, to take other paths. When we're walking, he'll say, "Oh, we walked this road already. Let's go a different way this time." When I'm with James, I'm always seeing a new place, bumping into new people, experiencing a city from a different perspective. My friend Casper Marney has an equally effective and very generous approach: every time we go to an event or are surrounded by a group of people, he finds a way to share an amazing story, generate a laugh, and always give something—be it a round of drinks, sneakily paying the bill for everyone, an introduction or a connection to someone useful, or even his signature red rose made out of a white paper napkin should the occasion call for it. Casper knows that the secret of building rapport and networks of friends is in how he gives—not how he receives. His generous approach is also a brilliant way to ensure that he will generate appreciation and build a solid foundation for future connections as a result.

James and Casper are each engineering opportunities for lucky encounters by changing the scene or playing with the criteria by which we connect with other people.

Increasing your network, your connections to other people, can directly increase your opportunities for luck. Even if that strikes you as obvious, there are yet several things you can do when building your networks to ensure that they work to your best advantage and help you become as lucky as you can be.

Albert-László Barabási has written much about the network science of communities. He argued that networks are everywhere—influencing everything from biology to the internet—and that they are fluid and fluctuating. One of Barabási's more surprising insights is that networking in the modern world is in a sense more challenging than it might have been in earlier times: "Once upon a time people were born into communities and had to find their individuality. Today people are born individuals and have to find their communities."[11] In the contemporary world, we need to focus on identifying, relating to, and integrating with a multitude of new and changing communities, using each to further expand and strengthen the fabric that connects and surrounds us.

Today, we're seeing just how much networks matter to advancing a field; whole industries rely on communities working together to arrive at insight and innovation. We may still admire da Vinci and other individual thinkers, but today, innovation isn't so much about individual great minds as much as collaboratives that can sometimes span the entire globe. Crowdsourcing/crowdfunding is one example; the phenomenon we call Wikipedia (and how it hands-down beat Microsoft Encarta) is yet another example, as are entities such as the decentralized international hacktivist group known as Anonymous.

My point is that we can't just think in terms of individual innovation anymore. And that means we have to think even more carefully about our connections to others. In addition to asking, What can I do to influence my outcome? we must also ask, What communities do I create or involve myself in to ensure that I continually increase and reinforce my bonds with others so as to have the greatest propensity to increase luck?

I encourage you to think *way* outside the box about the constitution of your networks. As an example of what I have in mind, I'll share with you a great story about how one of the large Boston-based

---

11   Albert-László Barabási, "Normcore," Network Science Communities 9, accessed November 2020, https://pdfs.semanticscholar.org/b511/685af740da12d444c875 789e629f385ac6a3.pdf?.

hospitals succeeded in solving an issue with post-op infections in their emergency rooms. To begin, they brought in post-op specialists from all over the world. But doing that only marginally improved their rate of post-op infection. It wasn't until they created a com-pletely diverse group of advisors, which they'd been encouraged to do as part of a pilot project with MIT Media Lab, that real change became possible.

> We can't just think in terms of individual innovation anymore. And that means we have to think even more carefully about our connections to others.

Among that new set of advisors was a world-class fashion designer and a Formula 1 pit boss.

The Formula 1 pit boss reviewed the operating room procedure and said, "I don't know much about bodies, but in Formula 1 when the car comes in and stops, we all jump on at the same time because the less time it's in the pit, the quicker it's back on the track. Maybe you all want to work on the body simultaneously rather than in order so that less bad stuff might get inside the body." That advice contributed significantly to procedural changes that shortened the length of the time insides of bodies were exposed during surgeries.

The fashion designer was less interested in the surgery and noted that the surgical gowns had poor quality seam finishing with loose bits of frayed hems and edges. She said to them, "I don't know anything about surgery, but I'm pretty sure that if little bits of foreign material fall inside a body, it might result in an infection. Maybe you want to invest in higher quality hemming and other finishes of the gowns." Taking her advice dramatically reduced the number of post-op infections as well.

That's the value of deep diversity of thought and personality within our networks.

EXPLORATION: THINK LIKE GERBER AND PAUGH

Is it better to have a few deep connections or a lot of superficial connections? Ideally, you want depth over breadth. I'd add here that you also want giving over taking. The most important consideration is what you can do for others, what *you* have to offer. The second is to consider what others can do for, or give to, you.

In their book *Superconnector: Stop Networking and Start Building Business Relationships that Matter*, Scott Gerber and Ryan Paugh focus on the idea of surrounding ourselves with "information brokers" at the highest level, people who are constantly learning about others and constantly making good judgments about how to connect people to one another in mutually beneficial ways. I've always called these people *rainmakers*; maybe you've got your own name for them. They're the people who form the basis upon which genuine communities are built.

Each of us has likely met someone with this amazing ability; we reach out to them with questions like *Do you know …?* or *Can you put me in touch with …?* They are high touch, high relationship people. Besides thinking of them as a Superconnector, you probably also think of them as a close friend, a confidant, part of your inner circle, someone in whom you happily invest time, visit in person, and so on. Superconnectors have three main practices:

1. **The art of selectivity.** Likely you've heard phrases like "You are the company you keep," or "Show me your ten best friends, and I'll tell you who you are." Superconnectors aren't playing numbers games when they accumulate con-

nections. They're focused on quality above all else.

2. **The power of association.** Superconnectors know the power of being anchored to people that are solid and trustworthy. Often, they are mentors or gatekeepers, adding credibility and value by effectively linking trustworthy people to other trusted people.

3. **Habitual generosity.** Our biggest and best Superconnectors are believers that what you put into the world is what you get out of it. They're not thinking about that in a quid pro quo sort of way but rather in terms of sheer generosity with their time, positivity, and energy. They know that what they put into the system will manifest back positively in some way or other.

One of the greatest Superconnectors I know from my days in Silicon Valley is Adam Rifkin, cofounder of PandaWhale, an online community of interesting people; and of 106 Miles, a meetup group of over eight thousand start-up founders and engineers. Adam was named Best Networked in Silicon Valley by *Fortune* magazine in 2011, and he swears by what's called the *Five-Minute Favor*, which is essentially anything that you can do in five minutes for the benefit of another person. Adam reminds us that it's not as quick as a ten-second favor, but it's also not something that consumes hours of our day. The favor's central aim is to give something meaningful and valuable to another person as part of building out that relationship. One of Adam's greatest bits of advice is this:

> "It is better to give than to receive. Look for opportunities to do something for the other person, such as sharing knowledge or offering an introduction to someone that person might not know but would be interested in

knowing. Do not be transactional about networking. Do not offer something because you want something in return. Instead, show a genuine interest in something you and the other person have in common." [12]

I could not agree more, and in fact I regularly describe the process of building networks like this: it's not "take as much as you can get"; it's actually "take as much as you can give." Build out your networks based on how much you're able to put into developing them rather than how much you might take from them. If you're going to do a Five-Minute Favor or follow some other guideline for building relationships, what you do should be defined first and foremost by your ability to give meaningfully, openly, and generously.

> It's not "take as much as you can get"; it's actually "take as much as you can give."

I decided I wanted to share two Guest Stars with you in this chapter. The first speaks on how we network, and the second speaks on how we connect.

GUEST STAR: JARED KLEINERT

Jared Kleinert started his first company when he was just fifteen years old. From there, he went on to work as the first intern, and then one of the first ten employees, for an enterprise SaaS company called

---

12   Adam Rifkin, "Silicon Valley's Best Networker Teaches You His Secrets" interviewed by Eric Barker, bakadesuyo.com, accessed November 2020, https://www.bakadesuyo.com/2013/02/ interview-silicon-valleys-networker-teaches-secrets-making-connections/.

15Five, which today has raised over $40 million and has over two thousand forward-thinking companies as monthly recurring clients.

Given his unique start and his early recognition that young people's power is greater today than ever before, Jared has spent years identifying and connecting the world's smartest millennials—all of them concerned with breaking down barriers and having a positive impact—to collaborate at mass scale for the sake of solving big problems.

Jared went on to become a delegate to President Obama's 2013 Global Entrepreneurship Summit in Malaysia, speak at TED@IBM the day before he turned twenty, and write multiple books including *2 Billion Under 20: How Millennials Are Breaking Down Age Barriers and Changing the World*. In his books, Jared profiles young leaders across diverse industries to collect their stories of joining together outside the bounds of traditional methods and institutions.

It's no surprise that Jared was named *USA Today*'s Most Connected Millennial.

Today, he also leads a mastermind community that brings together top entrepreneurs, CEOs, and business owners for quarterly summits. Members of this network enjoy more predictable revenue, increased profitability, and sustainable growth for their companies in addition to the lifelong friendships and long-term business partnerships they develop as part of the group. In the last three years alone, Jared has invited hundreds of diverse Superconnectors and subject matter experts to participate and share their experience and knowledge.

Jared and I sat down in Bermuda in August 2019 following a series of meetings he'd organized in advance of the first-ever Bermuda Entrepreneurship Summit in November 2019 (Jared is a cofounder of the conference).

SL: You were named the world's most connected millennial. That sounds like a numbers game, but from what I am learning about you, it's more about quality. Can you elaborate?

JK: I focus on the quality of connections over the quantity, and over time, I've been able to build up the quantity of quality relations I have. My process is that one at a time, I build relationships with very influential, very well-connected people whom I like. Then, over time, those people connect me to dozens of other very well-connected and very positive individuals.

SL: A well-regarded friend of mine, Verne Harnish, who wrote two best-selling books called *Mastering the Rockefeller Habits* and *Scaling Up*, advises to make a list of the top twenty-five people you want to meet that can help you go big. Then, put the names of those you want to reach into a Google alert so that you are notified every time they are in the news. When they pop up, follow up with them and find a way to build rapport and a relationship. Verne calls these people *gatekeepers*. You have your own approach to this, Jared, and can you share with us how you identify and nurture such relationships?

JK: Of course, I call them Superconnectors. They're people that are really well connected in their industry or in their community. Everyone in their network looks up to them and is influenced by them in a positive way. If you're talking mathematically, I think those connections hold more weight than others. The secret to building a relationship with Superconnectors is to provide value before you ask for value. When you're offering value up front, you can focus on your strengths. A lot of times it's your time or it's your effort, but over time as you develop your network, it becomes easier to offer additional resources to people that you meet. One of the easiest ways I know, for example, is to introduce them to one another.

SL: My experience is that many people seem to approach networks as a necessary means to an end and perhaps don't bring the best versions of themselves to the effort. Would you agree?

JK: Absolutely. It's about authenticity and intentionality. Be intentional about who you meet and how you deepen your relationships with them. I think it's the most authentic expression of yourself to invest time and energy into the people you care about most. This doesn't have to be time intensive, though. For every hour I invest, I really focus on how I can connect with them on an emotional level and offer value to them. How can I showcase their work to other people in my network? I like to create moments of connection where a year could go by, but we'll still feel strongly about our relationship and would be happy to help one another in the future.

SL: You refer to a term called *social proof* in some of your videos. Can you share your best practices with us please?

JK: Social proof is the transference of trust. If you come across someone in the business world who's been featured in major media outlets that you respect, and they have received awards that have meaning, other people that you admire have written testimonials about them, then you're naturally going to trust that person more. Social proof can happen in a lot of ways. It can come through an introduction via word of mouth. It can come through getting press and having a respected media outlet talk about your merits. It could be awards or other industry recognition. It's anything that another person or entity you're trying to connect with would see as a stamp of approval.

GUEST STAR 2: CHRIS TRAUB

Chris Traub is a successful entrepreneur, published author, adventure athlete, accomplished musician, yoga instructor, meditator, and transformation facilitator. He has been a pioneer in executive search and human capital advisory for the past thirty-two years. Born and raised in Connecticut, Chris received his degree in East Asian studies and cultural anthropology from Oberlin College in Ohio, but on the way to earning that degree, Chris spent a year studying Mandarin and fine arts in Taiwan, delivering forty-four-foot sailing sloops between Taiwan, Hong Kong, and the Philippines, and trekking in the Everest Himalaya. During that time, he also spent a summer in the Alaskan wilderness with the National Outdoor Leadership School program.

After graduating from college, Chris returned to Taiwan and two years later founded Strategic Executive Search, the global Asian executive search firm. While building his business, Chris became a regular member of global leadership communities including Forbes Global CEO, World Economic Forum, TED, and Summit. Through his adventures and business connections, he has developed an extraordinarily rich and broad global network.

Chris's interests are characterized by two major themes: communication and connection. The idea for his personal development program, Vortex, for example, came out of his early participation in the leadership wilderness training expedition in Alaska. From that experience, he learned the joys of being fully present, playful, and achieving a state of flow in nature. Vortex features and develops these abilities in its participants, drawing from both Western and Eastern philosophical and leadership principles. Its central aims are to nurture a close-knit community and create a shared transformational space where leaders can grow together and level up both personally and professionally.

Chris and I met through helping evolve a global youth hackathon and advising a number of start-ups and ventures. He's without a doubt the best communicator I have ever met in terms of building deep and meaningful connections.

SL: What are the three things that you do the first time you're meeting someone new?

CT: One is offer a warm, sincere, clean-energy greeting. Two is establish context. Three is extend an invitation in a warm but genuine way that is noncommittal. Rather than seeking a meeting, you're extending an offer. I might say, "I came across your profile." (*I wasn't hunting you.*) "You're clearly doing cool and interesting things." (*Everybody likes to feel validated, but they don't want to feel fanboyed.*) "I believe we have common interests and common friends." (*We may have a friend we know in common. If not, I know some cool people, and it would be great to connect you if you'd like.*)

I want to make my intention clear. I'm not forceful, because I believe there's common interest or common friends and because I'm appreciating the context in which we've met.

SL: Basically, what you're saying is "We might be in the same tribe"?

CT: Exactly. It's a much more genuine, authentic, and intentional approach than any other because it's not focused on a specific outcome. I am seeking a long-term connect regardless of whether or not there are transactions. I'm basically saying, "Let's connect and see if there is something there."

SL: What about the times when you are there to transact and possibly others are as well?

CT: I call that working with the filters in the system. If I'm fundraising, and I am with one thousand potential investors at an investment conference, then this particular group of investors has a filter that aligns with what I'm doing. If what I'm doing is front and center and square with those who are there, and they're oriented toward that, then we can all relax and hang out and just be vibrant. When you become transactional, people feel and smell your hunger.

SL: And when you want to establish a true lasting connection, what is your process?

CT: It is a continuum of conscious and subconscious awareness meets intention meets energetics—the eyes, the voice, body positioning, all of that, but particularly the eyes. I hold eye contact with everybody, and operate with a layer of presence, availability, and compassion. I'm present to you and nonjudgmental, unconditional, and compassionate. I'm holding space and welcoming you in without inserting an agenda or judging you. This gives the people I'm with the opportunity to be gifted with what people crave most, which is being seen, heard, and respected. That gives us both joy, too, because it's a moment when the heart is not alone.

IN BUSINESS: GROWING DIVERSE NETWORKS

Superconnectors, rare as they may be, have other counterparts in business that can help tremendously when it comes to expanding one's networks. We're going to look briefly at four of those counterparts here: (1) *influencers*, (2) *social proofs*, (3) *advisory boards*, and (4) what I call *LIT Loops*™.

- **Influencers**. Influencers are a social media phenomenon with an ability to generate a broader list of connections for a business. Influencers are trusted by a large number of often quite loyal social media followers; their endorsement of your business or product can shape the opinions of their networks in your favor. A decade or two ago, influencer marketing was still relatively little known, but today given the success of YouTube and Instagram, it's mainstream business. One should, of course, choose influencers wisely. Take the recent Fyre Festival in the Bahamas, for which influencer marketing was used to build the brand for a VIP music festival. The Fyre Festival turned out to be a fraud and a massive disaster that hurt both the brand and the influencers who got involved.

Influencer marketing has become an established business. It's projected to be a $15 billion industry by 2022, and that means that the returns on investment are hard to ignore.[13] In fact, the current ROI for influencer marketing is eleven times higher than for digital media alone: brands earn $2 for every $1 spent on ad words, compared to $11.69 for every $1 in influencer marketing.[14]

- **Social proofs**. Social proofing is a process that entails the transfer of trust. We look to certain others around us assuming they know more than we do, and we trust their advice and recommendations. Think about the authority we grant to experts, product users, even the wisdom of crowds. Having relevant social proofs encourages people to have confidence in your brand; if you're trusted already by experts, pundits, award winners, or people you admire and want to be associated with,

13 Audrey Schomer, "Influencer Marketing: State of the social media influencer market in 2020," *Business Insider*, December 17, 2019, https://www.businessinsider.com/influencer-marketing-report.

14 "Influencer Marketing Effectiveness: Key Survey Finds, Facts & Figures," mediakix.com, accessed November 2020, https://mediakix.com/blog/influencer-marketing-effectiveness/#gs.8tczun.

why shouldn't others trust you too? Social proofing can happen through word of mouth, but it can also come through actively going after press and respected media outlets and working with them to emphasize industry recognition, product merits, and other qualities that might attract third-party stamps of approval.

One of the great ways to engage in social proofing is to be considered the authority on a subject. From personal experience, I can say that the moment I became a TED fellow and TED speaker, I was ushered into a different league. The general consensus among people, magazines, and media outlets was "Oh, if you're good enough for TED, you're probably good enough for us." Another great way you can be recognized as an authority on a subject is to write the book on it. From a network-building perspective, your name will carry more weight, and you'll probably find yourself on other people's short lists more often than not.

- **Advisory boards**. Putting together just the right group of people on an advisory board can boost your business dramatically. One strategy is to surround yourself with a who's-who list of referenced brand names in the market as well as people representing a diverse background of skill sets, whether that's security, technology, politics, marketing, sales, or whatever else. Three things are likely to result from this effort: One, you'll be well advised because you've made yourself the least intelligent person in the room whenever you have a board meeting. Two, you'll have a better reputation by association. When people take a look at the company and see all the amazing names associated with your business, they'll likely have more interest and more faith in you. Third, you'll have serious diversity of input by age, gender, background, and ethnicity.

To be sure that you'll stay focused on the value of what you have to give to your networks and not simply what you might take from them, I'll remind you of an adage that I think is particularly relevant to assembling advisory boards: "Ask for money, get advice; ask for advice, get money twice." Young start-ups might find it impossible to raise money, but seeking advice—and genuinely looking to build and share knowledge with advisors—is often the fulcrum point at which the scales tip in their favor. I've seen it happen time and time again that a young company offering to share its learnings and soliciting only advice from potential investors will be met with the response "How interesting! Can I invest in your company?"

- **LIT Loops**. You may have heard these called Needs and Leads sessions; I call them LIT Loops—after my coaching and consultancy company LIT Leadership. LIT stands for Luck, Innovation, and Thought Leadership. In a Lit Loop, a facilitator gathers a group of people into a circle, and everyone gets to make one ask (identify one need); then everyone else in the group in turn is invited to generate their absolute best response to that need (a lead). Say someone's got an ACL injury and is looking for the best knee surgeon. Responses might begin like this: "Oh, I know this surgeon …" "My friend had ACL surgery …" "A great hospital for that procedure …" "I read a book that gives great advice…" Once everyone has responded and the loop is closed, the person who made the ask recognizes each and every lead, and the group builds accountability pairs for follow-up; then the pairs then work together to determine the best answer or solution. Then it's on to the next person.

You can conduct LIT Loops within subsets of expertise (say everyone in the group is an event planner) as much as among groups with more diverse skills and interests. LIT Loops are amazing ways for groups or communities to build off each other's knowledge and connections and solve their own problems. By learning the problems raised by others, individuals can find answers to questions that they didn't think they had or had forgotten to ask. LIT Loops are a powerful technique for building networks of solutions and creating concentric circles of luck.

In addition to the strategies I've mentioned here, there's an overarching analogy worth keeping in mind when it comes to enhancing networks and Connectivity: businesses are built much like sports teams. You've probably heard that already when it comes to talking about coaches putting team members in a position to perform, and teams needing a clear playbook of rules and procedures and a diversity of playing strengths. But the part of the analogy that speaks most to our insights in this chapter, especially when it comes to millennial and younger generations, is this: the players on sports teams come in for contracted periods of time. There's a benefit to having employees move on after a contracted period of time. They might share with their networks how amazing a few years at your company was for their development. Acknowledging shorter time spans up front and offering employees an amazing experience after which you'll help them find their next jobs is fast becoming a new way of promoting employees and expanding business networks in the process.

IN PRACTICE: WORK ON GROWING AND TRIMMING YOUR SUPERCONNECTOR LIST

- **Step 1: Identify Your Current Superconnectors**

  Write the names of **five** people that you think are the most- and best-connected people you currently know.

- **Step 2: Grow Your Superconnector List**

  Next, write the names of **twenty-five** companies or individuals you would like to connect to; but for any that are companies, you will then have to find the individual at that company with potentially the greatest benefit for you to connect with.

- **Step 3: Trim Your Superconnector List**

  Remember the art of selectivity and the importance of curating your networks. Be mindful about others' limitations as well as your own ability to give meaningfully to relationships. **Strike through the names of five of the thirty** total names that are unrealistic, unreliable, or least likely to result in value.

- **Step 4: Prioritize Your Superconnector List**

  Now **identify and rank the top ten** that you will commit to meaningfully reach out to in the next week. Think of what you can add/give to offer value (i.e., take only as much as you can give). Set a deadline and a calendar reminder, and get cracking!

5 SUPERCONNECTORS YOU ALREADY KNOW	1	2
3	4	5

25 NEW SUPERCONNECTORS YOU WOULD LIKE TO KNOW		6
7	8	9
10	11	12
13	14	15
16	17	18
19	20	21
22	23	24
25	26	27
28	29	30

NEW PRIORITIZED LIST OF YOUR TOP 10 SUPERCONNECTORS		1
2	3	4
5	6	7
8	9	10

IN PRACTICE: ESTABLISH AND
EXPAND YOUR SOCIAL PROOFS

We learned that social proofing is a process that entails the transference of trust. List your current social proofs and note opportunities for improvement or gaps where you need to invest energy to build more proofs.

TYPE OF SOCIAL PROOF		DESCRIPTION
Expert's Stamp of Approval	Description	An industry thought leader or influencer approves of your product via blogging, social media, or being quoted as a product user.
	Your Examples	
Celebrity Endorsement	Description	A celebrity uses your product and promotes it on social media or in public (especially meaningful if the endorsement is unpaid).
	Your Examples	
User Testimonials	Description	A vote of confidence in your product's value, preferably from well-respected websites indicating positive feedback from actual users.
	Your Examples	
Business Credentials	Description	Information about how many customers you have, which well-known businesses are your customers, or the awards and certifications you have received.
	Your Examples	
Earned Media	Description	Published positive reporting about your brand that builds awareness and shows your business is worth paying attention to.
	Your Examples	
Social Media Shares	Description	Positive shares of your content on social networks that encourage people to invest in your product or service.
	Your Examples	

Now identify and highlight the top three categories that you believe will add the most value over the next six to twelve months and to which you will commit to meaningfully focus on developing further. Complete the below summary table and write down a SMART goal for each category; be specific in what you will do.

		GOAL 1	GOAL 2	GOAL 3
SPECIFIC	Exactly what is it you want to achieve? A good goal statement explains the what, why, who, where, and when of a goal.			
MEASURABLE	To track progress and measure the result of your goal (i.e., how much or how many). How will you know when you have achieved your goal?			
ACHIEVABLE	Your goal must be relevant and realistic. Is your goal achievable in the time and budget allocated? (Insert confidence percentage here.)			
RELEVANT	Your goal should be a stretch but realistic. Make sure the actions you need to take to achieve your goal are things within your control.			
TIME-BOUND	Goals must have a deadline as well as some short-term milestones and critical dates along the way to help you measure progress.			

SUMMARY

- Connectivity's Operator is additive ✚, which means that growing networks not only adds to our ability to generate luck and thus results in a larger coefficient of luck but it also does so by strengthening bonds. The focus here is on a systematic and continual process of widening and honing our networks.

- Connectivity's Function is infinite ∞, meaning that we are always able to generate new connections. That said, we must ardently remember that it is not just a numbers game and that while we are building our networks, we also need to be trimming and focusing on quality. Remember that the limit on the number of connections is defined by how much we can give into the system, not take from it.

- Superconnectors are people with networks that are both broad and deep. They establish and sustain these networks by three primary means:

  1. *The art of selectivity*. Superconnectors focus on quality above all else.

  2. *The power of association*. Superconnectors know that the power of a network is reflected in the trust that's possible within it.

  3. *Habitual generosity*. Superconnectors are generous with their time and energy, knowing that what they put into the system will manifest back positively.

- When building out your networks, remember to "take only as much as you can *give*."

- Guest Star Jared Kleinert emphasizes intentionality and

authenticity in building out a network: "Be intentional about who you meet and how you deepen your relationships with them."

- Guest Star Chris Traub reminds us of the importance of connecting with others in the absence of any focus on a specific outcome: "I am seeking a long-term connect regardless of whether or not there are transactions. I'm basically saying, 'Let's connect and see if there is something there.'"

- Tap into the power of *influencers, social proofs, advisory boards,* and *LIT Loops.*

  □ *Influencers* can deliver loyal followers to your brand through trust built on social media platforms.

  □ *Social proofs* are those authoritative third-party stamps of approval that generate trust in your brand.

  □ *Advisory boards* should be composed of a who's-who list of referenced brand names in the market as well as people representing diverse skill sets and perspectives.

  □ *LIT Loops* offer the opportunity for individuals to build off each other's knowledge and connections to solve their own problems.

- This chapter's personal exercise uses a Superconnector identification tool inspired by Verne Harnish to encourage you to identify, prioritize, and focus your energy on your top twenty-five most important Connectivity relationships and commit to meaningfully reaching out to those people on a regular basis.

- This chapter's business-focused exercise encourages you

to identify and expand your social proofs by identifying any areas you are missing or not sufficiently focusing on, and then writing down an accountability schedule (using SMART goals) to measurably improve your ability to transfer trust and build a stronger brand. (These and other exercises are available in the *FFL Workbook* by download from www.formulaforluck.com.)

STUART'S SECRETS

- For a lesson on how *not* to build and leverage connections, check out the documentary *Fyre: The Greatest Party That Never Happened*.

- Verne Harnish's book *Scaling Up: How a Few Companies Make It ... and Why the Rest Don't* offers insight into the importance of people to growing your business.

- Build a winning culture in your business with Jack Daly's book *Hyper Sales Growth*.

- Check out *USA Today's* Most Connected Millennial Jared Kleinert's book *3 Billion Under 30: How Millennials Continue Redefining Success, Breaking Barriers, and Changing the World*.

- Try out my LIT Loops worksheet at www.litleadership.com.

CHAPTER 8

THE FOURTH PRINCIPLE: POSITIVITY

Think Optimistically about Outcomes

Operator: **+ (additive)**

Function: **∞ (infinite)**

Luck Mindset Category: **Habit**

Shift: **Moving from pessimist to optimist, from no to yes, from half empty to half full**

On Twitter: **#powerofpositive**

> *Life is a hell of a lot more fun if you say yes rather than no.*
>
> —Richard Branson

INTRODUCTION

Sometimes we choose our circumstances, and other times the circumstances choose us. This was no truer than in May 2011 when one of my closest friends, Rob DeVries, heard the words no one wants to hear: "You have stage four cancer, and the success rate is less than 25 percent." The diagnosis was followed by two months of aggressive chemo and six weeks of radiation. While all of us who were part of his support system quietly worried about the worst, Rob assured himself and us of a different reality. He called the cancer "an alien that does not belong" and said that he would stop at nothing to defend his body because, as he put it, "I have never doubted, not once, that I will prevail."

I called Rob as I was writing this chapter and asked him to reflect on his journey. He said, "Stuart, two things were responsible for my survival. I took the initiative to invest in my fitness, and I was lucky to be in some of the best shape of my life when cancer came knocking. This and my genetics were about a third of my success. I believe my mindset and attitude were responsible for the rest." It is incredible to note that out of his cohort of thirty-six such patients under the care of the same doctor, Rob is the only person still alive today. And he's not merely alive: for the past five years we have skied fifty-degree slopes from Zermatt to Vail with me (an ex–ski racer) still chasing Rob down some crazy lines. Just recently, I remember Rob disappearing over the lip and carving down the almost vertical face of Corbet's Couloir in Jackson Hole—ranked one of the eight most difficult ski runs on the planet—whooping and hollering as he cut tracks through the powder. Just attempting that alone requires no small amount of Positivity, but watching him do it after winning a seven-year fight against "the alien" is one of my happiest memories of all time.

Optimists have a way of dealing with change that sets them apart from others. First, optimists are very clear about their goals, and they're confident that they will accomplish them either sooner or later. They keep their minds focused on what they want and keep looking for different ways to get it. Second, optimists know to look for what's good or beneficial in *any* situation. Even when things go wrong or they face difficulties or problems, they'll find, talk about, and amplify the good rather than the negative.

How we see and deal with the challenges around us is a very important part of our overall happiness, as well as our ability to generate luck. Quite simply, lucky people are positive, optimistic, and expect good things to happen. They follow through on what they've started, guided by the belief that they're going to succeed.

Thankfully, optimism is a learnable quality. One of the best ways to shift your mindset from pessimism to optimism is by following the example of people you consider to be truly, and admirably, optimistic. If you do and say what happy people with positive attitudes do and say, you can come to share their optimism—to feel the same way they do, experience what they experience, and get the same results they get.

Dan Harris, ABC *Nightline* coanchor and *Good Morning America* weekend star, is a great example of learning to be positive.

> How we see and deal with the challenges around us is a very important part of our overall happiness, as well as our ability to generate luck.

Dan had a panic attack on live TV during one of his morning segments. For Dan, that attack was a clear sign that he needed to change something about his overall approach to living. He decided to learn how meditation could help, especially when it came to quieting the incessant and anxious voice in his head. The product of his learning was the award-winning book *10% Happier*.

Dan's biggest insight is that changing one's thoughts to become more positive is an iterative and incremental process but worth the effort in the long run. If we stick with a practice long enough, we will see positive change.

EXPLORATION: THINK LIKE NAPOLEON HILL

Maybe you're already familiar with Napoleon Hill's 1937 book *Think and Grow Rich*. That book has sold over fifteen million copies and is easily the most famous business success book of all time.

Hill wrote about using the power of thought to manifest desired outcomes. The process by which thoughts become reality was something Hill called *transmutation*. One easy way to understand his idea is to consider the placebo effect. Picture a scientific study in which all the patients believe that they are receiving medication that may help or cure their illness. Some people are given actual medication, and other people are given pseudomedication, like a sugar pill with no active ingredients. The placebo effect happens when some of the people who were given pseudomedication experience the same health benefits as those who took the actual medication. Because they *believed* that they were taking actual medication, they became healthier.

Now, I'm not saying that if we all believe that we will become healthy, we all will become healthy. But I'd ask you to consider the opposite point of view and its potential placebo effects. If you believe you're going to fail or if you believe you cannot do or achieve something you've set out to do, more often than not you actually will fail at it just because you believed that you would.

Therein lies the value of taking control of our thoughts, especially when it comes to shifting them toward Positivity.

We don't even have to think in terms of big life goals in order to see the Power of Positivity in action. Think about what happens every January, when New Year's resolutions bring a lot of people to the gym. Optimistic people often will stay with a new gym program and work out for the remainder of the year, becoming fit and happy. Those that are pessimistic, who don't believe that they're going to see a change, will not be comfortable with the incremental pace of change and are likely to fulfill their own prophecy of not becoming healthy. More likely than not, they'll stop going to the gym after a handful of weeks or months.

Positive people aren't always lucky, but they handle adversity differently than others. The one thing they all do is actively turn their bad luck into good luck. The most important insight that positive people offer is that when things get tough, there are always two options. We can either fold our tents and go home, or we can keep on going. Positive people keep going. They're resilient under pressure and very adaptable to whatever comes their way. Winston Churchill summed it up nicely: "The pessimist sees difficulty in every opportunity, and the optimist sees opportunity in every difficulty." In other words, optimists seek out the valuable lesson in every setback or reversal, asking themselves, What can I learn from this to take with me on my journey?

> "The pessimist sees difficulty in every opportunity, and the optimist sees opportunity in every difficulty."
> —*Winston Churchill*

GUEST STAR: TRAVIS ROY

Travis Roy grew up in Maine and played hockey all the time at the local ice arena his father managed. At age fifteen, he wrote down his dream goals, the first of which was to play Division I college hockey for Boston University (then the top program in the country). To get to BU, Travis determined that he would need to maintain a B average and score over 1,000 on his SATs. He told himself that he could achieve these things, and he did.

Travis's perseverance came to a culmination at a BU/North Dakota game on October 20, 1995. When his coach tapped Travis to enter the game, he knew this was the moment he had been waiting for his whole life, the moment he had always dreamed about.

After the initial face-off at center ice, the puck got shot into the offensive zone. A North Dakota player attempted to get the puck up against the boards, and Travis followed through to check his opponent. When the opposing player attempted to avoid the check, Travis lost his balance and fell headfirst into the dasher boards.

As he lay on the ice unable to move, Travis asked for someone to get his father from the stands and bring him down on the ice.

"Dad, I made it," he told his father as he lay motionless.

Travis's college hockey career lasted only eleven seconds. He had broken his fourth and fifth vertebrae and would spend the remainder of his life as a quadriplegic. He credits his core belief in a positive attitude to everything that occurred prior to and since that fateful night and has dedicated his life to building and supporting the Travis Roy Foundation, which helps to enhance the lives of individuals living with spinal cord injuries.

I caught up with Travis in Boston in September 2019 at Warrior Ice Arena, where he was leading a fundraiser for his foundation. We had an incredible conversation about the power of Positivity and its transformative influence in his life.

SL: It's amazing how people can view incidents as either lucky or unlucky. Where does your strength come from?

TR: First, there's energy. There is clear energy that I feel within myself—and I sense it very quickly in others—that accompanies a positive attitude. That energy exudes confidence. It is something that people gravitate to, and when I communicate that energy, there seems to be this echo back. And that echo gets enormously magnified in my life as a whole. I feel like I attract a lot of positives from people. I am an optimist. I embrace that positive energy, and I can even see the opportunities in horrible situations. Also, I have a natural instinct to put myself around people that give off similar energy.

SL: What words of advice would you give people to start developing their Positivity?

TR: It starts with the way you frame or look at every situation. You can either make decisions based on how you're going to make this challenge, this obstacle, this unfortunate event better, or you can spend the time just thinking how bad you have it. You've got to be aware of that moment of decision. Even that little bit of wallowing and that little bit of self-pity is the opposite of a positive attitude. For me it's become reactive, almost instinctive, in that I think, "No, that's not going to get me anywhere. How am I going to mold this outcome so that it becomes favorable to me and those around me?"

SL: And I guess to your point, on that pivotal night, you could've said, "Oh my God, worst thing ever." But definitely worse would have been if you fell down the stairs on the way to the hockey stadium and never got on the ice, right?

TR: Exactly. Be grateful about how your situation could have been a hell of a lot worse, and exhibit gratitude in that moment.

Literally you're putting gasoline, you're fueling and feeding the positive piece of it. And you just say, "OK, if I go the other way with this, all 'woe is me,' that feeds into pessimism, that feeds into blame." Because sometimes you choose your circumstances, and other times the circumstances choose you. It's what we do in the face of challenges that defines who we are. It's that simple. There are opportunities to move forward if you choose to see them, and there are opportunities to just sit there the rest of your life in that negativity and with that energy, and let it compound and bring on total misery. It's a choice, your choice.

SL: So when it comes to this power to choose, is it reflexive like muscle memory, or is it actually instinctive?

TR: I like the way you differentiate those words. I think it's more reflexive. I think it does become muscle memory. It's something that you slowly and with practice train yourself to do until it becomes more reflexive.

SL: What experiences would you bring to bear to help people bring the best version of themselves a little bit more center stage?

TR: My primary insight for people, whether you are recently paralyzed or dealing with your own challenge, is to recognize that in that moment things may be difficult, but from then on it's your responsibility to frame how you are going to respond. It's one decision or choice at a time. Don't let your limitations get in the way or focus too much on things that didn't go right. Once you realize, "Wait, this fear that I have, this negative perception I've created that there is no way out, it's generally false; it doesn't have to be this way," there is always an opportunity to frame your choices and their outcomes in a positive way.

IN PRACTICE: THE POWER OF POSITIVITY

This exercise is based on a practice in which my son Max and I engage every morning. For us, practicing awareness and gratitude sets us off on our day full of energy and optimism.

- What are you grateful for? **Write down five things** that make you extremely grateful and bring you immense happiness.

- Then consider the why. Practicing some curiosity here will help us focus on the root of why we are grateful.

- Then, write down some positive ways in which it makes you feel (be sure to use descriptive/feeling words in this column).

	WHAT AM I GRATEFUL FOR?	WHY IS THIS IMPORTANT TO ME?	HOW DOES IT MAKE ME FEEL?
1			
2			
3			
4			
5			

- Once you've done that, step away from wherever it is that you composed your list; if you can, find an outdoor area to take in some fresh air and pause in nature—perhaps on a park bench or in some other quiet place. From that spot, take one minute to reflect on each of the things on your list, replaying as many details as you are able. For example, if one of your things is a place or an event, what did it feel, smell, or taste like? Which emotions were most present? Emerge yourself briefly in those joys one by one. Once you've finished, notice the release of endorphins or "happy hormones," and take that good feeling with you throughout the rest of your day.

- Keep a gratitude diary in which you do this exercise regularly. The best time is at the end of the day and right before bed. You need only find three small things each day to be grateful for. Science shows that doing so has immense benefits for the quality of your sleep and the enjoyment of your dreams.

IN BUSINESS: POSITIVITY AND IMPROV

There's a well-known improv technique called "Yes, and …" Imagine two performers onstage. Each one needs to be carefully attuned to the words and gestures of the other so that they can take a scene that's developing in real time to a place of entertainment, learning, or both. One actor begins with a line or a gesture, and the other accepts the premise as true (no matter how absurdly funny) and adds to it, seeing what develops from there. "Yes" is about being receptive to and affirming the other person's ideas. "And" is about expanding on the proposed story line, heightening it, taking it further, being open to seeing where it goes.

Now contrast that technique with the traditional way in which a business or work environment typically functions. Consider how frequently ideas presented by team members are greeted with "no, because" or sometimes "yes, but" when presented to management. Consider, too, that "yes, but" is simply another form of "no, because" insofar as it eliminates the value of new ideas and innovation before they even have the time to truly be considered.

Applying the "Yes, and …" technique can make us better communicators and can be particularly helpful when it comes to group brainstorming or other moments that require us to share ideas freely. We needn't act on every idea that comes up, but we should try to hear every idea and to entertain what's best in each. Imagine if we all went into our meetings welcoming others' contributions instead of shutting down specific ideas or lines of thought. Or imagine if our own willingness to share ideas was welcomed by our colleagues! The most important personal learning that comes from creating a culture of improvisation is that it allows us to suspend our judgments and be present in the moment. Work cultures that embrace a "Yes, and …" approach are usually more inventive, solve problems more quickly, and have high levels of engagement. "Yes, and …" is ground zero for creativity and innovation.

In a corporate environment, "Yes, and …" can take effort to put in practice; it requires tremendous trust in working with others, and the recognition that trust is always conditional. When we trust, we relinquish some control. Cultivating a "yes" culture requires company leadership to model receptivity and Positivity. In a "yes" culture, leaders of all levels are committed to building on people's individual contributions and acknowledging their worth.

"Yes, and …" can be utilized in four key scenarios at work:

1. *Coaching and feedback.* Instead of interrogating, telling, or criticizing, those who are effective coaches try to understand, learn, and explore in conversations. They ask probing questions; they try to consider new approaches. They help their mentees discover what will work well for them and for the company overall.

2. *Brainstorming and ideation.* Instead of a culture in which people value their own ideas most or put their effort into being right or best, effective brainstorming relies on creating a safe environment in which people can say what comes into their heads without worrying about being brilliant or best.

3. *Problem-solving and conflict resolution.* When working toward compromise or win-win solutions, instead of assuming that one person must be right and another wrong, embrace differences of opinion and perspective. Trying to look at the same situation from different points of view encourages understanding, compassion, and cooperation.

4. *Overcoming objections.* Instead of "Yes, *but* …," saying "Yes, and …" to objections is a means of validating what is best

in them and sets you up to work together to meet or reduce the needs they address.

Practicing "Yes, and ..." is like practicing meditation and mindfulness insofar as both are incremental processes yielding incremental but potentially tremendously valuable gains. Both processes are focused on the slow build, brick by brick, of new habits and ideas, new ways of seeing what's right in front of us every day.

SUMMARY

- Positivity's Operator is additive **+**, as the power of optimism clearly transfers to others around you. As the saying goes, "Your attitude determines your altitude."

- Positivity's Function is infinite **∞**, as there are no real limits on how much optimism and energy can be harnessed in order to maintain and grow momentum toward any goal you put your mind to. It's not about the size of the glass or the amount of water in it; it's about how quickly you pour the water in and how thirsty you are.

- Positivity begins with the recognition that it is possible to train one's mind to approach every situation with an eye to its good or beneficial—even lucky—outcomes.

- Unlocking the tremendous value of Positivity requires a capacity to recognize and accept incremental change. True Positivity is the product of constant and rigorous practice.

- Guest Star Travis Roy encourages us to think about how we frame our experiences and take responsibility for ourselves: "There is always an opportunity to frame your choices and their outcomes in a positive way."

- "Yes, and ..." is a well-known approach in improvisational theater that can help generate Positivity in personal life and in the workplace. With *yes* we affirm others' ideas. With *and* we run with those ideas, expand on them, stay open to seeing where they lead.

  - In coaching and feedback, "Yes, and ..." makes for joint learning and exploration of solutions.

- In brainstorming and ideation, "Yes, and ..." creates safe space for risk-taking and sharing ideas that may be not yet fully formed.

- In problem-solving and conflict resolution, "Yes, and ..." opens us up to consideration of different points of view.

- In overcoming objections, "Yes, and ..." acknowledges concerns and moves them toward resolution and partnership.

- This chapter's personal exercise on the Power of Positivity encourages you to practice awareness and gratitude and to identify the root feelings and *why* statements behind what you are most thankful for. This is a fabulous and simple tool to share with friends, as it helps with positively beginning your day and sleeping better at night.

- This chapter's business-centric exercise (available in the *FFL Workbook* by download from www.formulaforluck. com) invites you to be inspired by the genius of Second City Improv to practice using the "Yes, and ..." technique. At work, this technique can improve communication and cultivate a culture in which company leadership models both receptivity and Positivity.

STUART'S SECRETS

- If you struggle to see the positive or if it's your tendency to see the glass as half empty, look instead for "neutral." Don't think about having to go all the way to positive, but at least try to shift your thinking away from negativity and toward neutrality.

- Since the best ideas usually come from within the company rather than from external consultancies, experiment with a default "yes" response for a while. You'll likely increase engagement and generate great new ideas.

- Read and apply the useful and learnable hacks in Dan Harris's book *10% Happier: How I Tamed the Voice in My Head, Reduced Stress without Losing My Edge, and Found Self-Help That Actually Works—A True Story*.

- Consider applying the seven principles in Shawn Anchor's *The Happiness Advantage: The Seven Principles That Fuel Success and Performance at Work*.

CHAPTER 9

THE FIFTH PRINCIPLE: EMPATHY

Empathy Matters

Operator: **+ (additive)**

Function: **∞ (infinite)**

Luck Mindset Category: **Habit**

Shift: **Moving from selfish to selfless, from thinking to feeling, from jealous of others to in service of others**

On Twitter: **#empathymatters**

> *People don't care how much you know until*
> *they know how much you care.*

> —Theodore Roosevelt

INTRODUCTION

Not that long ago, I was outbound on Icelandair, flying from New York to London via a connection at Reykjavík, Iceland's main airport. Unfortunately, stormy weather and high winds kept us from landing in Reykjavík, and we circled that airport for over two hours. Our plane eventually detoured and landed, along with about four others, in a little airport called Akureyri in northern Iceland.

After about five hours on the ground, with the little airport getting low on supplies and people getting grumpy, we finally flew out. We arrived in Reykjavík only to discover we were among twelve planes that had come in from nearby airports, all of us recently disembarked after the wind subsided.

Half the people were going on to other places, such that there were about nine hundred people that needed a seat on a plane. All of us had missed our connecting flights, and all of us were about eight or nine hours past the time originally set for our arrival.

As you might imagine, there was a premium on available seats. There were also just a few gate agents still working at three o'clock in the morning to reseat us.

I waited in line with my number; the scene unfolding in front of me involved a lot of very angry, loud, and aggressive people making demands of all kinds, including behind me a young anxious family with three very overtired little kids. The poor gate agents were getting more and more tired, more and more frantic. One of them was clearly losing her voice.

When I stepped away to get myself some water, I also bought a bottle of water for the agent at the head of my line who was now struggling to talk. When it was my turn next to approach the ticket counter, I first turned to the family behind me with the three young kids:

"Hang on a second," I said to them. "Why don't you go ahead of me?" They did and thanked me.

When it was my turn again, I gave the agent the bottle of water, and she croaked out a thank-you. "No worries," I responded, "I can only imagine the day you've had. You have a lot of very needy people here, and I'm just traveling for business—not a big deal. Happy to put my name in line wherever you can."

"Thank you, Mr. Lacey" was her reply.

Not less than thirty minutes later, they called the next flight to London. The few people who had gone off to restaurants or elsewhere started losing their standby seats. At one point, the same croaky-voiced agent walked right over to me with a ticket and said, "Mr. Lacey, please get in the line for this flight."

As I was walking onto the plane, the same agent was there helping people as they entered. She stopped me: "Oh, Mr. Lacey, I think I've got a problem with your ticket." I tried not to let my face drop. She then smiled. "We've just moved you into business class."

"That's very kind of you" was my reply. Just after I took my seat, the family with the three kids walked past. The father paused at my seat.

"You're the gentleman that let us in front of you at the gate."

"Yes sir."

"Listen, here's my card. I own the largest ticketing agency for Broadway shows in London, and if you ever need a ticket, just call me. I'll get you set up."

I'm guessing that arguing and yelling and screaming probably didn't help many of the people trying to find new flights. Some might call me lucky to have found myself sitting on the next flight in business class with the promise of tickets to a London show. But all I did was behave empathetically, with some care for the experiences of other people around me.

EXPLORATION: THINK LIKE BELINDA PARMAR

Empathy is feeling that you understand and perhaps even share another person's experiences or emotions. It's your capacity to put yourself in someone else's shoes. Empathy stems from understanding the emotional rationale as much as the logical rationale driving other people's decisions.

Increasingly, business leaders are thinking about how to cultivate the skills (both "soft" and "hard") that people need in order to be successful in the world. In a *Harvard Business Review* article, Belinda Parmar—founder and CEO of the Empathy Business—wrote, "I believe that empathy should be embedded into the entire organization." She also argued that there's nothing "soft" about empathy: "It's a hard skill that should be required from the boardroom to the shop floor."[15]

What I find most interesting about Parmar's argument is that it stands in stark contrast to more traditional tenets of business and life success. We've likely all learned at some point about the need to take a cutthroat approach to competition and the need to climb over others on our way to the top. To the contrary, Parmar makes the case that every single one of us needs support to achieve the results that might drive us forward; we can't go it alone.

In my view, there's a link between Empathy and a biological concept called *coevolution*. Coevolution explains how organisms adapt as they are triggered by changes in the other organisms and in their environments. From a biological standpoint, that means living things have a reciprocal effect on each other's evolution. They influence, shape, and reshape one another.

---

15   Belinda Parmar, "Corporate Empathy Is Not an Oxymoron," *Harvard Business Review*, January 8, 2015, https://hbr.org/2015/01/corporate-empathy-is-not-an-oxymoron.

Recognizing this exchange of energy—our shared capacity to affect one another—helps explain what it means to live empathetically. Some of the most truly empathic people are those who are able not only to take account of the changes around them but also to adapt themselves to those changes so as to strengthen their interactions with others.

I hope we all know someone who has a real talent for truly understanding how other people are feeling. I'm reminded of when my wife and I were on our honeymoon in Laos. We were in the old historic city of Luang Prabang, and I was wandering through a little curio shop, the upstairs of which was a photo gallery with some incredible photographs in it.

To my right, there was a gentleman looking at the photos and smiling. He asked me, "Which one resonates best with you?" And I replied, "Oh, these are all fantastic, but I specifically like the light in this one." And then I asked, "What about you?" His reply: "Well, that's a little hard for me. I'm biased. They're all my photographs."

I laughed, not having realized I was speaking with the photographer. I laughed again when I learned that the photographer was Tony Wheeler, cofounder with his wife of Lonely Planet, the guidebook about traveling the world. I took advantage of an opportunity: "Sorry, forgive me, but if I were to ask you for one piece of advice about traveling, what would that piece of advice be?"

"It's actually quite simple. Get out from behind the glass."

Besides the amazingly insightful reference to his own penchant for photography, I sensed that Tony meant something more: that we live whole portions of our lives literally behind panes of glass—from cameras to planes, cars to buildings—and we live whole other portions of our lives *as if* behind panes of glass, by being disengaged or otherwise protected from genuine human contact, shared experience, and the possibility that others might affect us as much as we might affect them. If we don't get out from behind the glass, we could end up being world travelers who've rarely risked exposing ourselves to the real humanity of others. To really "be" in another place, another country, it's imperative to have met and known the people. That requires putting yourself into their world and trying to understand their thoughts, needs, loves, and fears. Empathy has humility at its heart because it teaches us to get out of our own shoes and imagine what it might be like in someone else's.

Empathy begins from vulnerability, from opening ourselves up to others. To quote Leonard Cohen, "Our cracks let the light in."

GUEST STAR: BOBBY SAGER

Bobby Sager made a fortune buying troubled companies, perhaps most notably Polaroid, where he served as chairman of the board for eight years during its recent historic revival. Then he decided to spend his life traveling around the globe, giving his money away and using street smarts and an entrepreneurial attitude to make a difference in some of the most devastated places on the planet. Bobby established the Sager Family Traveling Foundation, which has allowed him and his family to spend their lives in the most difficult places in the world.

"It's all about looking people in the eye," he says, "feeling their humanity and connecting with them on a level they never thought possible." For Bobby, this is the greatest return on investment ever imaginable. As he writes in his book *The Power of the Invisible Sun*: "My family and I live in such close contact to the ground that we truly understand what's going on. And I use my entrepreneurial ability, instincts, and tenacity to get the really tough stuff done.

Money certainly matters, but when we make ourselves a currency, that matters even more."

For Bobby, the most transcendent moments arrive when least expected. "They've risen out of the joy and frustration of sharing in ordinary people's everyday lives." Bobby's not someone who seeks the limelight, not someone whose name we quickly recognize. He does, however, among his closest friends count both the Dalai Lama and Sting, which is just a small indication of his incredible journey of giving and caring. His impact is the result of a very personal choice: the decision to be empathetic and to respect the life of each and every soul around him.

I last sat down with Bobby in the summer of 2019 in his apartment in Boston, which has as flooring the original wood of the Boston Garden on which the Boston Celtics won sixteen championships. Neatly emblazoned in the center is the Celtics logo—a large leprechaun. Bobby had started his business life as a fifteen-year-old ticket scalper outside the old Boston Garden. I could tell this would be one wild and appropriate interview.

SL: Could you share some learnings from conflict zones you've lived in where you have an opportunity to try building a bridge? How do you approach that?

BS: If you start by looking at someone as an object, that will never work. The first connection point has to be as living, breathing, feeling human beings. I'm always asking myself, even if I'm meeting a little kid, "What can I learn from this person?" Most people will look at someone who's downtrodden or a refugee as an object to be dealt with instead of a person to gain insight from.

SL: Can you share with us the idea behind your Hope Balls project—the indestructible soccer balls made from the same material as Crocs shoes?

BS: Well, when you're trying to help somebody, the first thing to think about is the dignity of that person. You see, if I simply gave a ball to a little kid and gave him a pat on the head, I would not be recognizing that kid's dignity. In fact, I would be taking that dignity away. When I talk to a child, I say, "Listen, I have an indestructible ball. A ball that can be in your life for a long time. A ball that one day you may use to play football with your sons and daughters. If you want, I'll trade my ball for your ball." What gives dignity is making that more of an even swap.

SL: Spending so much time in war zones must have taught you some incredible lessons on how to truly communicate with another human. Can you share some of these please?

BS: You have to get up and close and personal. The closer you get, the more you can find the light. When it comes to understanding someone, when it comes to figuring something out, everything comes down to being a great listener. And the only way that you can be a great listener is if you're really present and you are rid of your disruptive emotions.

SL: Can you tell me a little bit more about your chats with His Holiness the Dalai Lama on the power of truly listening?

BS: Well, Tibetan monks talk about the importance of taming disruptive emotions like greed, anger, jealousy, and fear that keep you from being truly in the moment as an open-minded, open-hearted listener. Whatever your biases are or whatever your distractions are, unless you find ways to control them, there's always going to be this very loud static when you're trying to listen and understand.

SL: His Holiness has a tremendous capacity to just draw you into complete confidence. I remember when he walked on the stage in LA in 2014 in front of several thousand people. The first thing he did was say, "Please turn up houselights. I cannot see who I'm talking to." Do you remember that?

BS: He wanted to look directly into everyone's eyes. People were at the edge of their seats involved in a one-to-one conversation but at scale. His idea is not talking at people but talking *to* people—no matter how many.

SL: What is one thing that you would encourage anyone to do that would give them a greater sense of purpose and meaning in their lives?

BS: There isn't any question that if you don't have gratitude in the day, you're not going to have a full day. Gratitude is basically not taking things in your everyday life for granted. It needs to be a daily practice and a very conscious effort.

IN PRACTICE: PUT YOURSELF IN ANOTHER PERSON'S SHOES

Empathy isn't just good for understanding how families or teams and the complex relationships within them work; it's a critical element of developing caring, supportive, and independent circles of trust. Role-playing lets us explore empathetic approaches by allowing each person to have at least one turn placing themselves in a seat representing a different point of view from their own. In this way, each person can explore how someone else feels and consider how that person approaches problem-solving. This exercise is designed for a family group but works just as well with small groups of all kinds.

Describe the problem/
opportunity the group
is facing:

- In the boxes below (if there are not four family members, only use what you need and/or add), write the names of each family member, and then, given the above problem/opportunity statement, have each family member identify which responsibilities they would typically take on and the desired outcome from their perspective.

- Now put everyone's names on slips of paper and randomly draw names (ensuring you do not get your own name). You now need to assume and play the role of the person whose name you've drawn during the problem-solving session. Set a time limit, like three to five minutes per person for round one, and include a summary round where each person can reflect on the others' comments and make a one-minute summation of their position.

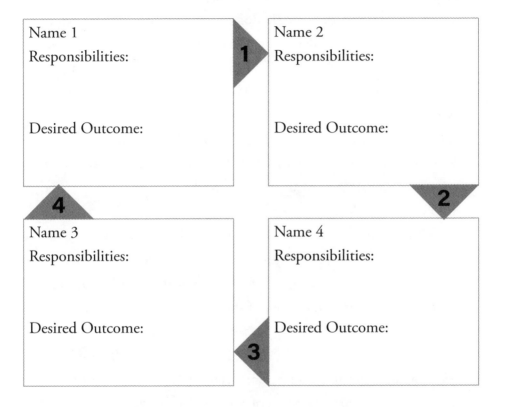

Once you've completed the problem-solving session by arriving at a shared plan or compromise, return the roles to their original owners, and now retry the exercise while continuing to practice Empathy for the other members. See if you can find new compromises that work even better.

IN BUSINESS: EMPATHY AND
RELATIONSHIP BUILDING

Clay Christensen devised the *Jobs to Be Done* framework of innovation. He claimed that people don't actually buy things by demo-
graphic (e.g., age, gender, geographical location, education level,
marital status, household income, occupation, or hobbies) so much
as they make purchases that solve problems they encounter as they're
living their daily lives. When they encounter a problem, they essentially "hire" a product to do the job of taking care of that problem.
When people have a need, or what we sometimes call a *pain point*,
a successful business will listen to it, understand it, frame it, and
supply a savvy solution.

Christensen wrote about how neither Akio Morita of Sony nor
Steve Jobs of Apple ever commissioned any market research. Rather
they just walked around the world watching what people did and
putting themselves in the shoes of their customers. To the contrary,
we often see businesses trying to sell to customers what they *think*
customers want rather than what those customers actually need.

Empathy isn't just good for understanding a business's customers;
it's become a critical component of good leadership within a company
and of the way leaders educate and develop their teams.

One direct challenge to applying Empathy within our businesses
is that male leaders have often been discouraged from showing, let
alone talking about, feelings. Many men have been told to "man up"
or "grow some balls" at some point in their lives. To the contrary,
not only is suppressing or turning away from emotions harmful to
health and well-being, but if men are not able to ask for help in the
workplace, they're also missing out on huge opportunities for self-
development and improvement. Having their more aggressive characteristics called to the fore can actually damage work productivity

and relationships with colleagues and among teams.

Women, too, have suffered from the implied or explicit requirement in some business environments to suppress emotions and adhere to a more aggressive model of behavior. A study of one thousand 360-degree feedback forms on female executives in the United States found that 41 percent of women have cried at work, while only 9 percent of men have done the same.[16] The result? When rejected for promotion or more senior leadership posts, more often than not, women are deemed to be "too emotional."

Belinda Parmar and others have shown us that Empathy can be fostered in ways that improve business environments. When businesses bring Empathy to the fore, they help to increase the happiness, engagement, and productivity of their workforces.

> **Empathy isn't just good for understanding a business's customers; it's become a critical component of good leadership within a company and of the way leaders educate and develop their teams.**

For those interested in cultivating Empathy, evidence shows that active listening and role-playing are some of the best techniques for helping people put themselves in others' shoes.

- **Active Listening**

Quite naturally, human beings tend toward selfishness and

---

16   Kathryn Heath and Jill Flynn, "How Women Can Show Passion at Work Without Seeming 'Emotional,'" *Harvard Business Review,* September 30, 2015, https://hbr.org/2015/09/how-women-can-show-passion-at-work-without-seeming-emotional.

have low attention spans. We spend most of our time in a conversation preparing what we will say next, waiting for our turn to talk, and being distracted by our environments. To help ourselves listen actively, we need to focus in on our conversation partner's physicality, their body language or positioning, their facial expressions, and the subtext of what is and is not being said.

Other active listening techniques involve repeating what we've heard beginning with phrases like *Let me see if I've heard you right* to check that what we believe we've heard or understood matches the speaker's intent. Another practice is to put aside the need to respond immediately or to engage immediately in problem-solving. Instead, think about what the other person is saying and register how it lands on you. The more present we can be, the more we improve both our own and others' experience of the conversation.

- **Role-Playing**

  Switching roles can allow for new and unexpected dialogue among colleagues and, when enacted in front of groups, can also help those who witness the role-play identify direct and indirect cues that reveal the attitudes and feelings of the players.

  Role-playing games and activities might focus on challenging scenarios (imagined or real), such as team members failing to fulfill their responsibilities on time or conflicts centered on sparring or talking over one another in meetings. Explore empathetic responses by allowing employees to have at least one turn placing themselves in a role representing a different point of view from their own.

In addition to these exercises, it's worthwhile to consider the value of *modeling* Empathy in work environments. Thoughtful and keenly attuned leadership can go a long way toward creating an environment in which people are looking out for rather than competing against one another.

SUMMARY

- Empathy's Operator is additive **+**. With practice (intentionality, mindfulness, and gratitude) it can be developed, and it can also be called upon situationally in order to further add to the potential upside/luckiness of an outcome.

- Empathy's Function is infinite **∞**. There is no upper limit on how empathetic you can be or on how much emotional intelligence you can express.

- Empathy is the capacity to imagine what it might be like to be in someone else's shoes.

- Empathy begins with carefully noticing the signs other people give of their emotional states.

- Guest Star Bobby Sager reminds us of the immense power of being a great listener: "The only way that you can be a great listener is if you're really present and you are rid of your disruptive emotions."

- The majority of leadership personality tests now clearly indicate that EQ (emotional quotient) and Empathy are the top leadership traits and in almost all cases exceed the values of IQ (intelligence quotient).

- Empathy can be fostered in business environments through exercises like active listening and role-playing.

  - In active listening, we do our best to whittle our focus down to the physicality and words of the other person. That means keeping distractions of all kinds at bay.

  - In role-playing, we imagine and enact the physical and emotional states of people in various scenarios. That might mean stepping into the shoes of someone whose experience—or opinion—is quite different from our own.

- Consistent demonstrations of Empathy from people in top leadership positions can reset the tone of corporate culture, taking it from cutthroat to compassionate.

- This chapter's personal exercise asks you to "Put Yourself in Another Person's Shoes" to help develop more caring, supportive, and independent circles of trust within your family and close-knit circles. This fabulous exercise is especially valuable to practice with your children, as it gives them and you much greater insight into how the family unit can run more smoothly and with greater compassion and understanding for one another.

- This chapter's business-focused exercise (available in the *FFL Workbook* by download from www.formulaforluck.com) begins with the observation that people act either to move toward gain or away from pain. If you're looking to influence your customers by addressing those needs, this exercise encourages you to identify, name, and then reflect on what your customers really want.

STUART'S SECRETS

- Download the app Headspace and start your day with a gratitude session and five minutes of calm breathing and mindfulness.

- Develop an "active listening feedback loop," and use it in conversations with colleagues and employees. It might sound like this: "Thank you for sharing; I just want to restate what

I believe I heard you say ..." Doing so shows others that you listened and that their time is valuable to you, reinforces what was said, and enables you to double-check with others that their message came through clearly.

- Remember what we learned from Chris Traub in the chapter on Connectivity: Hold eye contact with everybody, and operate with a layer of presence, availability, and compassion. Be present and nonjudgmental, unconditional, and compassionate. Hold the space, and be welcoming without inserting an agenda or judging. This gives the people you are with the opportunity to be gifted with what people crave most, which is being seen, heard, and respected.

$y^2 = \frac{2}{\pi m}$

$y = \sqrt[3]{3+1}$

$1.3 = c\,005$

SO_4

$y = \sqrt[3]{1}$

$\left(\frac{2}{3}\right) = x_7$

$\frac{a}{m}$

$1.3 = c\,005$

$1.3 = c\,005$

$1.3 = 0.005$

$x_7 = \left(\frac{2}{3} \times 2x\right)$ $a^2 = b^2 + c^2$

$N^2 \times H^3$ $\frac{a}{\sin d} = \frac{b}{\sin d}$

$f(3) = 2^{-3}$

NH_3 y

$2x \left(\frac{2}{3} \times 2x\right)$ SO_6

$\frac{a}{\sin d} = \frac{b}{\sin d}$ $f(3) = 2^{-3} + 1.3 = c\,005$

$a^2 = b^2$ $x_7 = \left(\frac{2}{3} \times 2x\right) a^2 = b^2$

$6c$ $= + x_7$ $\frac{a}{\sin d}$

$\frac{d}{\sin}$ $\frac{t}{\sin}$ NH_3

CHAPTER 10

THE SIXTH PRINCIPLE:
ADAPTABILITY

Shift Happens

Operator: ✖ (multiplicative)

Function: ♥ (finite)

Luck Mindset Category: **Behavior**

Shift: **Moving from the routine toward the random, from rigidity toward flexibility, from frozen to rapid adjustment, from fragile to antifragile**

On Twitter: **#shifthappens**

> *Treat yourself like a series of two-week experiments.*
>
> —Tim Ferriss

INTRODUCTION

In February 2020, the world was just beginning to come to grips with how big an effect COVID-19 might have. That same month, I was in San Diego in leadership meetings with YPO (the Young Presidents' Organization). At that time, YPO had a membership of 29,000 CEOs who collectively employed 22 million people with a GDP of $9 trillion—effectively making it the third largest economy on the planet. After being in YPO for a decade, I had been elected to a regional chair position, overseeing about 1,500 CEOs covering the US Eastern Seaboard from Washington, DC, to Boston. The other regional chairs and I, along with the organization's international board, were in long meetings trying to figure out how we should best respond to the rapidly changing landscape. It is noteworthy that these meetings occurred just ten days *before* the first confirmed COVID-19 case in the United States and not long before California would commence the first statewide lockdown, and the Centers for Disease Control and Prevention would declare a pandemic.

Our immediate challenge? Once per year, YPO hosts an international leadership conference called the Global Edge at which about three to five thousand CEOs gather from all over the world. The Edge had hundreds of confirmed speakers, and over one thousand contracts had been signed with service providers including airlines, hotels, venues, food and beverage, and entertainment. The upcoming event had been eighteen months in the planning and was due to start in San Diego just four days after that leadership meeting! Hundreds of CEOs were already airborne, and thousands more would be within forty-eight hours. Thousands of hotel rooms had been booked and paid for, and more than one hundred thousand individual meals had been organized and food procured. Our choice was simple—on the one hand we could cancel and face the frustration and angst of thousands of CEOs and incur cancellation fees and costs amounting to over $20 million in liabilities (all without the right to invoke force majeure and claim on insurance contracts) because a pandemic had not yet been declared. On the other hand, we could move forward with existing plans and more than likely put at risk the lives of all the attendees, hosts, and service providers, possibly spreading the disease across the entire event as well as into San Diego, California, and well beyond. Such a tragedy would later be called a *super-spreader event*. Despite the immense risk, worry, and invested effort, YPO had to adapt in real time and make a firm decision. The organization canceled the entire event.

Not only were all fees refunded and expenses covered for any CEO attending out of pocket but, more important, a volunteer committee was also assembled to determine how best to repurpose everything that could be repurposed for charity. Tens of thousands of meals were redirected to the homeless; clothing and bags intended for attendees were given to shelters and others in need. Contracts were canceled where possible, in a way that recognized and attempted to minimize providers' losses by means of defrayal, rebooking, or postponement. Communications were critical; they needed to be kind, thoughtful, caring, and inclusive but also clear and definitive. Where needed, payments were extended, terms offered, and compensation provided. YPO chose not just to do the right thing by canceling but also to cancel in a most considerate way. Not only did the organization's members understand but they also appreciated the proactive stance. The No Member Left Behind policy enabled the organization to respond with dignity and speed in a way that only reinforced its celebrated brand and increased the loyalty of its members and the community.

COVID-19 has been referred to as a *black swan event*—something that is extremely negative, rare, and almost impossible to predict. The seminal piece of work in this space was conducted by Nassim Taleb in his five-volume essay *Incerto* (written between 2001 and 2018), specifically in his 2007 book, *The Black Swan*. I was fortunate to catch up with Nassim in April 2020, when we discussed his views on the global response to COVID-19, the importance of Adaptability, and how preparation can help make a person, a company, or a community "antifragile" (that happens to be the title of the third book in the Incerto series). Quite simply, Nassim reminds us that we can divide the world and all that's in it (people, things, institutions, ways of life) into three categories: the fragile, the robust, and the antifragile. We are *fragile* if we avoid disorder and disruption for fear of the mess they might make of our life. In so doing we may believe that we are keeping safe, but really we are making ourselves vulnerable to shocks that can tear everything apart. We are *robust* if we can stand up to shocks without flinching and without substantially changing who we are. And we are *antifragile* if shocks and disruptions make us stronger and more creative, better able to adapt to each new challenge we face.

EXPLORATION: THINK LIKE DIAMANDIS

A high IQ shows you're smart, a high EQ shows you care, and a high AQ (Adaptability quotient) shows you're flexible and resilient. We might have some sense already about how to recognize and develop the first two qualities, but how about the third?

Peter Diamandis, the founder of Singularity University, has pointed out that "We're living toward incredible times where the only constant is change, and the rate of change is increasing."[17] Our ability to respond to constant change is the biggest differentiator for

---

17　Peter Diamandis, "Peter Diamandis Quotes," BrainyQuote.com, accessed November 2020, https://www.brainyquote.com/quotes/peter_diamandis_690476.

our future success and for increasing our capacity for luck. In today's world more than ever before, strength is a matter of flexibility. That's something of a shift from the old adage that to bend is to break or the idea that strength is a kind of superheroic imperviousness. Instead, Diamandis and others suggest that to bend is itself a way of not breaking, of withstanding pressures by fully acknowledging and even accommodating them.

The world of design offers us a model for thinking about Adaptability, especially over the long term. Design flexibility is what enables a building or other structure to evolve over time as users' needs change. It's what makes the building more efficient as it ages and diminishes the chances of obsoles-cence. A similar concept is part of the world of computer programming, where flexible code is designed to maximize its utility. TOM and Python are great examples of ways that computer languages are structured almost like Lego blocks, minimizing refactoring or the need to discard all the code as different use cases arise.

> Our ability to respond to constant change is the biggest differentiator for our future success and for increasing our capacity for luck.

Of course, the greatest models of adaptability can often be found in the natural world. We all know that Darwin was a keen observer of the role of adaptation in genetic survival and species propagation. But we can look to nature for still other models of flexibility. Bamboo, for example, is one of the most flexible and resilient plants on the planet and has been used regularly for scaffolding and construction. That's because it grows quickly to great lengths (some species even grow up to thirty-five inches in only twenty-four hours), and it flexes instead of breaks under load. Bamboo has one of the highest strength-to-weight ratios in the world—a higher compression strength than wood, brick, or concrete—and a higher tensile strength than steel. In addition to all that, if bamboo stems are cut, the plant regenerates, heals, and grows again.

From nature's models, we can see some of the features or characteristics that comprise our *human* adaptability: the ability to withstand pressures and challenges as well as the abilities to recover from setbacks and adjust to changed circumstances.

GUEST STAR: DAVID BREASHEARS

David Breashears is one of the world's most award-winning filmographers. In addition to summiting most of the major mountains in the world, he filmed the IMAX movie *Everest* on the summit attempt that claimed the lives of twenty-three climbers in May of 1996.

During climbs, David witnessed and regularly had to cope with the result of poor decision-making under stress. He's drawn attention to those moments when even with the most nimble and elegant of plans, climbers can become unable to adjust course. Their judgment might become clouded by raw ambition, arrogance, fear, or any number of other factors that keep them stuck taking actions that no longer suit changes in weather, terrain, or other obstacles that crop up along the way. David learned from personal experience that inflexibility in those moments can quickly become life threatening.

When his IMAX team was on Everest in 1996, the team ended up saving many lives by deciding to forgo its chance to summit the mountain as storm conditions threatened. As Breashears's team descended the mountain, they passed several other teams still on their way up. By nightfall, eight people on those other teams had already perished, including Rob Hall, a world-renowned climber and friend of Breashears. Hall was leading a group of individuals who had paid a substantial fee to be guided to the top. Jon Krakauer, a writer and outdoorsman who was on Hall's team, would eventually write the best-selling book *Into Thin Air*, chronicling in heartbreaking detail what had gone wrong.

In September 2016, I had the opportunity to attend an amazing lecture Breashears did on adaptability and other lessons learned at high altitude about leadership and decision-making. Thanks to him making time to chat with me afterward, and to my copious note-taking, I'm able to share with you here my learnings and some of the biggest insights and takeaways he offered on the topic of adaptability.

• • •

Breashears's view on the subject of what qualities a team needs to take on a serious challenge safely and successfully:

- Trust is the glue that makes it possible for a team to take on challenges safely and successfully. And trust is more easily established if team members share values like selflessness, kindness, and generosity. Those values have to be almost immutable, or else trust can't be built.

His view on the fateful climb of Everest in May of 1996, when he had to make the difficult decision to abandon the goal of summiting the mountain:

- The decision to abandon a goal is hard to make. It's easy to be so much into the climb that you don't know when to stop. The temptation to go on is immense, even when things are falling apart. There's a similar pressure on businesses to always push for results and nonstop success—that's a version of "summit fever."

His view on the dangers of ego in leaders:

- The day we abandoned the climb was one of those times when having trust among team members who share a common vision made all the difference. No one's ego could take precedence. A leader who puts his interests first can be a highly demoralizing force, as can the individual who responds to crisis by falling away from the group and focusing only on their own survival.

His view on making critical decisions as a team:

- We came to the decision as a group through open discussion of everyone's concerns and hesitations, and we had to adapt *all together* under rapidly changing conditions. To accomplish that, we needed to be a truly collaborative team—one that could communicate well and plan together under life-threatening pressure.

His view on what makes a great plan under any circumstances, whether on Wall Street or on a cliff:

- One of the primary characteristics of a great and elegant plan is that it's flexible. A good plan makes you nimble, keeps you from getting stuck. Our plan gave us wiggle room, options for this or that unanticipated situation or obstacle. Before we even got to the mountain, we ran through an extensive array of what-if scenarios.

His view on assembling a team that's capable of adapting under rapidly changing circumstances:

- There is a key requirement to look for talented people who believe in their craft, not those who are looking for praise. Look for people who are already very clear and fearless communicators. In groups, unconscious collusion occurs when no one feels either empowered or responsible for calling out red flags that could spell trouble. Try to find people who are less likely to tolerate or succumb to that pressure but who are also good team players capable of putting the group's needs ahead of their own.

IN PRACTICE: THE A, B, C, D, E OF ADAPTABILITY

Life is full of ups and downs. Part of being adaptable is being able to get through the tough parts, recover from them, and carry on. Both Adaptability and resilience have a lot to do with changing our negative assumptions and beliefs so that we can take positive action. Resilient people tend to have several things in common:

- They are hopeful but also realistic and are able to keep their emotions from overwhelming them.

- They are able to think through problems and can reach out to others for support when they need it.

The following exercise will help you to develop this skill.

Think of a recent event that called up negative feelings for you and that required you to adapt significantly:

A, B, C, D, E	QUESTIONS	ANSWERS
ACTIVATING EVENT	What happened? (Include some words that describe your feelings.)	
YOUR **B**ELIEFS	What negative stories were you telling yourself about this event?	
CONSEQUENCES OF YOUR BELIEFS	How did your beliefs make you feel? What did they make you want to do?	
DISPUTE YOUR BELIEFS	Were your negative beliefs really true? Could you restate them here as positive ones?	
EXTRAPOLATE	In the future when similar events occur, what key learnings from this exercise will you apply?	

Dr. Nassim Taleb wrote about this subject in his books *The Black Swan* and *Antifragile*. The reality is that none of us is resilient all the time. We may be very resilient in some parts of our life but struggle with others. Similarly, if we face many challenges at one time, we may temporarily run low on our capacity for Adaptability and thus resilience. Focusing on developing these behaviors helps make us and our businesses antifragile.

IN BUSINESS: ADAPTABILITY IN CONTEXT

Jim Collins is an international superstar and author of books like *Good to Great, Built to Last,* and *Great by Choice.* But Jim Collins got something wrong.

In each of his books, Collins used the same basic approach: he began by looking at factors like share price and dividend data to identify excellent companies. Having identified those companies, he then tried to pinpoint what made them so wonderful. His aim was to provide a formula for their excellence so that other companies could put those same practices into place and arrive at equivalent performance results.

Phil Rosenzweig, in his 2014 book *The Halo Effect,* wrote about the pitfalls of this approach. He pointed out that in the excitement of the day, the companies Collins identified were indeed outstanding performers. They had widely admired leaders, great office cultures, and other markers of success. But when we look at these companies today, we discover that almost all of them are no longer as great as they were when Collins first evaluated them. In fact, of the fifty or so companies identified across Collins's three books, current performance indicators are almost embarrassing.

The companies reviewed in *Good to Great* only beat the S&P Index by 2.6 percent, and those mentioned in *Built to Last* only beat the S&P Index, at large, by 1.6 percent. More notably, there were many more big losers than big winners among them; if we were to remove Walmart, Intel, and Phillip Morris from the lot, the remaining companies are now part of a tragically badly performing group. As we've heard it said: if it weren't for cigarettes, Jim Collins's predictions would have gone up in smoke.

What happened? One of the biggest measures of a company's greatness comes down to business context and to people's capacity to bend and flex in response to shifts in that context. Chris Bradley of McKinsey & Company has put the context issue like this: "It was good to be great. But the external environment in which these companies found themselves mattered far more. The biggest dividing lines seemed to be their position in relation to a megatrend—either a good or bad one—and the skill to ride it and stay on it."[18]

Bradley's point reminds me of my days running a hedge fund where we built trading models that were back tested using historical trading data. As many of you know, one of the biggest dangers in predicting future performance is taking an old set of data, plugging it into a model, shaping the curve until you have a perfect 12 percent annual return, and then investing in that exact same set of stocks and expecting the same 12 percent going forward. That practice overlooks the need to understand and validate a rapidly changing business environment—or the context in which it is operating. Rather than look at measures such as stock price, I posit that Collins's evaluation could have been a more subjective evaluation of the decisions made by key leadership in relation to changing circumstances.

That said, I do want to pick up on something vitally important to long-term Adaptability that Collins identified in his book *Great by Choice*, where he refers to a company's "return on luck." Companies that were successful in moments of big operational change had the highest return on luck, by which Collins meant that their success had to do with making good use of what came their way. In other words, these companies weren't clearly "luckier" than others so much as they simply made good on whatever happened—whether positive or negative. We know that bad circumstances might yield a good

---

18   Chris Bradley, "Surprise: Those 'Great' Companies Generally Turn Out to Be Meh ... Or Duds," MarketWatch.com, August 31, 2017, https://www.marketwatch.com/story/great-companies-are-more-likely-to-do-really-badly-over-time-than-really-well-2017-07-12.

outcome just as good ones might end up being squandered. The primary differentiator in these companies was the ability of management to adapt to new trends and new ideas, leaving old legacy thoughts and habits behind and pivoting without losing sight of the business's strengths and goals. As if foreshadowing the contents of this book, Jim wrote, "The evidence leads us to conclude that luck does not cause 10X success. People do."[19] What was not yet clear to Jim at the time was that it was the mindset of these business leaders that in fact was at the core of this incredible growth.

As Collins noted, it takes incredible discipline to be able to rebound or pivot, especially in the face of circumstances that threaten a company's well-being. Discipline helps companies pull through when the path to their goals demands everything from minor adjustments to significant shifts. In the end, it's disciplined self-awareness and a disciplined support network that matter most to long-term success and foster the ability to iterate and pivot both quickly and wisely.

Adaptability comes down to the company's people. Yes, adaptable and antifragile businesses must have the right people in management positions. Without good, clear guidance from leadership, even business-enhancing technologies and processes can still bring all manner of ills upon a company—from data breaches to privacy abuses, and the like. But just as important is building a company-wide culture in which employees at all levels have (1) well-developed knowledge of processes and operating systems, (2) the skills necessary to address issues with ease, and (3) a share in the vision and values that make for business consistency over time. Adaptability, in other words, must include our values, our focus and commitment, and our faith

---

19   Jim Collins, "Return on Luck," JimCollins.com, accessed November 2020, https://www.jimcollins.com/concepts/return-on-luck.html.

in ourselves. That's what turns "bad luck" into growth and progress.

True Adaptability is not just about risk management or disaster preparedness. Sure, it's absolutely the case that a business needs to identify clearly how it will respond to security breaches, IT outages, supply chain disruptions, health and safety incidents, and natural and other disasters—just as it needs to have clearly identified plans for recovering quickly from financial and other difficult-to-foresee challenges. But, in a world characterized primarily by rapid change, companies need to develop—in all sorts of everyday circumstances— employees' capacity to withstand change, to recover quickly from setbacks and shocks, and to adapt to new demands.

The chapter on how companies weathered and came back after COVID-19 is yet to be written at the time of this book being published. How will remote workers remain engaged; how will the use of Zoom affect in-person relationships; how will mental health and welfare be affected in the long term? What will corporate social responsibility look like after COVID-19? What is the future of commercial office space? These and other big questions are those that demand CEOs make decisions in real time and adjust their business plans rapidly not just to survive but also to thrive. How much your business can bend before it breaks is directly related to the individual abilities of the people who comprise it.

What companies must do on a daily basis is help employees accept changed realities, find meaning in hardship, think positively about setbacks, recover essential functions, and improvise when the playing field has changed. Many of the

> How much your business can bend before it breaks is directly related to the individual abilities of the people who comprise it.

techniques we are encouraged to use when it comes to *introducing* change into business environments can also be used on a regular basis to develop the habits of Adaptability over the long term.

SUMMARY

- Adaptability's Operator is multiplicative ✖. The preceding Principles have all been additive; however, should the additive value of them (or you) run into an event or situation that demands rapid adaptation, not adapting will quickly deplete or void the value of all the other additive Principles, even if they are all acting in concert. The effect could be to render those Principles valueless. Alternatively, should you adapt quickly and appropriately, the value of all those Principles would be magnified considerably.

- Adaptability's Function is finite ⬤. Our ability to adapt to significant events always comes with opportunity cost and often requires substantive effort to achieve. As such, although microadjustments are relatively easy and always useful, it is the triage and speed with which we react and adapt to the large changes that really makes the difference.

- Adaptability is our capacity to adjust to difficult situations in order to create a positive outcome.

- Antifragility is a state in which shocks and disruptions make us stronger, more creative, and better able to adapt to each new challenge we face.

- Highly adaptable people spend less time feeling sorry for themselves and more time making good on their circumstances, whatever those may be.

- Guest Star David Breashears reminds us that a great plan is a flexible plan. "A good plan makes you nimble, keeps you from getting stuck. Our plan gave us wiggle room, options for this or that unanticipated situation or obstacle."

- This chapter's personal exercise addresses life's ups and downs. Part of being adaptable is being able to get through the tough parts, recover from them, and carry on. Use this A, B, C, D, E exercise to help you identify and challenge any negative assumptions and beliefs you might have, thereby enabling you to take positive action and become more antifragile.

- This chapter's business-focused exercise (available in the *FFL Workbook* by download from www.formulaforluck.com) asks you to assess your key team members' Relative Adaptability as well as to consider opportunities for improvement, to identify those who are most likely to be able to adapt to rapidly changing scenarios, and to identify those on whom you can rely when the going gets tough or in times of crisis.

- From Jim Collins we learned to (1) take prescriptions from prior greatness with a grain of salt; and (2) above all identify and respect the big trends, and then surf on them or get ahead of them if you can.

- Adaptability can be fostered every day by clearly stating and showing change, by explaining why change is necessary or unavoidable, by inviting and acknowledging feedback, by defining clear roles in light of changes, and by rewarding strong performance.

STUART'S SECRETS

When you prepare to deliver a presentation, workshop, or talk, consider the following preparations:
- Carefully consider all questions that might come your way so that you are prepared to speak to them should they arise.

- Consider what to do if technology—your microphone, the projector, the battery in your pointer—dies or fails to advance. Smoothly flowing into plan B shows your mastery of the subject and that you are an authority without in any way diminishing yourself as so many others unfortunately do when technology fails them onstage.

- If you'll be speaking with a large audience, remember that you are not addressing the room but rather are entering into a number of one-on-one conversations with selected people around the room.

- Ask yourself which animal you are or wish to be: (1) a turtle—quick to hide and evade (equals *fragile*); (2) a hedgehog—puts head down and sticks at tasks (equals *robust*); or (3) a fox—resilient and rapidly adapts and changes direction (equals *antifragile*).

CHAPTER 11

THE SEVENTH PRINCIPLE: SITUATIONAL AWARENESS

Pay Attention, 007

Operator: ✖ **(multiplicative)**

Function: ◉ **(finite)**

Luck Mindset Category: **Behavior**

Shift: **Moving from blinders on to radar out; moving from being unaware to preemptive action, from internal approach to systemic approach**

On Twitter: **#payattention007**

> *Awareness is the greatest agent for change.*
>
> —Eckhart Tolle

INTRODUCTION

On February 17, 2011, I was visiting Manama, Bahrain, to give a keynote speech at the Capital Club. The club is on the fifty-first floor of a building in downtown Manama, right near Pearl Roundabout. On the evening of my speech, in a taxi from my hotel to the club, I noticed a very celebratory-looking event at the Roundabout with about a thousand people in attendance. On the trip back to my hotel later that night, the crowd appeared to have changed. There were more flags and banners, and people were blocking the road a bit. "What do you think?" I asked the driver, wondering if we should change directions. He offered either to take the same route, which would bring us right alongside the event, or to take a ring road. I selected the ring road. From the ring road, we were able to see a long line of armored personnel carriers lining up just outside of view of Pearl.

The next morning, I was awakened by the sound of helicopter gunships in the air and looked out the window to see smoke rising from Pearl. As you may know, security forces had launched a raid that night in Pearl Roundabout to clear protesters participating in a national uprising. Some news reported it as a massacre. My immediate question to myself as I looked out the window: "Do I stay, or do I flee?" I asked for an official car, and against the default "shelter in place" instructions of the hotel, I left. I decided against the short route to the airport to avoid the violence at Pearl. That meant having to take another long ring road. On that road, I watched helicopter gunships flying above and saw an armored personnel carrier drive right over the top of a barricade in front of me. When I made it to the Bahrain International Airport, I got on the very next one-way flight out—a flight to Qatar. Within an hour, we were wheels up.

In that situation, I made decisions without time to spare and well before a full accounting of the facts was available to me. I made those decisions based on a strong internal sense of what I needed to do, a combination of my instinct, my training, and what I saw happening around me in the moment. That's the essence of Situational Awareness—quickly recognizing and assessing one's environment to maximize decision-making ability.

EXPLORATION: THINK LIKE ARISTOTLE

Aristotle had a lot to say about our moral development, but it turns out he also talked a good deal about something called *situational luck*.

For Aristotle, all our habits—good or bad, learned or not—contribute to our moral development. The sum of those habits can help explain how one child develops in ways that encourage stealing or some other vice while another develops into a virtuous and charitable person. Our natural tendencies affect our moral development, but so do external influences like education, role models, and other opportunities that come from family or community. These influences are the product of what Aristotle called *developmental luck*: maybe we have wonderful family and community influences that mold our natural tendencies in ways that encourage virtue, or maybe we don't. What's really interesting about Aristotle's account of developmental luck is that he also accounts for the influence of crises—and here's where situational luck comes into play: those moments that require us to choose, immediately, between more and less virtuous alternatives.

A good example of situational luck (or lack thereof) occurs in the movie *Titanic*. We all remember the scene with Kate and Leonardo at the ship's helm, but do you remember the scene where a man pushes a child and woman out of the way so that he can secure himself a spot cowering under a cloth on a lifeboat? He's forced by the situation to decide, under duress, how he should act. Aristotle recognized the potentially profound influence of situations like this one that put our habits to the test. The man's actions highlight elements of cowardice and fear—not so good for becoming a good human being.

In my opinion, at the heart of situational luck is Situational Awareness. Bad things happen; dangerous situations abound. But becoming situationally aware allows you to quickly recognize threats and either avoid them entirely or make smart decisions in real time about how to proceed in order to maximize good outcomes.

Granted, Situational Awareness should not be thought of only as a means of avoiding danger. It's also at the heart of noticing positive and potentially life-shaping or even life-changing opportunities. Imagine yourself at a friend's backyard barbeque, when you momentarily catch the eye of a stranger across the yard. Is it something about the way they are smiling at you, or did you notice that their eyes linger a moment longer than needed? Fortunately, you were neither glued to your phone nor the game on TV, and you were aware and open-minded enough to catch and act on the possible invitation. Moments like these—the basis of many "how I met your mother/ father" stories we heard while growing up—are sadly becoming less frequent in the days of swipe-left dating, with its emphasis placed largely on one's ability to be a master of photo editing on social apps.

Quite simply, the skill set required to make sure your radar is up and cast wide enough is vital for you to capture and capitalize on many of the most serendipitous and delightful opportunities that will cross your future path. I remain optimistic that most readers are fairly well versed in the positive aspects of Situational Awareness and will hopefully enjoy the fruits of it as much as they can when it comes their way. Some of the learnings in this chapter and the next one on Serendipity will help you hone this skill. However, it's my experience that the average reader is far less prepared to be aware of potential dangers or to know how to act in response to them in life-saving ways. So in order to maximize the remaining value of this chapter for readers, I'm going to focus primarily on aspects of Situational Awareness aimed at avoiding harm.

At the heart of Situational Awareness is flexibility. Training to be more flexible and responsive is different from training to repeat the same behaviors no matter what the circumstances. The former is about careful assessment and decision-making—even if it feels more like habit when it's happening—while the latter is about unthinking habit or complacency, falling back on responses that have worked for us in the past regardless of whether or not they apply to the present. The best we can do is see to it that our deepest inclinations are aligned with a capacity for flexibility so that we can be responsive to whatever situation we find ourselves in.

When it comes to developing Situational Awareness, the real challenge is that it's not easy to go against an inclination to take the path of least resistance. Sometimes when we do what's most comfortable, we are *putting* ourselves at risk instead of avoiding risk. Think about all the people caught and injured in stampedes running for the closest and most obvious exit during a fire or threat. For example, not long ago, I toured twenty-one different countries in Africa. I had a high level of Situational Awareness everywhere I went. The only time I was robbed was in the Johannesburg airport in South

> The best we can do is see to it that our deepest inclinations are aligned with a capacity for flexibility so that we can be responsive to whatever situation we find ourselves in.

Africa, which I understood to be the safest place in all twenty-one countries. What happened there was that I let down my guard for the first time on that trip; you could say I was influenced by my prejudices, by my belief that I would be safe in that space. My sense of security was a kind of complacency; it made me most vulnerable in that situation.

The bottom line is that the more information we can process, the more informed our decisions are or can become. Of course, there's a limit to how much we can do. Imagine yourself sitting in a restaurant. As a situationally aware person, you probably want your back against the wall. You want to know where the exits are. And yes, if a funny-looking fellow comes in the front door carrying a large duffel bag, you might want to pay a bit more attention.

Now, James Bond or Jason Bourne might map the eyeballs, clothing, history, and food orders of everyone in the restaurant, noticing every detail from how they walked into the room or even lip-reading to understand what they're saying to one another. But you can't do that for all the people there. That's why they are fictional characters and why James and Jason also rely on a bunch of fancy technology: because in reality, only technology can process that much information that quickly.

The important thing is to make a determination about how much information we need to take in and how we should prioritize that information to maximize our awareness. The secret is to balance the greatest amount of visual information with a minimum amount of exposure.

Training of any kind is about creating some hard wires within us that we can rely on to serve us well in the future. What Situational Awareness asks of us, what it needs to develop and grow, is that we train ourselves to make the best decisions we can with the information we have, as quickly as we are able.

Think about even our earliest training in developing Situational Awareness—noticing and assessing similarities and differences. Remember those games we played as children where we were encouraged to look at a group of objects for the one thing that didn't belong with the rest? Maybe there was a pencil, a crayon, a ruler, an eraser, and a hand grenade. Guess which one doesn't belong! Situational awareness depends on that ability to be attentive enough in general that you can quickly recognize what doesn't make sense or doesn't fit.

Happily, as the children's games suggest, this is a skill we absolutely can develop. With practice, we can train ourselves to possess a mindset in which more and more accurate Situational Awareness is our default behavior, our habit—we might even say that with practice, Situational Awareness becomes our instinctual response.

The more quickly we can read the scene and focus on

> **What Situational Awareness asks of us, what it needs to develop and grow, is that we train ourselves to make the best decisions we can with the information we have, as quickly as we are able.**

aspects that stand out or "don't fit," the more quickly we can evaluate our options and select an appropriate response.

Imagine that someone approaches you looking for directions. Typically, people with an intent to engage in open, honest dialogue might approach by making eye contact, smiling, or indicating awkwardness or embarrassment about asking for help. As this person approaches you, you would want to be thinking about those outward signs. Are they actively scanning the horizon, potentially looking for police or bystanders? Are they fumbling with stuff in their pockets, looking away from you while also closing in fairly quickly? The more you are able to notice about how this person moves toward you, the more well positioned you are to focus in on what may be unique or odd about their behavior. And the more you can focus in on those oddities—even if the oddity is them seeming to be "too normal"— the more time you grant yourself for assessing the scene, deciding how to respond, and responding appropriately.

GUEST STAR: KRISTINA ANDERSON

It was eight thirty in the morning on April 16, 2007, and Kristina Anderson's friend Colin Goddard called to offer her a ride to their French class at Virginia Tech. She got dressed quickly and almost put on flip-flops but, seeing a few lazy snowflakes falling through the air, chose her blue Puma sneakers instead. On the way to campus, Colin and Kristina discussed skipping class to get bagels and coffee, then decided against it.

While sitting in class doing a grammar exercise, Kristina heard noises in the hallway—like an ax chopping wood—and felt echoes of pressure through the wall. As her professor stepped into the hallway to investigate, Kristina saw fear on her face.

"Call 911!" the teacher shouted. Kristina got under her desk because there was no time to move. Then there was shot after shot. She turned and saw the shooter, face blank, walking over from the other side of the room. A bullet pierced her back. Play dead, she told herself.

Just as soon as the shooter seemed to have left, another bullet hit her—lower this time. Both wounds burned. One more bullet struck the wall above her head, and then the noise stopped. Pain overtook her, but she sensed that it had become safe enough to push herself away from the desk, stretch out on her back, and wait for help to arrive.

On that day, a student used a semiautomatic pistol to kill thirty-two people and wound seventeen others. As a result of her experience, Kristina started the Koshka Foundation for Safe Schools, which advocates for student safety awareness and healing after mass shootings in the United States.

Kristina and I first met in 2012 when I invited her to speak at an event about school safety. Her commitment to education, support, and healing brought her immediately to mind as this chapter's guest. She and I caught up again for me to ask about her views on modern best practices for Situational Awareness and response.

SL: I know you're not defined by that day, Kristina. But if we revisit it for just a moment, how did luck play into your survival?

KA: Although I don't think about luck very much, I very much benefited from luck in that classroom. I had the advantage, for instance, of where I was sitting. On the other side of the classroom, there was very little chance one could survive. But I also did some things. I moved very quickly. I couldn't identify what it was, but I knew that something very dangerous was happening, and my best instinct was to stay low. I basically tried to stop breathing and become invisible. I was shot three times, but I'm very lucky that most missed.

SL: I am amazed how many people are heard saying, "I thought the sound was firecrackers," and as a result were slow to react. With terrorism being a larger threat these days, what advice can you offer?

KA: I always tell people to quickly get out and away from any situation like that. You may have to help someone, depending on where you are, but if you make no choice and freeze, you're just kind of letting it happen. If you exercise some choice, you can minimize some of the risks. Have a plan if you are with your family because that would be very different from being alone. And always pay attention. That starts with learning how to assess your environment. No matter where you're sitting, for example, look for where the exits are or where someone might come in from. How would you get out of a space quickly? It's important to remember that you're allowed to break the rules—break a window, for example, or exit through the kitchen. Finally, start paying attention to things that stick out or seem unusual.

SL: That's helpful, thank you. What about in the workplace? I have read that companies should appoint a crisis management lead to assess threats, locate escape routes, identify risky customer types, and create best practices.

KA: Yes, absolutely. Most important, give your crisis management leads direct access to the CEO. You can even build security into how you design spaces without negatively impacting culture. There are companies and consultants that help with planning, but most people don't seek them out until after the fact. ASIS and SHRM wrote comprehensive guides that are the gold standard for workplace violence prevention. It wouldn't take long for any company to do all those things, including training employees, which is a very big part of it.

SL: Can you help us understand how to avoid workplace violence?

KA: The big step is to know your sources. There are four types. The first one is customers who might be walking in to steal your property. Next there are those that might harm your people because they are angry about something your company did or took away from them. The third is former or current employees, people who are upset because they were fired or shamed. The fourth type is domestic violence, which statistically is both under-reported and always at a very high rate regardless of industry. That could even happen in a parking lot. Imagine a really contested divorce. It's very unlikely that one of your employees would say, "Hey, if my husband shows up, please don't let him in the front door." Some companies do have programs in place and inform security at the front desk; it's called a BOLO—"be on the lookout" for this person.

SL: I recently read a quote of yours: "You wake up, and you decide the world is good." Is that about how victims recover after devastating incidents?

KA: Because language is a very important part of this, I use the term *survivor*. When we call someone a *victim* or say they've been victimized—even five, ten years after the event—it does not help their emotional healing. Regarding that quote, I think survivors, intentionally or not, make that decision every day. And I think it's applicable to all of us. We all decide each morning if we're going to give 110 percent and be the best person we can be. That's an intentional decision regardless of what people have been through. That quote is from my response after the San Bernardino shooting on the need to never give up.

SL: We get to control the story we tell, right?

KA: Absolutely.

IN PRACTICE: TEST YOUR AWARENESS

Check out your score on this quick test of your Situational Awareness during a potential active shooter event. And consider this: if you can ask the people in your company to assemble outside every couple of months for a fire drill, why not also create for them a drill or plan focused on other workplace threats?

ACTIVE SHOOTER AND WORKPLACE VIOLENCE QUIZ

Circle your responses to the following questions. Check your responses against the answers in the key below.

---

1. It is not always possible to predict when someone is going to become violent.

a. true

b. false

---

2. Workers who are susceptible to violence often talk about

_____

a. problems at home

b. firearms

c. violent crime

d. all of the above

---

3. You should not report indicators of violent behavior if you don't want to get involved or if you are reluctant to report a coworker to management.

a. true

b. false

---

4. How many feet should you try to keep between you and a person displaying violent behavior?

a. 2 feet

b. 3 feet

c. 5 feet

5. When confronted with an active shooter, you should leave your personal belongings behind and alert others to the danger as you exit.

a. true

b. false

6. If you see an active shooter, you should sound a fire alarm to alert others of the danger.

a. true

b. false

7. If you and your coworkers decide to hide from an active shooter, it's better to spread out than to huddle together.

a. true

b. false

8. Fighting back against an active shooter is your last resort in an attempt to survive the situation.

a. true

b. false

9. What should you do when you first notice law enforcement on the scene with an active shooter?

a. ask for help

b. raise your hands and spread your fingers

c. point toward the area where you last saw the shooter

Answer Key: 1. a 2. d 3. b 4. c 5. a 6. b 7. a 8. a 9. b

IN BUSINESS: SITUATIONAL AWARENESS
AND THE OODA LOOP

Situational Awareness is key to personal protection; it's also the key to business in an increasingly fast-paced market insofar as it makes smart speedy decision-making possible. To be as flexible as possible in our thoughts and actions, we have to be able to update and revise our awareness on the regular.

Air Force military strategist John Boyd developed a process known as the OODA loop. OODA stands for observe, orient, decide, act. The basic idea behind the OODA loop is that we can face situational threats, even overcome them, with well-practiced agility. Though it got its start as a military tactic, the loop has been translated into business environments to encourage our ability to make complex decisions with greater and greater rapidity. That process involves collecting data, turning it into insight, and acting on it—in a constant loop.

Observe. Gather your data. Get as much accurate information, or feedback, as is realistic or necessary so that you have the correct information from which to learn.

Orient. Analyze and assess the information or the relation between actions and results. Set aside your prejudices, shift your perception, and try to attend to the evidence that's in front of you.

Decide. Clarify the options and predict the impact of each decision.

Act. Implement a decision with confidence, but stay open to new information and input.

Think of the OODA loop as a way of focusing your attention in an ever-changing environment.

The OODA loop opens up possibilities for you to act. It actually gives you the opportunity to consider more options than you might otherwise. The more you practice using it, the better—and faster—you'll get.

SUMMARY

- Situational Awareness's Operator is multiplicative ✘. The absence of Situational Awareness will quickly deplete or void the value of all the additive Principles acting in concert and could render those Principles valueless. Alternatively, should you apply Situational Awareness and respond appropriately (or take preemptive action as required), the value of all those Principles will be magnified considerably.

- Situational Awareness's Function is finite ♥. We are neither James Bond nor Jason Bourne. The secret is to make a realistic determination about how much information we are able to take in and how we should prioritize that information to maximize our awareness and minimize our amount of exposure.

- Situational Awareness begins with noticing and assessing your environment. The faster you can take in and evaluate data, the more likely you are to make decisions that increase your chances of a good outcome.

- Unlocking your capacity for Situational Awareness takes practice predicting outcomes: you filter out what's unnecessary so that you can focus in on what demands your attention. Whether in terms of personal safety or in terms of finding solutions to business problems, Situational Awareness is about becoming more flexible, more agile, more capable of responding cleverly in the face of rapid change.

- Guest Star Kristina Anderson reminds us of the importance of exercising choice in a threatening situation: "If you make no choice and freeze, you're just kind of letting it happen.

If you exercise some choice, you can minimize some of the risks."

- This chapter's business-focused exercise offers an active shooter test of your Situational Awareness and encourages you to learn some key skills that will serve you well in the event you become exposed to violent behavior. This is a key exercise to share with all your employees and teams.

- This chapter's personal exercise (available in the *FFL Workbook* by download from www.formulaforluck.com) utilizes Air Force military strategist John Boyd's highly regarded process known as the OODA loop (observe, orient, decide, act). Use this exercise to practice facing situational threats and to learn skills to manage and overcome them.

STUART'S SECRETS

- Flying on an airline that's unfamiliar to you? Visit www.airlineratings.com for up-to-date information about airline safety and flight reliability.

- Taking the subway? Know that the survivability ratio of a subway bombing or mass shooting is ten times higher if you're in the first or last carriage and not in the center of the subway. So walk to one or the other ends of the platform to get on either the first or final car.

- Headed to the airport? Do not stop for your latte or otherwise choose to hang out before passing through security; this is the most vulnerable location in the airport. Get out of your car and through security as quickly as you are able, and get your latte on the other side.

- Going to the movies? The large majority of all fatalities and injuries that occur in a cinema shooting happen to those front and center, because the most light is cast on them from the screen. Your survival ratio is going to be dramatically higher if you sit in the back, where the visibility is low, or near an exit.

SO_4 $2 \times a^2 = b^2$

$\left(\frac{2}{3} \times 2x\right)$ $\dfrac{a}{\sin} = \dfrac{b}{\sin}$ H^3 SO_4

$z^2 + xyz = 2$ $y = \sqrt[2]{3+1}$

$= 2T^3 + 1$ $\mathcal{E} = c\,005$ SO_4 $y = \sqrt[2]{3+1}$

$\left(\frac{2}{3}\right) = x_7$

a^2 H^3 $\dfrac{a}{\sin}$ $1.\mathcal{E} = c\,005$

$+1\,\mathcal{E} = 0.005$ $1.\mathcal{E} = c\,005$

$xyz = 2$ $x_7 = \left(\frac{2}{3} \times 2x\right) a^2 = b^2 + c$

$N^2 \times H^3$ $\dfrac{a}{\sin d} = \dfrac{b}{\sin}$

$2x)$ $f(3) = 2^{-3}$

$+c^2$ NH_3 y

$x^2 - 2x \left(\frac{2}{3} \times 2x\right)$ SO_4

$\dfrac{a}{\sin d} = \dfrac{b}{\sin d}$ $f(3) = 2^{-3} + 1\,\mathcal{E} = 0.005$

$(a^2 = b^2)$ $x_7 = \left(\frac{2}{3} \times 2x\right) a^2$

$b^2 + c^2$ $6c$ $\sin$ x_7

CHAPTER 12

THE EIGHTH PRINCIPLE:
SERENDIPITY

Hunch Forward, Not Back

Operator: ✖ **(multiplicative)**

Function: 📍 **(finite)**

Luck Mindset Category: **Behavior**

Shift: **Moving from analytical to instinctual, from avoidance to embracing, from ignoring to exploring**

On Twitter: **#hunchforward**

> *I've always been in the right place at the right time. Of course, I steered myself there.*
>
> —Bob Hope

INTRODUCTION

My wife, Lisa, and I and our two boys always do a summer trip, the more off grid and non-touristy the better. In April 2018, we rented a four-wheel drive Toyota 4Runner and were exploring the southern coast of Iceland both on and off the road. One afternoon we found ourselves on the immense volcanic plains leading from the black sand beaches of Vik toward the massive Katla volcano. Before our vacation, I'd been contemplating whether to pair up with a business partner in order to launch a global electronic identity platform. The trip was essentially a break from work and an opportunity to get some perspective before making any commitments.

At around mile 280 at two o'clock in the afternoon, I picked a random iTunes radio station to play in the car. The first song that came on was Steve Aoki's "This Is What We Started." The song rang in my mind as an anthem for the proposed new venture and as a call to action. That night, at the small hotel, I typed a quick note to my potential business partner and attached the link to Aoki's song: *Hey bud. On vacation. Back in a week. Thought of you when I heard this song.*

The next morning, I received a reply: *Love the song. The video is awesome. Where are you? Iceland?*

How had he known that? It wasn't until that evening that I had a chance to look on YouTube and watch the video I had sent. I was shocked and amazed. Steve Aoki and Don Diablo had recorded the video on the exact same stretch of road in Iceland that my family had been driving on the day before—I mean, within a mile of where we were driving when it came on the car radio. I was overwhelmed by a sense of connectedness, purpose, and the beautiful coincidence of it all. I was also compelled to act, and did so without hesitation, by reaching out to commit to my partner and launch the joint venture.

Swiss psychologist Carl Jung coined the term *synchronicity* to describe meaningful coincidences—when events are not connected by causality, yet we take them to be meaningfully associated with one another. Jung wrote that "Synchronicity is an ever-present reality for those who have eyes to see it."[20]

What Jung was explaining is the way that our minds are capable of seeing significance where there may be only randomness or mere chance. His essential point is that we humans see meaning in one instance and randomness in another based largely on our subjective personal experiences and beliefs. So a meaningful coincidence is an event that speaks to something inside us rather than to some external causal connection.

Scientists have come to call this *confirmation bias*, our capacity to find in the world validation for the beliefs that we already hold, and sometimes hold dear. But what I think is quite interesting about serendipity is the underlying experience of interpreting a situation in a way that makes it meaningful and perhaps even motivates us to act in particular ways. So long as our experiences of synchronicity lead us toward, rather than away from, further investigation and learning, they may have an interesting role to play in increasing serendipity.

It's that additional factor—the inclination to further investigation and learning—that ultimately separates serendipity from synchronicity. Serendipity is instructive or repeatable and not just a matter of mere coincidence. Even my experience corresponding with my business partner from Iceland—moving and remarkable and oddly synchronous as I found it—wasn't just a happy accident.

---

20 Georgia Bamber, "What is the universe trying to tell you?," *Medium*, December 2, 2019, https://medium.com/@GeorgiaBamber_64526/ what-is-the-universe-trying-to-tell-you-814c1365a0f3.

That's to say, I think it's worth asking: How can we repeatedly put ourselves in the right place at the right time? How, like Bob Hope, can we *steer* ourselves there?

EXPLORATION: THINK LIKE A PRINCE

To begin, we need to investigate the shifting meaning over the years of the term *serendipity*. Sometimes, the emphasis is put on the *unexpectedness of the event*, as when one comes across good fortune by sheer accidents of circumstance. Other times, the emphasis is put on *an innate ability*, as in Edward Sully's 1849 article "The Notes and Queries," where serendipity is identified as natural cleverness, a trait, or even a gift. The ambiguity between personal attribute and unanticipated event has been propagated through many redefinitions over the years.

In 2004, Robert Merton and Elinor Barber devoted a book to investigating these alternatives.[21] As they outline in the book, after some research into the matter, they came across a text by Horace Walpole, an eighteenth-century aristocrat and the fourth Earl of Oxford, who was both an architect and quite a gossip. In 1754, Walpole wrote a letter to his friend and distant relation Sir Horace Mann in which he recounted a discovery he'd made. To help explain his experience, Walpole referred to a Persian fairy tale called *The Three Princes of Serendip*, in which the titular characters are "always making discoveries by accident and sagacity, of things which they were not in quest of."[22] What I think is phenomenal about Walpole's "definition" is that it emphasizes both accident *and*

---

21   R. K. Morton and E. Barber, *The Travels and Adventures of Serendipity: A Study in Sociological Semantics and the Sociology of Science* (Princeton: Princeton University Press, 2004).

22   Ibid.

sagacity. Serendipity may seem to be synonymous with accidental discovery, but I would say that's impossible to achieve without a keen eye, skill, and/or the wisdom to recognize what has been stumbled upon.

Serendipity is quite at home in science. Scientists have to try to understand the conditions under which discoveries are most often made. This helps both to ensure that studies are replicable and to facilitate future discoveries. You might think that this requires processes in which nothing is left to chance, but in fact, there's something quite different going on.

Many have described scientific inquiry as hunting a hare (searching for a specific theory) with a rifle (a scientific rule). But there's yet another element to scientific discovery: while you're out looking for hares, you might have the opportunity to catch a fox.

> **Serendipity may seem to be synonymous with accidental discovery, but I would say that's impossible to achieve without a keen eye, skill, and/or the wisdom to recognize what has been stumbled upon.**

We have some amazing examples of serendipitous discoveries in science. We need look no further than Fleming's discovery of penicillin or Nobel's discovery of dynamite. These were not possible without a measure of intentional action, but they also required a learned ability to notice and recognize novelty and then explain it. Let's focus on Fleming's discovery of penicillin in 1928, which was triggered by a spore of penicillium fungus contaminating his petri dish while he was growing staphylococcus bacteria. Now, it was an accident that the mold spores landed in the dish. But the discovery was serendipitous in several ways. First, had Fleming not been culti-vating bacteria, he wouldn't have had the opportunity to notice the stray mold spore. Furthermore, had Fleming not had a deep and full understanding of how bacteria develops—and this is the element of sagacity—it's unlikely he would have even noticed the antibiotic properties of the penicillium and therefore develop what was, at the time, the single most important advance in health technology in the twentieth century.

Sagacity—the keen eye, the skill in perceiving, or the astuteness on which the serendipitous moment relies—is emphasized also by Louis Pasteur, who observed, "In the fields of observation, chance only favors the prepared mind."[23]

If sagacity is the handmaiden of serendipity, what can we do to become more sagacious? This was first and best explained by Max Gunther in 1977 in his book called *The Luck Factor*. Gunther proposed thirteen criteria, five of which he groups together under the title "The Luck Adjustment." These five techniques are the spiderweb, the hunching skill, boldness, the ratchet effect, and the pessimism paradox.

- **The spiderweb** is the process of building out your network, a topic we covered in detail in chapter 7.

- **The hunching skill** involves acting on our intuitions by following three rules: One, learn to assess the available data. Two, don't confuse a hunch with a hope. And three, make room for hunches to grow and prosper.

- **Audentes fortuna juvat** or, roughly translated, "fortune favors the bold." If you've got a spiderweb and strong

---

23   R. M. Pearce, "Chance and the Prepared Mind," *Science New Series* 35, no. 912, June 21, 1912, https://www.jstor.org/stable/1638153?.

hunching skills, now you're ready to take the next step: pouncing on opportunity quickly and effectively.

- **The ratchet effect** is, effectively, the capacity to recognize sunk costs. We all know the story of the gambler who couldn't quit when ahead. If there are signs that you're about to have a change in good fortune, you should probably cut your losses. If you're able to notice carefully and act quickly, you'll minimize potential risk or loss of money, time, or love. This principle applies not just to actions but to words: important as it is what you say and when you say it, it's equally important that you don't say the wrong thing at the wrong time.

- **The pessimism paradox** is the one element of the Luck Adjustment criteria with which I strongly disagree. Gunther recommends that we approach all things pessimistically. You know that I argue strongly in this book for both Positivity and optimism. That said, I do think there's a useful interpretation of Gunther's approach, and that's the idea that we should always have a fallback plan should things go wrong. But that's not the same as having an essentially pessimistic approach. We should *not* assume that the worst will happen. Instead, we should simply develop our capacity to survive, and make success of, those moments when things inevitably go awry.

You cannot plan a serendipitous discovery or event. What you *can* plan is careful work that will probabilistically lead to discovery, and you can also plan to track well the processes that are in play. Be an astute and conscientious observer, make room for hunches, expect some mistakes, and work collaboratively to facilitate success.

I've come to think that there are three variants of serendipitous occurrences—three *types* of Serendipity, if you will. For all that we have been told over the years by parents and teachers about looking for a certain something in the right place, I invite you to consider that solutions to problems you're not currently trying to solve might be discovered in the most unexpected places.

Serendipity Type A: Actively looking for a solution for a problem, you find something else in an unexpected place that solves that problem (think of getting a flat tire, and then a tow truck happens to drive by and helps you out).

Serendipity Type B: Actively seeking a solution for a problem, you find in an expected place something that you were not looking for that solves for an entirely different problem (think of how penicillin or Post-it Notes were discovered).

Serendipity Type C: You stumble upon something that you were not actually looking for and which was in an unexpected place. However, you are open to it, curious enough to investigate it with a keen eye; you apply knowledge (maximize its potential) and in so doing realize it can solve another entirely different problem that you were not even looking to solve. (Think of Newton sitting under a tree and discovering gravity after an apple fell on his head.)

I happen to think that Type C is Serendipity in its truest form, the absolutely unanticipated thing upon which one stumbles, accompanied by the ability to recognize and capitalize on it.

GUEST STAR: VANDANA HART

Vandana Hart was born in Russia at the peak of the Cold War. From her parents she inherited her mother's fire and her father's diplomacy; from both, a sense of adventure and risk-taking. Her passion for dance led her around the world exploring cultures and making connections to people and places that have repeatedly reoriented the trajectory of her life. Just a few of the things Vandana has achieved include dancing for the Alvin Ailey Company in New York City; becoming a UN ambassador for women's rights working for the United Nations to cofound UNIFEM and launch their Safe Cities Global Initiative in India, Rwanda, Egypt, Papua New Guinea, and Ecuador; studying international relations at the London School of Economics; and hosting a top-ten Netflix series showcasing cities and cultures around the world through dance.

All of Vandana's pursuits are held together by two interwoven threads: interest in effecting structural changes that alleviate human suffering and a willingness to say yes to challenges both small and large. In fact, what her father said to her every day when he dropped her off at school as a child has become a central component of her approach to life: "Take a risk today." Vandana attributes her success to the skill she has developed in identifying and inviting Serendipity and flow into her core decision-making processes. For Vandana, saying yes and taking risks is a way of following her deepest intuition. "I was never trying to calculate things," she says of her attitude toward change and adventure. "I wanted to soak up as much knowledge and skill and experience as possible—and go where the flow leads me."

How entirely appropriate to this chapter's theme that Vandana and I met early in 2020 via an uncanny collision of people and circumstances that literally implored us to connect!

SL: Flashback to your origin story, where your father drops you off at primary school each day and his final parting words are "Take a risk today." How has that shaped you?

VH: He was not talking about extreme sports or any kind of obvious risks but instead what happens when you come face to face, eye to eye with something in the world that feels uncomfortable and unknown. How we decide to act in those moments defines us. Because each time we feel that tension or little bit of fear, it's an invitation to break through. What's on the other side is really the magic. If we feel that wall of fear and we just stay there, we miss out on the opportunity for magic.

SL: In your twenties, you were on a pickup truck bouncing through the townships outside Johannesburg, South Africa, heading to a late-night dance event. What was going through your mind then?

VH: I was in a community an hour outside of Johannesburg. There were no lights, just darkness, and little concrete and tin houses for miles. I was with a bunch of men, thinking to myself, "This is a horrible idea." But something inside me also said, "Go on this adventure." For me, there was this really deep sense of trusting myself to navigate that experience. Learning how to tell the difference between true intuitions and stupid decisions is very important.

We have an invitation every day to push through our hesitation. In interactions with people that are different than us, that have different values, different mindsets, if we can create joy, we can learn so much. Where richness and even a kind of flow state have happened in my life are in talking to strangers, punching through walls of fear, and seeing what's on the other side.

SL: Does punching through fear also entail growth?

VH: Absolutely, it's not about overcoming or boosting adrenaline. It's about getting closer to your life's purpose—why you're here and what your mission is.

SL: So as you become better attuned to what your life's purpose is, then there's an alignment; there's a spark. What does that feel like, and what do you do in those moments?

VH: Serendipity typically doesn't happen when you are alone—most of the time, it's relational. The Serendipity amplifier is our interaction with other people. Serendipity is only possible in its full magnitude in interactions with other people—and more often than not with new people. If I hadn't really been fully present in some of my most serendipitous moments, I would've missed out on some of the most magical things in my life. Being present is foundational when it comes to recognizing Serendipity.

> Serendipity is only possible in its full magnitude in interactions with other people—and more often than not with new people.
> —*Vandana Hart*

SL: OK, so one of the biggest things someone can do is to work on being present. It's sort of a foundational element for Serendipity. For example, if you're stuck in some story, some emotion, some ego-driven trip, if you're not present in the moment and present with other people, it's pretty hard for Serendipity to occur or be recognized. What do you recommend for people who might feel stuck in a rut or in need of a change?

VH: I recommend being like a snake. We have to constantly be shedding our skin because part of Serendipity is knowing when it's time to let go of one of your identities, one of the layers of your ego, to then be able to be present when the new stuff shows up. You know, we have golden handcuffs in so many different parts of life that give us comfort—and Serendipity really does not like comfort! Whenever I've let go of something I thought I needed or was really attached to, magic happened, including loves of my life.

SL: One closing question. People can manifest downward (vicious) cycles as well as upward (victorious) cycles. When you are in a moment that feels serendipitous, how do you direct your energy?

VH: If an encounter is going my way, I press on. I actually swim harder, deeper into that wave, because I know that's a move that has served me well. It doesn't always work, but more times than not, I get the most out of that moment. If it's going the other way, I cut. It's kind of like a gambler at the poker table. If it's going well, you double down, and if it's going poorly, you walk away. With practice that becomes a reliable reflex. That's a key to success—not just surfing but swimming into the Serendipity waves.

IN PRACTICE: THE THREE
TYPES OF SERENDIPITY

Identifying the three different variants of Serendipity and what we can do more of to manifest them is as important as understanding what is not Serendipity but just regular discovery. Remember our review of Serendipity from earlier in the chapter:

NOT SERENDIPITY: Actively looking for a solution to problem ❶ and finding solution ⓪ in an expected place that solves for problem ❶.

A. SERENDIPITY TYPE A: Actively looking for a solution for problem ❶ and finding something else ① in an unexpected place that solves for problem ❶.

B. SERENDIPITY TYPE B: Actively looking for a solution for problem ❶ and finding something else you were not looking for ② in an expected place that solves for an entirely different problem ❷.

C. SERENDIPITY TYPE C: True Serendipity—stumbling upon something else ③, which you were not actually looking for and which was in an unexpected place. However, you are open to it, curious enough to investigate it with a keen eye; you apply knowledge (maximize its potential) and in so doing realize it can solve another entirely different problem ❹ you were not even looking to solve.

NOW: Fill out boxes A, B, and C with an example of each type of

Serendipity you have had.

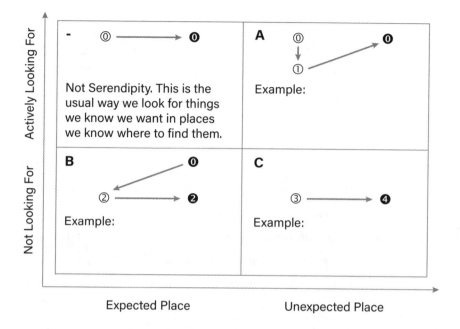

NEXT: Answer the following: What enabled each of the three types of Serendipity to occur? What did *you* do or not do to encourage or take advantage of the situation or opportunity?

IN BUSINESS: SERENDIPITY AND INCENTIVIZATION

We are, as individuals and as business leaders, often encouraged to set goals and single-mindedly pursue them, plowing through obstacles and avoiding distraction. Equally we're told that business is largely about conducting thorough rational analysis of data. These might be some of the most counterintuitive ideas to success, as they limit, even devalue, following gut instincts and pursuing chance encounters. In the real world, opportunities surround us and pop up at all different moments. If you're driven in only one direction and not tuned in to your instincts, you're going to miss out on interesting opportunities.

In business environments, we've seen the rise of paradigms intended to facilitate serendipitous outcomes, like rapid prototyping or pivoting in response to incremental change. These, and others, have been detailed in seminal books like *The Lean Startup* by Eric Ries. We've also learned that it's critical for HR departments to help create an inclusive environment that attracts a diversity of team members and enables them to feel comfortable sharing opinions. It's those differences of opinion that challenge the echo chamber of homogenous ideas and invite serendipitous encounters among people and perspectives.

I want to suggest one other strategy to stimulate Serendipity in business environments, and that's performance incentivization. We need to engineer into our businesses alternate ways of recognizing and rewarding performance so that we open up more diverse, and perhaps also more unlikely, opportunities for discovery.

Consider this question: If you had a ton of money and wanted to achieve the greatest global impact, would you give large grants to a few previously proven successful applicants, or would you give a larger number of small grants to many average, unsuccessful, or unknown people?

If you're trying to engineer creativity, innovation, or outside-the-box thinking, allocating resources solely on the basis of prior star performance will be less impactful to your organization than spreading those resources among a broader group.

A study conducted in 2013 by Jean-Michel Fortin and David J. Currie looked specifically at whether larger grants given to a few elite researchers led to larger discoveries overall.[24] They learned that the scientific impact of large grants is positively, but only weakly, related to funding. They concluded that funding targeting diversity would likely be more productive than funding targeting only excellence. As a result of their and others' studies, there has been an ongoing debate within scientific communities about transforming a system that is currently highly competitive into one that is more egalitarian. Most seem to agree, however, that the least-effective funding strategy for global grants is one in which a larger percentage of the funding is given only to those who already have been successful. A mixed strategy may be a suitable compromise, but, quite strikingly, the most efficient way to generate outcomes is likely to involve distributing funds at random.

In complex social and economic contexts, where chance and Serendipity are more likely to play a role, strategies that allow for and incorporate randomness perform better. Equal funding to an equal number irrespective of prior performance is the best funding strategy. When that comes to the distribution of business resources and opportunities for professional development, an egalitarian approach is more likely to yield maximum results.

The bottom line is this: instead of thinking of Serendipity as mere happy accident, focus on the element of sagacity, the preparation, resource allocation, and positioning of employees within business structures to the benefit of everyone.

---

24 Jean-Michel Fortin and David J. Currie, "Big Science vs. Little Science: How Scientific Impact Scales with Funding," PLoS ONE 8, no. 6, June 19, 2013, https://doi.org/10.1371/journal.pone.0065263.

SUMMARY

- Serendipity's Operator is multiplicative **✖**. Doubling down when Serendipity is going your way (i.e., when you are in a flow state) can create victorious cycles and be an exponential multiplier for luck. In the same way, cutting your exposure when Serendipity sends you downward is a way to significantly limit or eliminate loss and avoid vicious cycles.

- Serendipity's Function is finite **♥**. We can manifest more Serendipity by casting our radar wider and looking into unexpected places, being more respondent to unforeseen events, and acting rapidly through applying wisdom. However, there is simply a limited number of times this can occur. That limit reinforces just how important it is that we miss as few such opportunities as possible.

- Serendipity is a combination of happy accident and sagacity. It is neither a natural gift nor a matter of mere situational fortune.

- Unlocking your capacity for recognizing and acting on serendipitous events requires practice becoming sagacious. It's our sharp powers of judgment and keen mental discernment that enable us to take advantage of unexpected, and lucky, opportunities.

- Guest Star Vandana Hart reminds us that Serendipity is often relational: "The Serendipity amplifier is our interaction with other people. Serendipity is only possible in its full magnitude in interactions with other people, and more often than not with new people."

- This chapter's business-focused exercise invites you to train yourself and your team to better identify the three different variants of Serendipity and what you can do to take full advantage of Serendipity when it appears.

- This chapter's personal exercise (available in the *FFL Workbook* by download from www.formulaforluck.com) asks you to focus on your aha moments by identifying a handful of your own serendipitous events and their outcomes. Using the benefit of hindsight, you'll identify commonalities in order to improve and document new best practices that enable you to make the most of serendipitous events to come.

- In a business environment, explore HR practices that welcome diverse experiences and points of view, and create practices that encourage quick pivoting in response to changed circumstances and feedback.

- When it comes to providing resources for your employees, set up performance incentives that reward *potential* victories. When allocating resources, instead of rewarding only star performers, spread resources among a broader group to invite greater opportunities for future success.

STUART'S SECRETS

- For further study of the idea of Serendipity, check out Robert K. Merton and Elinor Barber's *The Travels and Adventures of Serendipity: A Study in Sociological Semantics and the Sociology of Science*.

- For tracking what stands out to you about your days and weeks, try the Five Minute Journal app. It allows you to begin each day with intention and end each day with gratitude. You can use the photo function to tag moments during your day that you want to reflect on as you work toward inviting Serendipity into your life.

- If you've been reading these chapters in order, then you're already familiar with this one, but it's worth repeating here: Carry a "book of bad ideas" for writing down *all* of your ideas—everything that comes to mind! The goal is to memorialize all the transient thoughts and signals that you come across. You can reflect on your ideas at the end of any week or month and begin to notice that amid all that noise may be some serendipitous insights.

$$H_2SO_4 \quad 2x \quad a^2 = b^2 + c^2 \quad \mathcal{E} = C005$$

$$\left(\frac{?}{?} \times 2x\right) \quad \frac{a}{9m} = \frac{b}{9m} \quad H^3 \quad SO_4$$

$$y^2 + z^2 + xyz = 2 \quad y = \sqrt[2]{3+1}$$

$$= 2^{-3} + 1 \quad \mathcal{E} = C005 \quad SO_4 \quad y = \sqrt[2]{3}$$

$$\left(\frac{2}{3}\right) = x_7 \quad 1.\mathcal{E} = C005$$

$$a^2 \quad H^3 \quad \frac{a}{m} \quad 1.\mathcal{E} = C005$$

$$1.\mathcal{E} = 0.005$$

$$xyz = 2 \quad x_7 = \left(\frac{2}{3} \times 2x\right) a^2 = b^2 + c$$

$$N^2 \times H^3 \quad \frac{a}{9md} = \frac{b}{9m}$$

$$f(3) = 2^{-3}$$

$$NH_3$$

$$x^3 - 2x \quad \left(\frac{2}{3} \times 2x\right) \quad SO_4$$

$$\frac{a}{9m} = \frac{b}{9m} \quad f(3) = 2^{-3} + 1 \quad \mathcal{E} =$$

THE NINTH PRINCIPLE:
CHOICE

Choose Wisely

Operator: ✖ **(multiplicative)**

Function: **0 1** **(binary)**

Luck Mindset Category: **Action**

Shift: **Moving from reactive to proactive, from procrastination to getting on with it, from rest to motion, from no control to control, from no choice to choice, from passivity to activity**

On Twitter: **#choosewisely**

You are not the victim of the world but rather the master of your own destiny. It is your choices and decisions that determine your destiny.

—Ray Bennett

INTRODUCTION

It was a cold evening in October 1993, and I was on the double-decker Go Train heading home from downtown Toronto. I had just delivered to my boss my learnings and recommendations from reading the first edition of *Internet for Dummies*, which had been released a couple of months earlier. In my recommendations, I suggested that we buy our company's domain name, which at the time was available for $29. Sitting on the train, I had the sudden idea that I should go to the bank, borrow a few thousand dollars, and then buy domain names for every Fortune 500 company that hadn't yet purchased one, as well as domains for the most common search terms and major brands.

At that time, the vast majority of these domains were available for that $29 price. Here's just two examples of top search terms and their eventual worth: cars.com is valued at $872 million today, and sex.com sold twice, once for $13 million and then again for $14 million. Had I acted, my life might have been very different. There's a quote from Bill Gates that I've often thought stands against my experience at that time. Gates says: "I was lucky to be in the right place at the right time. But many others were also in the same place. The difference was that I took action."[25] I, too, was lucky to be in the right place at the right time, but I did not act. And I can say that I have regretted that lack of decisive action since.

That was my hundred-million-dollar mistake. I promised myself that I would not make that mistake again.

In 2012, when I had an idea about how to positively impact the lives of over one billion people (what Salim Ismail, in his book *Expo-*

---

25   Bill Gates, quotefancy.com, accessed November 2020, https://quotefancy.com/quote/775298/Bill-Gates-I-was-lucky-to-be-in-the-right-place-at-the-right-time-But-many-others-were.

nential Organizations, calls an MTP—a Massive Transformational Purpose), I acted decisively and started on a seven-year journey to change the world with the company I founded called Trunomi. I did not hesitate to act on my hunch that the largest asset class in the world was personal data and that data ownership and data self-sovereignty would soon become some of the largest industry disruptors in decades.

EXPLORATION: THE PARADOX OF CHOICE

> "I was lucky to be in the right place at the right time. But many others were also in the same place. The difference was that I took action."
> —*Bill Gates*

We humans are not very good at making decisions. It may be some consolation to learn that our ineptitude stems from several million years of genetic coding. During the Paleolithic era, around three million years ago, humankind did not have innumerably many choices to make. Humans hunted to eat and to survive, and when they finally killed an elephant or a mammoth, that was all they ate for breakfast, lunch, and dinner until it was completely gone, and its indigestible parts were put to other uses. Even during much of the time since then, humans continued on in the world with relatively few choices. Reasoning did not really enter our lives until the last few thousand years, and the rationalization of choices and consequences came along even more recently.

From a twenty-first century point of view, early humans might seem to have had it good insofar as they were not faced with having to make so many choices on a daily basis. Between 1975 and 2008 the average number of products in supermarkets alone rose from nine thousand to almost fifty thousand.[26] Today, we are even more inundated with options. And some of our choices have big consequences. Every time you go to a doctor, for example, you're likely to be presented with more options than solutions—alternatives from which you are invited to pick. Our options may have grown in number, but our brains have not evolved to be much different from those of our early counterparts. And today's science has confirmed the very thing many of us experience regularly—that it takes significant cognitive energy to make thoughtful decisions.

With so many choices before us, making decisions can become a source of significant mental stress, the effects of which can be dramatic. Did you know, for example, that Formula 1 drivers can lose up to four kilograms of body weight and burn over 1,500 calories during a single race?[27] That's the product of incredibly high levels of cognitive functioning, heart rates of over 170 beats per minute, and the number of choices being made at every acceleration, break, and corner under the duress of high g-forces and in superheated cockpits. It's not just Formula 1; World Chess grandmaster Vladimir Kramnik lost nearly ten kilograms during a November 2000 match in which he defeated chess king Garry Kasparov—all of which was attributable to nervous tension and immense mental focus.[28]

Very few of us may be Formula 1 drivers or chess grandmasters, but we all still need to figure out how to manage and even decrease

---

26   "What to Do When There Are Too Many Product Choices on the Store Shelves?," ConsumerReports.com, January 2014, https://www.consumerreports.org/cro/magazine/2014/03/too-many-product-choices-in-supermarkets/index.htm.

27   Jordan Golson, "F1 Drivers Push Their Bodies to Extremes in Malaysia's Heat," Wired.com, March 27, 2015, https://www.wired.com/2015/03/f1-drivers-push-bodies-extremes-malaysias-heat/.

28   "Kramnik Lost 10kg Playing Kasparov," News24.com, December 20, 2000, https://www.news24.com/xArchive/Archive/Kramnik-lost-10kg-playing-Kasparov-20001220.

our stress in the face of all the choices on offer today. In his book *The Paradox of Choice,* published in 2004 by Harper Perennial, author Barry Schwartz uses the term *choice overload* to explain that our minds simply cannot cope with the vast number of options. That inability to cope leads us often to feelings of suffocation, exhaustion, and anxiety—in addition to decreased satisfaction when we do make decisions. In a TEDx presentation on the same topic, Schwartz offers the example of going into a store to purchase new running shoes and seeing rows upon rows of alternatives. Given that no one shoe offers everything, we can be left unhappy with our final choice. Schwartz concludes that "the secret to happiness is low expectations." Much as I find that take humorous, you know by now that I also disagree with that approach overall. I think the real question about Choice is this: How do we do a better job of rewiring our neural pathways so that we can trust our most basic choices to align with the outcomes we most desire? With that question in mind, I'd like to suggest some alternatives to low expectations that I think go a long way toward mitigating choice overload and helping improve decision-making.

1. **Avoid homophily**. Homophily names our tendency to associate with others who are like us. Ethan Zuckerman of MIT Media Lab is known for his groundbreaking observations about the way that homophily characterizes our approach to news, information, and social media outlets. All the information and news around us makes it difficult to see outside our circles of comfort or entertain other points of view. On top of that, algorithms guide our search engines to offer us more of what reinforces what we already know or believe. Zuckerman used that insight to found Global Voices as a means of countering the threat of information isolation. Zuckerman reminds us: if it looks like me, acts

like me, lives like me, and thinks like me, it's probably only going to reinforce whatever ideas I had already. Homophily, says Zuckerman, "can make you really dumb."[29]

(This first recommendation may seem like it would open up more choices rather than reduce or help us negotiate them. But widening your view and being well informed can actually aid decision-making by helping you better weigh options against one another and even anticipate options so as not to be overwhelmed by them. It takes practice, but you can train your ability to choose so that it becomes like instinct, a gut feeling guiding you toward the best choice.)

2. **Set clear priorities**. Having a clear goal or outcome in mind helps determine what would constitute a minimum for satisfaction. Assess how relevant any choice really is to you. For example, are you choosing among heart surgeons or protein bar varieties? Are you hoping to pick up a fresh salad with chicken, but today's menu offers a similar salad with salmon? Considering the nutritional value and immediate availability, is that a "good enough" substitute for what you initially wanted?

3. **Steady your emotions**. Try to let strong emotions subside before making major decisions. A calm heart contributes to a level head. If you're writing an emotional email response, step away from it for a bit and then edit with perspective and a clear head before sending. If there is an imminent deadline, at least stand up and get some fresh air before

---

29 Vijaysree Venkatraman, "Ethan Zuckerman on How to Engineer Serendipity Online," *The Christian Science Monitor*, December 12, 2008, https://www.csmonitor.com/Technology/Tech-Culture/2008/1212/ethan-zuckerman-on-how-to-engineer-serendipity-online.

reviewing and hitting send.

4. **Ask**. Ideally, we make judgments and decisions about how to act based on as much useful information as we are able to gather and review. The key here is to avoid making assumptions in situations where simply asking about possibilities can lead to quicker solutions.

5. **Assess the risk of inaction**. What's the full opportunity cost of not acting? The risk assessment of not doing something is as critical as any assessment of the benefits of doing it.

6. **Sleep on big decisions**. Buying a house, getting engaged, or moving to another country are among the sorts of decisions that most deserve your time and consideration. Be sure at least to sleep on them, if not also to seek out the insights of trusted advisors.

7. **Don't second-guess yourself**. Once your choice is made, make good on it. Move immediately to action. Set SMART goals (specific, measurable, attainable, relevant, and time-based) to move forward.

The reality is that we need to train our impulses and use our daily activities to develop habits that nourish our capacity to choose wisely. The choices we make every day are powerful; they can bring us closer to illness or to health, connect or disconnect us, and ultimately shape the lives that we wish to live instead of lives characterized by regret or undue suffering.

There's a famous Cherokee parable about the incredible power of Choice. An old Indian chief is teaching his grandson about life. "A fight is going on inside me," he says to the boy. "A fight between two wolves. One is evil: anger, envy, sorrow, regret, greed, arrogance, self-pity, guilt, resentment, inferiority, lies, false pride, superiority, and ego." He continues: "The other is good: joy, peace, hope, serenity, humility, kindness, benevolence, empathy, generosity, truth, compassion, and loving awareness. The same fight is going on inside you and inside every other person in the world." The grandson thinks about it for a minute, then looks to his grandfather and asks, "Which will win?" The old chief's reply: "The one that you feed."

Insofar as they form habits within us, our everyday decisions ultimately help to establish our enduring traits or character, the very defining qualities of our humanity. That alone should make them worth training in the direction of our well-being and our good luck.

> The choices we make every day are powerful; they can bring us closer to illness or to health, connect or disconnect us, and ultimately shape the lives that we wish to live instead of lives characterized by regret or undue suffering.

GUEST STAR: McKEEL HAGERTY

When he was just entering his teens, McKeel Hagerty's parents started an insurance agency in Traverse City, Michigan, with a focus on collector wooden boats. Though he had earned his insurance license and was selling marine craft policies by the age of eighteen, McKeel hadn't planned to enter into the family business. If anything, his interest was in restoring classic cars. He also had a deep curiosity about the history of ideas. For nearly a decade, he studied English, philosophy, theology, and classics, even earning an MA in theology along his journey.

When McKeel eventually returned to Traverse City to join the family business, one of his first projects was to expand the focus to include classic and collector cars. From there, he created the Historic Vehicle Association, partnered to create the National Historic Vehicle Register, and turned the family business into the world's largest provider of specialty insurance to collector car enthusiasts; and he publishes a magazine called *Hagerty* that serves as the world's reference point for collectible cars.

As a leader, McKeel has incorporated his deep curiosity about big ideas into helping others think about how they approach life, human connection, and success in an increasingly technological age. Notably, he led the world's largest organization of industry leaders as its global chair from 2016 to 2017, where one of his headline phrases—"Yes, and …"—inspired more than twenty-five thousand CEOs not just to say yes but to be curious about how they could do even more.

For McKeel, the possibility of human growth is boundless so long as we measure ourselves by who we are and are becoming rather than by mere material externalities.

Our mutual commitment to YPO and its credo "Better leaders through lifelong learning and idea exchange" has united McKeel and me for almost a decade. I have stood next to him in formal roles like ringing the opening bell at the Nasdaq stock exchange as well as informal ones like the time we interviewed Howie Mandel in Los Angeles. He is an eloquent and impactful speaker and truly inspiring to chat with.

SL: We have spoken about Jim Collins's concept of return on luck. What are your thoughts on how you make the most of the "what" luck and "who" luck that comes your way?

MH: The most successful people tend to take greater advantage of the luck coming their way. I've always taken a "be ready for everything" approach in my life. So whether it's my physical training, whether it's the reading that I'm doing, I always want to be ready to go in any direction and ready to take advantage of opportunity as soon as it comes my way. Luck falls on all of us. The difference is who can take the most advantage of it when it hits.

SL: Earlier in this book I interviewed my mentor, James Donnelly. When we were discussing decision-making, he said to focus on the biggest decisions that have the most impact and approach them with a filter—either it's materiality or outcome. Then act swiftly. The reason why some people don't succeed in life, or don't get lucky, is that they wait for 100 percent of the information before making a decision. Do you agree?

MH: Absolutely! I've always taken a kind of 80-percent-ready-for-everything approach to life. I always want to be 80 percent ready to take advantage of opportunity when it comes my way. If you make a decision with 80 percent info and turn out to be right, by then you're far ahead of the next person who's still trying to research the last 20 percent. Leaders make the most with what information they have.

SL: What are some of your best practices for making the most of life's opportunities?

MH: First and foremost, you've got to know that the brain is a pattern recognition engine, and its primary purpose is to keep us alive. For these reasons, it tends to overreact to threats and can make us feel like there's somebody coming after us. It's important to learn how to use your mind in a way that takes advantage of the things that it's wired to do well and tamps down the overreaction to meaningless things. What I found is that a lot of people don't know how to tamp down those overreactions to take advantage of some opportunity that's happening now. We often overreact to risk or threat or we fear failure or shame/embarrassment because we're wired to the idea of belonging or not belonging to a tribe.

Also, I've discovered that people develop blind spots mostly because of their strengths and not because of their weaknesses. People get so good at something that they just keep playing to their strengths. Understanding the blind spots that result from their strengths will make it more likely for people to take advantage of luck when it comes their way.

SL: Once they decide to act, how do the best leaders deliver a message that's empowering and that people can connect to?

MH: You won't see me turning to a lot of spreadsheets! Of course, more and better data can inform decisions, but I've never seen data stand up in front of a room and deliver. Data always has to be the servant to the story. If you've spotted a good leader, you probably have found a good storyteller. Good leaders are very good at finding stories that connect people, bring them in, and create those unifying elements.

IN PRACTICE: KNOW YOUR REAL OPTIONS

Before reading anything below, cover the right-hand page (IN GRAY) with a piece of paper so it does not influence your thinking.

Imagine you arrive in New York City on a business trip, and a colleague tells you about a once-in-a-lifetime music event that's going on that night. Tickets sold out months ago, and you are envious because you really want to go too. Think through how you would feel after hearing that the event is sold out and what your default mindset would be about the likelihood of you being able to attend.

STEP 1: Complete the exercise below to see how your choices stack up to alternative possibilities. Once done, uncover on the facing page each set of Luck Mindset statements which indicate alternative choices that could profoundly improve your outcomes.

STATEMENT ABOUT THE SITUATION YOU FIND YOURSELF IN:	AGREE	DISAGREE
Tickets are no longer available, as event is 100 percent sold out		
You don't know anyone in NYC that could help you attend the event		
No ticket = no entry		
Missing this event means you will never see it		
Since you cannot go, it means you might as well go back to your hotel		

WHAT YOUR REALITY MIGHT LOOK LIKE
WHEN CHOOSING A LUCK MINDSET:

- Tickets are always available somewhere. Sites such as StubHub, Lastminute Tickets, and others usually have extra tickets; they will just cost a lot more.
- There will almost definitely be scalpers and profiteers selling tickets near the entrance to the event.
- Check at will call for resale tickets for no-shows.

- Ask: post your need on social media and in your networks. If you have a developed network, someone might just come to your aid or might introduce you to someone else who can assist you.

- Depending on the event, a ticket might not be needed. Grab some courage, show up, and be prepared to offer a bouncer, security member, or event staff some cash to let you in without a ticket.
- Sometimes a kind word, a smile, or a sincere ask for help might also get you access on-site.

- Typically, an event like this will occur another night and or in another city as part of a tour or series.
- Do some quick research online to check and see what alternative options really exist.

- Tell yourself a "different story" and make your night memorable by finding another amazing thing to do/see that night while in NYC.
- There are always other options to bring you joy, provide new experiences, and make amazing memories.

STEP 2: Identify any areas of your thought processes that you might wish to improve upon / work on for the future, and introduce some more optimistic problem-solving techniques. Remember, the key here is becoming more aware of your default thought process and paying closer attention to what you choose to do (and not do).

COUNT TO THREE

When I was living in Sarasota, Florida, in the late nineties, I met an amazing friend named Ross Bryans who would later serve as the best man at my wedding and my brother from another mother. In over twenty-five trips to travel, ski, and scuba destinations around the globe, a wonderful secret for success that Ross used rubbed off on me. Ross uses a hack called "one, two, three" each time he needs to work up the energy to just go do what needs to be done in the moment and without question. Here's how it works: If you need to act on a decision and you're just not ready yet to do it, say to yourself, "One, two, three," and then get to doing it *before* you get to *three*. If you can commit to never getting to *three*, this hack will spur you into action countless times and save your bacon at others. This very simple but powerful tool has given me the ability to face obstacles where I also felt I lacked either the courage or the ability to act or to choose.

If Ross's hack sounds familiar, that's because it's quite like the one that's used with reluctant children. When you're trying to get a child to do something they're resisting, you might say, "I'm going to count to three, and at three if you haven't done what I'm asking you to do, it's over." A lot of adults fail to follow through on this simple promise of consequences for the child's inaction. Instead, they might say, "I'm asking you again. One, one and a half, two, two and a half, two and three-quarters …," which defeats the whole power of the simple "one, two, three." There is no two and a half; there is no delay. If you hold the line repeatedly, the child realizes that shit hits the fan at *three*, and they always act before it, sometimes just on *one*. The inevitability of it is vital. The psychology is the same for adults as it is for kids, except that as an adult, you are both the resistant party and the authoritative one. By simply not giving your mind the opportunity to generate excuses, you generate velocity and train yourself to take action.

IN BUSINESS: FACILITATING DECISION-MAKING

Businesses offering goods and services to the public are essentially presenting people with a variety of options from which to choose. How do they help potential clients overcome a tendency toward decision paralysis? The answer to this question dictates the outcomes for most of the largest consumer brands in the world.

In 2000, psychologists Sheena Iyengar and Mark Lepper published a study about alternating jam displays in a supermarket by day: on one day, they would display a table with twenty-four different kinds of jams, and on another day, that table would have only six different kinds of jams. Iyengar and Lepper found that while the table with a lot more jams generated more interest, people were far less likely to purchase a jar of jam than when the table had a much-smaller display. In fact, they were ten times less likely. The results suggest that while choice might seem appealing at first, customers easily experience overload. Volume of sales was impacted, and the customer satisfaction rate was reduced as well—not just with the jam purchases but with their experience at that store overall.

In 2015, the *Journal of Consumer Psychology* presented an analysis of choice studies to help determine the extent to which reducing choice actually boosts sales.[30] They determined four scenarios in which reducing the number of alternatives motivates consumers to make purchases:

---

30 Alexander Chernev, Ulf Böckenholt, and Joseph Goodman, "Choice overload: A Conceptual Review and Meta-Analysis," *Journal of Consumer Psychology* 26, no. 2, April 2016, https://www.sciencedirect.com/science/article/abs/pii/S1057740814000916?np=y.

1. **Quick and easy**. Reducing the number of choices helps when people want to make a quick and easy decision, for example, at a gas station or convenience market. Offering fewer and simpler choices helps people when they need to move on to other things.

2. **Complex products**. When the product is complex, like a healthcare plan or a riding lawn mower, the fewer the choices you need to offer.

3. **Difficult to compare**. Fewer options facilitate decision-making when it's difficult to compare alternatives. Imagine the difference between researching alternatives on the internet (where product comparisons are ubiquitous) versus standing in the cereal aisle, attempting to read the backs of twenty boxes in order to compare their nutrition values.

4. **No clear preferences**. When your product is one for which consumers don't already have a clear preference, or they lack knowledge of the product, less is once again more.

Now, let me complicate this story a little bit, because although reducing the number of options is one trick, so is altering the order in which options are presented. We know, for example, that when a restaurant wine list has too many options, people spend 34 percent less money on a bottle. But we also know that when wines are inverted and listed from most expensive to cheapest, people spend 26 percent *more* on a bottle.[31] So, if you're running a restaurant, reduce your list to twenty bottles and put the most expensive first, and you could see a 40 percent increase in wine sales by doing nothing else.

---

31 Armando Maria Corsi, Simone Mueller Loose, and Larry Lockshin, "Let's See What They Have …: What Consumers Look For in a Restaurant Wine List," *Cornell Hospitality Quarterly* 53, no. 2, April 2012, doi: 10.1177/1938965511428448.

As business owners, besides considering the sorts of needs that guide consumers to our products in the first place, we must also look into how we're presenting our products so as to maximize consumers' capacity to move from decision to action.

A NOTE ON KNOWING ONE'S OPTIONS

My emphasis in this chapter has been on developing a capacity to reduce and prioritize one's choices in a world where options abound. But I would be remiss if I didn't acknowledge that we sometimes limit ourselves by making assumptions about our options instead of investigating them. I'll give you an example.

On a ski trip to Salt Lake City with my good friends Ross, Rob, and James, the first day was stormy and windy, and all the ski mountains were closed except for Deer Valley. When we showed up at Deer Valley, the parking lot was completely full. We appealed to the guard, who could only say kindly that he would be happy to help us were there any parking spots available.

Just as we were about to bail on our ski day, I proposed the following: "Let's just drive to one of the resorts at the top of the hill. I'm just going to go in and ask at the front desk if we can use the hotel parking lot." Ross and James were skeptical: "Why would they let us do that?" "I have no idea," was my reply, "but we're here, so why not ask?"

When we arrived, I explained our situation to the manager: "Forgive me, we're here on a ski trip. There's absolutely nowhere to park for Deer Valley, and I just want to ask if we could park in your lot."

"I can't tell you," he began, "how many people try to pirate our lot all the time. No one ever just comes in and asks! I appreciate you asking." And then: "Here's a sticker for your car. You can use the resort for the day. If you're hungry, I can have the chef make you some food. Lunch is being served right now, and you probably need to eat."

We had a fantastic ski day. Ross and James pointed out to me afterward what they called my "uncanny ability to ask." I hadn't thought about it before, but I suppose it takes both a certain confidence and a certain humility to ask about possibilities rather than assume they are not available to you. I'm comfortable with the thought that the worst that can happen is that my request is denied. If someone says no, that's fine, but I won't let that possibility stop me from asking.

SUMMARY

- Choice's Operator is multiplicative ✘. Like the Behaviors of Luck, which are all multiplicative, Choice is the fundamental differentiator between why luck seems to strike more often for some than for others. Because Choice is binary (see below), the formula is either multiplied by one or by zero.

- Choice's Function is binary **0 1**. It is neither finite nor infinite; it can only be a one or a zero. Realize however, that not all choices need to be big ones. We all make many choices multiple times a day, and these microchoices (like going to the gym each day) are fundamental to growing and sustaining good Habits of Luck.

- Choice should always be thought of as an action—in the words of Sartre, "If I do not choose, I am still choosing."

- Barry Schwartz used the term *choice overload* to explain our struggle to cope with many options and the feelings of suffocation, exhaustion, anxiety, and dissatisfaction that may result.

- Unlock your capacity to choose by setting clear priorities, steadying your emotions, making sure to ask for the information you need, and then refusing to second-guess your decisions.

- Guest star McKeel Hagerty recommends what he calls a "be ready for everything" approach to life: "I always want to be ready to go in any direction and ready to take advantage of opportunity as soon as it comes my way."

- This chapter's personal exercise asks you to test your assumptions against what your real choices might be in a given scenario. You'll identify any areas of your thought processes that you might wish to improve upon and learn some more optimistic problem-solving techniques to apply in the future.

- This chapter's business-focused exercise (available in the *FFL Workbook* by download from www.formulaforluck.com) uses the DRAGS technique (dependencies, risk, available data, gut vs. logic, speed) to help you to identify commonalities and differences in your decision-making process across five recent major business decisions. The results will dramatically increase your velocity and focus on key success criteria.

- For businesses that offer products and services, be sure to take into consideration ways of facilitating your clients' decision-making process. Recall the four scenarios that motivate consumers:

  □ *Quick and easy.* Reducing the number of choices helps people make a quick and easy decision.

  □ *Complex products.* Fewer choices need to be on offer when the product is one that most people struggle to understand.

  □ *Difficult to compare.* Fewer options facilitate decision-making when comparing alternatives would be complicated.

  □ *No clear preferences.* Less is more when you offer something that may be needed but about which consumers tend not to have particularly strong preferences or opinions.

STUART'S SECRETS

- Check out Dan Gilbert's TED Talk "The Surprising Science of Happiness" and his book *Stumbling on Happiness*. Dan argues that we "synthesize" happiness, which is to say that even though we may expect our happiness to come about naturally or in some particular way, we can synthesize it by choosing to make good on whatever does happen.

- Try out the power of "one, two, three" on any young ones in your care.

- Watch, or rewatch, the 2004 movie *The Butterfly Effect* for an exploration of choices and their consequences.

- Read Barry Schwartz's *The Paradox of Choice* for his argument about how eliminating choices can reduce consumer anxiety.

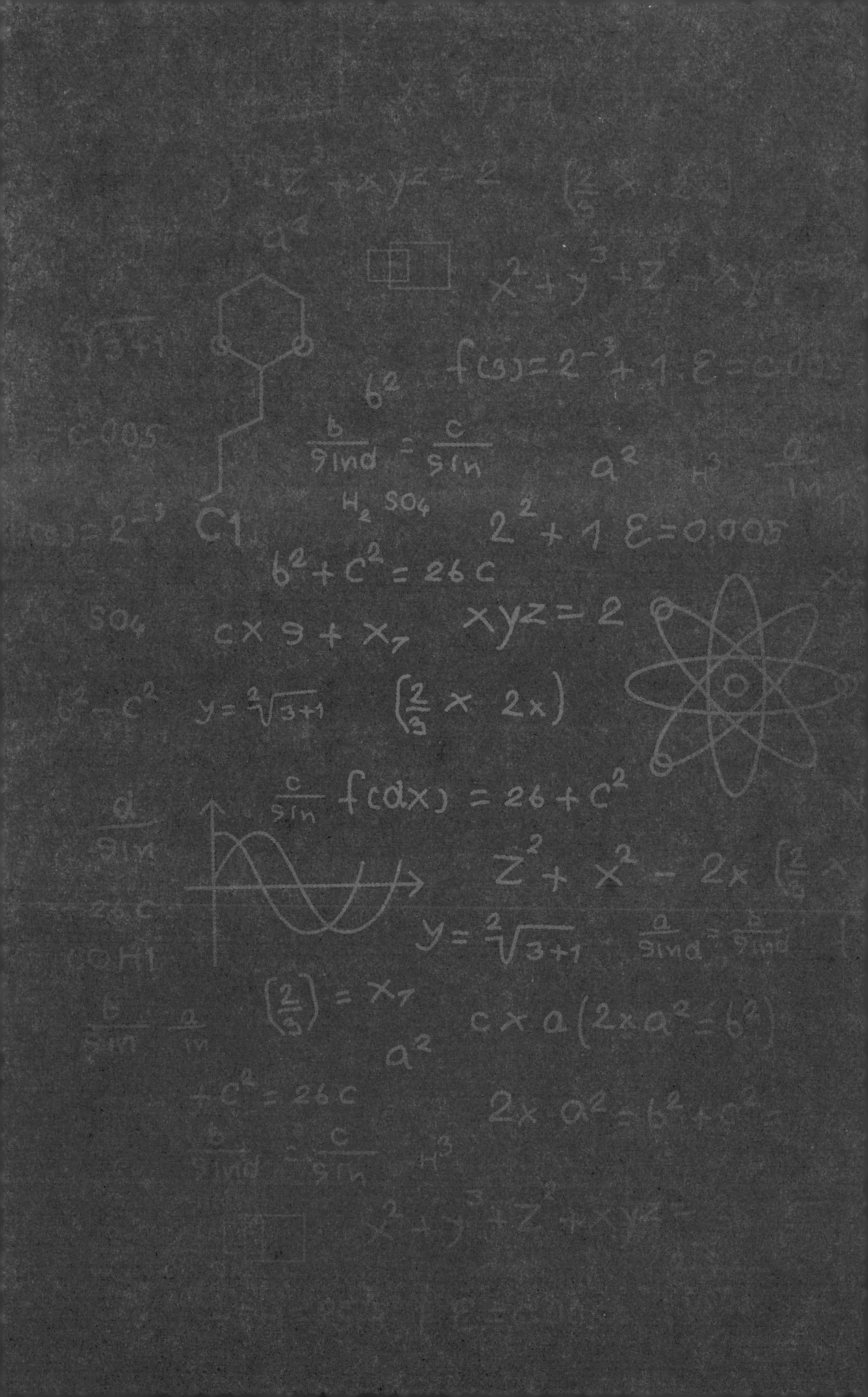

xyz = 2
C1
b² + c² = 26c
2² + 1 ε = 0,005
f(dx) = 26 + c²
z² + x² − 2x
cxa(2xa² = b²)
2x a² = b² + c²

CHAPTER 14

THE TENTH PRINCIPLE:
FAIL FORWARD

Keep On Swimming

Operator: ✖ (**multiplicative**)

Function: **0 1** (**binary**)

Luck Mindset Category: **Action**

Shift: **Moving from failure to learning opportunity, from impossibility to not yet done, from cover up to promote**

On Twitter: **#keeponswimming**

> *I didn't fail one thousand times. The light bulb*
> *was an invention with one thousand steps.*
>
> —Thomas Edison

INTRODUCTION

It was the summer of 1987. I was fifteen years old, racing sailboats for the Quebec sailing team and hoping to one day make the Olympics. Olympic fever had gripped Canada that summer as the country prepared to host the 1988 Calgary winter event. The main sponsor of the Olympic torch relay hosted a competition called *Share the Flame*, which would enable a handful of lucky Canadian citizens to win a chance to carry the Olympic torch for one kilometer of its journey across Canada. In order to qualify, applicants were required to complete a very long handwritten form including a paragraph detailing why they should be selected. The sponsor expected more than a quarter of a million applications and was careful to note at the outset that only 6,214 people would be selected to participate.

A few weeks after the start of the competition, having read that there were already a massive number of applications, I decided that the five applications I had written were insufficient. I figured my chances would be very low unless I tried more frequently. Over the next three weeks before the deadline, I spent time handwriting another seventy-five applications—a process that took me about twenty-five hours of handwriting (at twenty minutes per application).

In total, there were more than 6.6 million applications. My chances were less than one in a thousand, but as true chance would have it, I was selected. I ran one kilometer, 0.62 miles, in the falling snow on a late December evening outside the beautiful Château Montebello in Quebec, Canada. My efforts to keep trying had paid off. My success was a combination of increasing my odds and straightforward chance. Although persistence is an incredibly important part of our efforts toward increasing luck, persistence is also not the primary focus of this chapter. Instead, I want to focus on the critical importance of how we address failure and how those of us who lead lucky lives learn not just to deal with it but to overcome it.

Let's consider a more spectacular, and public, show of continued effort despite the odds. In the film *The Dawn Wall*, you can watch as one of its stars, Kevin Jorgeson, clings by his fingernails to the Dawn Wall of El Capitan. Along with Tommy Caldwell, Jorgeson spent seven years preparing to assault a 3,200-foot-high slab of granite wall that had never been climbed. Over nineteen days, the two tried and tried. Halfway up, Kevin found himself confronted by a class 5.14 D pitch, which is listed as the toughest on the planet. He faced a seventy-foot-wide strip of sheer vertical rock with the consistency of sandpaper and with tiny razor-sharp holes no bigger than the dimples of a golf ball. Both athletes had practiced their entire lives for this event and attempted these same moves tens of thousands of times. Tommy made it across, but Kevin could not.

Over the following seven days and eleven attempts, Kevin just could not complete the crossing. He kept tearing his fingers apart and continuing to fall. Then finally, in front of the world's media, battling fatigue and the fear of letting down his climbing partner, who was running out of time, something changed in Kevin's mind that enabled him to make the crossing. On his next attempt he succeeded, and he and Tommy went onward and upward to make history.

EXPLORATION: THINK LIKE DORY

Since we were children, most of us have been taught to avoid failure. In fact, if we ever received an F or otherwise failed at something, there's a chance we didn't simply feel that we needed improvement but, instead, that we had been labeled as failures in and of ourselves.

In this subtle way across countless experiences, it has become embedded in our mindsets from very young childhood to avoid making an attempt when we suspect we might fail. Two Nobel Prize–winning psychologists, Daniel Kahneman and Amos Tversky, actually studied this phenomenon. They set out to understand why we humans go to such lengths to avoid losing.

What they found was astonishing: the negative impact of a loss—that includes both the sense of loss and the memory of loss—has a greater effect on us (more than twice as great) than any positive impact of success. Zig Ziglar may have gifted us with the inspirational quote "Failure is an event, not a person," but what Kahneman and Tversky showed is that we have quite a lot of trouble separating the two.

> # Failure is an event, not a person.

Research also shows that fear of failure paired with feelings of incompetence leads to self-sabotaging activity, including procrastination.[32] We tend to think that not trying is a guaranteed protection from failure, but I want to suggest that when we don't try because we fear falling flat on our faces or otherwise embarrassing ourselves, we're failing by our inaction in that moment. The antidote to inaction in the face of failure is to understand that we never want to fail at failure itself.

In part, succeeding at failing requires us to maintain a positive attitude. We can choose to face failures as if they are ends, or we can treat them as steps along the way to eventual progress and success. In other words, we might all take a lesson from that plucky little fish Dory, the forgetful blue tang that was introduced to us in 2003,

---

32   Guy Winch, "10 Signs That You Might Have Fear of Failure," Psychology-Today.com, June 18, 2013, https://www.psychologytoday.com/intl/blog/the-squeaky-wheel/201306/10-signs-you-might-have-fear-failure.

swimming along with Marlin in the movie *Finding Nemo*.

Ellen DeGeneres, who voiced Dory's character in the film, revealed in a National Public Radio interview just how honored and awed she was to have been given the opportunity. In that interview, Ellen mentions that the opportunity to voice Dory came at a particularly difficult time in her own life. She hadn't worked for three years on the heels of publicly coming out as a lesbian and having the main character on her sitcom, *Ellen*, come out as well. Not long after these events, the sitcom's ratings dropped, and the show was canceled.

"I was being made fun of for three years," DeGeneres says. "I was attacked for being gay, and nobody would hire me, and so I was out of money … all of a sudden not being validated as a comedian or as an intelligent woman."[33]

> The antidote to inaction in the face of failure is to understand that we never want to fail at failure itself.

It should come as no surprise Ellen's attachment to the character of Dory, whose attitude in the face of adversity is to encourage Marlin to "just keep swimming." When we "just keep swimming," we're pulling on threads of optimism and positivity, literally deciding not to take no for an answer. For us humans, of course, "just keep swimming" might also translate to "keep your head above water," since by not continuing to swim we essentially give ourselves over to drowning.

Keeping going is both the practice and product of resiliency. In the face of difficult times, sometimes the only difference between those who succeed and those who don't is a matter of continuing the

---

33 Ellen DeGeneres, "'Just Keep Swimming': A Lesson In Fortitude From Dory And DeGeneres," NPR, June 16, 2016, https://www.npr.org/2016/06/16/482324585/just-keep-swimming-a-lesson-in-fortitude-from-dory-and-degeneres.

attempt again and again.

In my opinion, Winston Churchill summed it up best: "Success is stumbling from failure to failure with no loss of enthusiasm."

GUEST STAR: BARBARA CORCORAN

In her early twenties, Barbara Corcoran lost the first love of her life. The same man who had given her the seed money for her real estate business venture left her by telling her that she would never amount to anything without him. She swore that she would prove him wrong and that he would never see her fail. When she eventually sold the Corcoran Group brokerage for $66 million in 2001, it had become the biggest residential real estate firm in New York.

In all her business dealings, Barbara has been most appreciative of people who, like her, approach their work with a killer instinct, a sense that there's nothing to lose and much to gain from being absolutely tenacious about their goals. Just as at the start of her career she decided to convert her anger at sexist perspectives into a motivating force for her own success, throughout her life she has turned that competitive energy into opportunity. The desire to prove to others—successful business*men* in particular—that she should not be dismissed helped her build an empire.

In 2008, Barbara was given the opportunity to participate on the hit television show *Shark Tank* and accepted the invitation with excitement. Not long afterward, she received a notice from the producers telling her that they'd decided to go with someone else. She wrote them a long email with a very personal story, encouraging them to see her in person and let her compete for the position. She'd been given a no by the men in charge, but, as she had done early in life and so many times since, she refused to accept that no and ultimately convinced them to give her the gig.

Barbara, like me, is a TEDx speaker, and it's not surprising to me that her TEDx Talk was entitled "Rethinking Failure." We both love skiing powder, and although we missed each other in Colorado last winter, we connected later in the spring to chat about her learnings and insights.

SL: Without action there's no learning. Without learning we don't progress. But how does failing fit into this for you?

BC: I'm uncomfortable with sitting still. And so, I'd rather shoot at a lot and see what sticks rather than think things through or analyze them to death. That old expression "Ready, fire, aim" is the right way for me because I'm already firing, and if it doesn't work, I'll take another shot.

SL: Some of my research is on a subject called *flow*, which happens when luck and reinforcement circles build on each other. It can be a vicious cycle going down or a victorious cycle going up. Basically, you take existing energy, and you augment it, turning a bad day even worse or a good day into something even better. Is that something you would agree with?

BC: Yes. I also think it's always easier to bounce off of something than to create energy on your own. When someone insults you or when an obstacle comes your way, you have the advantage of bouncing off of it. I think by using the energy of a moment, it's easier to keep momentum going, to get a response, and to do something with it. Otherwise you are just playing by yourself.

SL: How do you make decisions?

BC: I always trust my gut because often I don't entirely know what the components are or how I would even approach analyzing them. But my gut says yay, nay, or maybe, and I just trust it. Those times when I have not trusted my gut, I've always looked back and realized I should have listened to myself.

SL: If you go after something so quickly, are you not sometimes unprepared? Do you have to, as some people say, "fake it till you make it"?

BC: Well, "fake it till you make it" sounds ingenuous. I don't like that expression, quite honestly, but some might say I've practiced it my entire career. For me, it's "act like you belong; act like you're capable," knowing full well you'll figure it out if you get the job. It's all right to fake it, but you'd better run like hell to make it really fast; otherwise it's not fair. I think of it more like an early vote of confidence in yourself that you're going to figure it out. Over time, you begin to trust yourself as a person who's capable of coming through no matter what. Once you get your confidence, you know you're going to find a way. You're going to borrow the talent, ask advice, get the right people, change the circumstances. You're going to do whatever you have to do to make it happen.

SL: We have spoken often about persistence and how it creates resiliency. What do people need to work on to be truly resilient?

BC: Whether you're talking about raising a child or getting an employee to become better than they thought they could ever be, I would say the most important thing is to not allow them to feel sorry for themselves. The minute there's any kind of setback, you've got to handle it like "Well that's to be expected. Now what do we do next?" The difference between successful people and others is how much time they spend feeling sorry for themselves.

SL: You are known for having amazing teams working for you. What are your secrets?

BC: You have to consciously promote failure to make sure people are at their creative best. And that's what I've done my whole career. In other words, "Here's some money; let's give it a shot and really go for it." I welcome failure because what I'm going to get are people willing to try. When you put a bunch of those people together, you have a creative organization. We were out first for everything, and it wasn't because I was smarter than anybody else or had the big ideas. I never did. We would just try stuff, move fast, and see what stuck.

If I had a spectacular failure, I would stand up and start talking about it. Then people would see how cool that was and would know it's OK in our company to try all kinds of things. I don't think you can have a creative organization unless you actively and publicly promote failure. Set that habit by your own example, and make it OK for everybody you work with.

IN PRACTICE: RAPID LOOP LEARNING

Most people spend too much time trying to know everything there is about the pros and cons of an opportunity before acting, rather than acting much sooner and proceeding in small increments, embracing any failures that might result and then making rapid micro-adjustments on each subsequent attempt. This form of rapid loop learning was born out of the Lean Startup approach and allows you to quickly prototype, learn from smaller, cheaper, and quicker mistakes, and iterate.

STEP 1: Below, identify a challenge you are currently facing and use this exercise as a tool to consider how you might tackle it, learning rapidly and iterating in loops.

STEP 2: After the first circuit, challenge yourself to find a smaller, quicker, easier and cheaper way to test the loop. Ask yourself, what part of the overall problem /opportunity that you are facing can you simply and easily test first.

STEP 3: If that result is positive, then start a second loop on the next incremental step.

LEARNING: Running these loops will enable you to utilize the benefits of multiple small failures that are constrained in size, effort, cost, and consequence. Rapid looping also enables you to keep up with the fast pace of modernization, exponential change in organizations, the market, and the competitive landscape.

Describe the problem/
opportunity you are facing:

6

Apply these learnings, and reformulate the
problem statement above. Run the cycle again.

1

What is the smallest
and quickest test you
can do to learn if you
are heading in the
right direction?

5

If successful, what
worked best, and
how can you use it to
inform the next test?

If unsuccessful, what
went wrong and how
can you use it to
inform the next test?

2

How will you measure
success or failure of
this test, and by what
date will you have
tested it?

4

3

Run the smallest and quickest test, and collect and evaluate the data.

Running these loops will enable you to utilize the benefits of multiple small failures that are constrained in size, effort, cost, and consequence. Rapid looping also enables you to keep up with the fast pace of modernization, exponential change in organizations, the market, and the competitive landscape.

IN BUSINESS: INVITING REPEATED ATTEMPTS

We're learning from Major League Baseball the value of rewarding our ability to keep trying. As of June 2019, annual MLB statistics showed that home runs *and strikeouts* were at an all-time high. There's certainly a difference in approach between today's players and those of the 1950s. As a rookie, and after striking out three times in a single game, Micky Mantle was demoted. But today, of the 163 qualifying hitters for the strikeout record, 99 of them have a strikeout rate equal to or greater than Mantle's.

Why have the number of home runs and strikeouts per game gone up? Fundamentally, today's hitters are freed of the shame of having to head back to the dugout with their heads bowed. Instead, they're in constant attack mode, hitting twice as hard, even with two strikes on the board. In other words, players are now encouraged to take risks. This alone contributes to developing the confidence to try and fail.

In business cultures, it's still the case that we penalize risk-taking more often than not. Kathryn Schulz, author of *Being Wrong: Adventures in the Margin of Error*, calls this our *method mistake*. Essentially, we are wrong about what it means to be wrong. Far from being a sign of intellectual inferiority, the capacity to err is crucial to human cognition and development. Failure and defeat are life's great teachers.

Sadly, most corporate cultures just don't encourage their people to risk failure. Instead, whether implicitly or explicitly, employees are encouraged to play it safe, believing that if they make no waves and attract no attention, at least no one will yell at them for messing up.

Breakthrough ideas, iterations, and innovations, however, have become the lifeblood for companies attempting to grow and thrive in today's world. Jack Ma (of Alibaba) and Jeff Bezos (of Amazon) have talked publicly and often about the importance of taking on risks and failures within an innovation culture. As a result, we're seeing a change in business culture, especially when it comes to more aggressive, innovative companies deliberately seeking out new hires with track records of both failure and success. The motivating belief in these cases is that those who've been in the trenches—have failed, survived, and gone on to do well—bring irreplaceable experience.

The same shift that's occurred in the MLB, then, has been occurring bit by bit in the business world. Of course, risk adjustment is critical. As Ralph Heath, author of *Celebrating Failure*, puts it, "One of the biggest secrets to success is operating inside your strength zone but outside your comfort zone." Although you might risk incredible failure, you might also succeed incredibly, assuming you begin from a place of strength.

That said, one significant issue raised by this shifting attitude toward multiple attempts and failures is that not everyone is an Edison—not everyone, or every company, has the time or the resources to fail as much as he did. This raises the question *Is it possible for us to build into our work cultures the resources and time to fail?*

In May of 2016, I spent some time at Adobe's headquarters in Silicon Valley with their vice president of creativity, Mark Randall. Adobe had recently launched a program called Kickbox, specifically designed to accelerate innovation. The company feared that the most creative ideas, to quote Randall, "weren't getting tested because they had to be sold to management first before even being given a budget for prototyping."[34]

Kickbox is literally a small red cardboard box containing everything employees might need to generate a prototype or test a new idea. The top of the box features the image of a fire alarm with the words

---

34   David Burkus, "Inside Adobe's Innovation Kit," *Harvard Business Review*, February 23, 2015, https://hbr.org/2015/02/inside-adobes-innovation-kit.

Pull in case of idea. When one breaks the seal, there are instruction cards inside along with a pen, Post-it Notes, notebooks, a Starbucks gift card, a bar of chocolate, and, most important, a $1,000 prepaid credit card. The card can be used for anything the employee needs to pursue the idea, and there's no requirement to justify spending or to complete an expense report. The simple goal is to take a concept from the ideation stage to testing without needing management's permission in order to do so.

Kickbox fundamentally changed the culture at Adobe by taking away any worry or fear of failure that might otherwise stop an employee from bringing an early-stage idea to management. The resources offer a way for employees to take thousands of little risks without any fear of reprisal. It's a way of giving employees a means of failing "with enthusiasm."

Beyond utilizing Kickbox or a similarly playful strategy, companies might also consider some of the following options for nurturing employees' efforts to keep trying:

> Cultivating a culture in which it is truly acceptable to take chances and court failure enhances employees' sense of engagement by recognizing attempts, discussing processes, and rewarding successes.

Coaching and Recognition

Cultivating a culture in which it is truly acceptable to take chances and court failure enhances employees' sense of engagement by recognizing attempts, discussing processes, and rewarding successes. Encouraging employees to recognize and support one another also goes a long way toward increasing positive attitudes toward calculated risk-taking. Equally much, discussing and analyzing individual or group processes can help teams move from being stuck to taking the next step in the iteration process.

Learning Opportunities

We've seen a fundamental shift toward greater velocity of change and innovation in business to the point where innovation has become de rigueur. It's commonplace to hear that if you're not disrupting yourself, someone else will come along and disrupt you. Given that the rate of change is increasing, our flexibility and ability to adapt to change need to increase along with it. Companies are being pressured to try and fail, learn and iterate, so that the best ideas will bubble up with good outcomes and a positive return in the market. Offering clear and directed learning opportunities for employees is one way of encouraging their growth and development while also making them sharper and less risk averse; the more they know, the wiser their decisions are likely to be when they are called on to adapt to changed circumstances.

Advanced Technologies

Today, with sandboxes, AI, and external resources, the costs of iterating are much lower, as are the barriers to doing so. This means that testing our hypotheses doesn't any longer require building out a full-scale model. For example, car companies no longer have to build prototypes and then put them into wind tunnels to determine aeronautical efficiency. Investment in supercomputers with advanced modeling technologies drives rapid iteration and allows us to try over and over again without our failures becoming cost prohibitive.

A FINAL WORD

I want to close out this chapter and our discussion of luck's Ten Principles by returning to a point I made at the beginning of this book. Earlier, you considered my proposal that Malcolm Gladwell's thesis about ten thousand hours of practice actually comprises about 25 percent of the Formula for Luck. We put Gladwell's thesis in the context of training and other forms of "muscle memory" or discipline development. What I've tried to clarify in this chapter on failing forward is something different: here we've looked at the mindset component of our response when the choices we've made don't have the consequences for which we had hoped. We've also touched on how best to respond, adapt, learn, and adjust so that our next attempts have a higher likelihood of a successful outcome.

That's a case I've tried to make throughout these last ten chapters: honing our skill sets and micromuscles is necessary but not sufficient for success. Despite years of training and practice, the fact that Kevin Jorgensen and Tommy Caldwell successfully climbed the Dawn Wall ultimately came down to a matter of mindset. It's even commonplace among climbers to say that the difference between one who falls and one who doesn't is not necessarily strength and not necessarily technique—it's all about confidence in sticking to the wall. Their attitudes are just as, if not even more, crucial influencers.

SUMMARY

- The Operator for Fail Forward is multiplicative **✖**. Each time you try, you multiply the other Principles in the formula by one more attempt, increasing your odds significantly of generating an optimal outcome.

- Fail Forward's Function is binary **0 1**. Think of failing forward as a longer string of choices, where each time you choose to fail forward. It is basically one additional choice to act off the back of another choice from before. Utilizing this Principle properly will in effect keep on repeat-multiplying the formula by one on each subsequent attempt. The idea is that with persistence and determination you will prevail. The secret to success in failing forward lies in downsizing the size, time, cost, and risk of each repeated attempt so that it becomes easier to learn and move on and does not result in you giving up.

- Unlocking your capacity to "keep swimming" or trying comes down to attitude; positivity and resiliency are two influencing factors.

- Guest Star Barbara Corcoran recommends encouraging failure within teams: "I welcome failure because what I'm going to get are people willing to try. When you put a bunch of those people together, you have a creative organization."

- This chapter's personal exercise invites you to learn how to use LIT Loops (inspired by the Lean Startup methodology) to help you rapidly learn from smaller, cheaper, and quicker mistakes and then iterate quickly to execute processes faster and with much less risk. This is a fabulous business tool as well and is the core operating system for most Silicon Valley high-velocity start-ups and unicorns.

- This chapter's business-focused exercise (available in the *FFL Workbook* by download from www.formulaforluck.com) encourages you to work smarter and not harder by using the Risk Appetite Assessment tool. This tool can help you and your business understand your resource commitments and sensitivity analysis when selecting among new projects based on their relative drain on finances, energy, governance, reputation, time, and your work/life balance.

- It's up to businesses to create opportunities to reward attempts and iterative processes. This can be achieved through coaching and recognition, learning opportunities, and funding opportunities for low-budget rapid prototyping in judgment-free zones.

STUART'S SECRETS

- Check out the documentary *The Dawn Wall* to see a live-action account of Kevin Jorgeson and Tommy Caldwell's record-breaking climb.

- Give a read to John Maxwell's book *Failing Forward: Turning Mistakes into Stepping Stones for Success* for a reminder that embracing possible failure is key to taking on new challenges.

- Find an accountability partner, especially when you're faced with a task that's going to take a little bit of extra effort on your part.

- Write down your goals. A goal written down is ten times

more likely to get completed than one not written down.

- It's just as important to have employees review management as it is to review employees themselves. If you're not already using them, try implementing 360-degree reviews, a process of allowing employees to evaluate themselves while also gathering feedback from their subordinates, colleagues, and supervisors. The 360-degree process encourages a more collaborative approach and recognizes that we all have something to improve.

- Locate apps and other resources that show incremental achievements. For example, if you're struggling with your health or weight, one amazing system is called Renpho and includes a scale and app that measure weight, BMI, body fat, fat-free body weight, subcutaneous fat, visceral fat, body water, skeletal muscle, muscle mass, bone mass, BMR, metabolic age, and more. Tools like these, while they might seem overwhelming at first, allow you to measure changes that you might not otherwise be able to recognize without them. Seeing your results at that level of detail can help you see that you're succeeding in ways not yet visible to the eye.

- Remember that the word *fail* stands for "first attempt in learning" and *end* in essence means "effort never dies"; and if you get no as an answer, remember no actually means "next opportunity."

CHAPTER 15

THE FORMULA FOR LUCK

In one of the most-well-known commencement speeches ever given, author Debbie Millman gave the graduating class of San Jose State University the following insight: "Do what you love, and don't stop until you get what you love. Work as hard as you can, imagine immensities, and if you imagine less, less will be what you undoubtedly would deserve."

I would like for you to be able to imagine more and do more.

You have just reviewed Ten Principles that make up the Formula for Luck. In this chapter, we'll move forward from our exploration of each Principle to suggestions for how they might overlap and fit together (hint: it's a bit like Lego bricks) to create the Luck Mindset—a kind of luck operating system. We'll look at how all Ten Principles come together to comprise the full Formula for Luck, and then we'll review some case studies to show how you can utilize different groupings of the Principles to adapt to any situation in which you want to create luck.

> The Luck Mindset is comprised of all Ten Principles in three key categories: **Habits of Luck, Behaviors of Luck**, and **Actions of Luck**.

Half of the Principles are best considered as everyday habits, qualities we can practice developing at any time and under most circumstances. Think of these like muscles that we build over time and which, through disciplined nurture, repeated effort, and greater flexibility, become powerful drivers of our daily lives. As a result, they are all additive (you will note that for all five their Operator is additive), and as such they are considered fundamental building blocks that we can continually aim to increase and improve upon. Because they can be practiced with great regularity, these Principles have the easiest chance of becoming almost instinctual or automatic. These five—the Habits of Luck—are Curiosity, Passion, Connectivity, Positivity, and Empathy.

These are distinct from the rest insofar as practicing and developing the Habits of Luck takes time, and their cultivation is much less situationally dependent. They are foundational, and your attention to them enables you to apply them with greater flexibility and in various combinations. They are the core building blocks of your Luck Mindset. Because there is no limit to the amount you can develop each of them, they are infinite. (You will note that for all five their Function is infinite).

THE BEHAVIORS OF LUCK

The next three—Adaptability, Situational Awareness, and Serendipity—are the Behaviors of Luck and act as significant force multipliers when they are called for. They can also multiply both upward and downward—where your Situational Awareness or lack thereof, your Adaptability or lack thereof, and/or your recognition and exploration of Serendipity or lack thereof, can significantly multiply their relative outcomes either positively or negatively. (You will note that for all three, their Operator is multiplicative.)

These Behaviors of Luck are also more bound than the first five Principles to situation and circumstance. These depend on our responses or reactions to outside stimuli within an overall system, and due to this responsive nature, are all finite (you will note that for all three their Function is finite). Many of you might consider the Behaviors of Luck to be closely akin to Jim Collins's idea of return on luck. You'll recall from an earlier chapter that what Collins had in mind is that lucky people have an ability to make more of opportunities that come their way. In other words, those who proved to be lucky weren't necessarily given more breaks or better chances, nor were their lives a series of fortuitous events. Instead, they simply did more with those opportunities that came their way.

Noticing and fully taking advantage of the opportunities before us can act as a huge lever for increasing our luck. Of course, there's a critical timing component when opportunities come our way; being able to act in a timely fashion requires us to have built reliable reflexes. It might not be every day that we have the chance to prove our Adaptability or deploy Situational Awareness in game-changing ways, but we can train and ready ourselves for when we *are* faced with opportunities. The same is true for a Principle like Situational Awareness. We can develop it in potentially lifesaving ways, like knowing the location of the movie theater exits or choosing the aisle seat on an airplane. To the extent that we regularly train ourselves to think in certain ways—to sit in the end carriages on the subway, to scan a crowded public gathering for abandoned bags or erratic behaviors, or to have the flexibility to take different routes in a city's crowded downtown—we can influence the reflexes on which we might at some point have to rely in order to reduce risk and maximize good outcomes.

> Noticing and fully taking advantage of the opportunities before us can act as a huge lever for increasing our luck.

For "opportunity dependent" Principles like the Behaviors of Luck, we have the ability to amplify our luck tremendously *if* we have readied ourselves internally by forming good habits. Adaptability, Situational Awareness, and Serendipity all have amazing knock-on effects for increasing luck and equally for minimizing downsides or even outright avoiding bad luck.

THE ACTIONS OF LUCK

The final two Principles, Choice and Fail Forward, are the Actions of Luck; without them, the others are likely to go unrealized. They are both quite obviously multiplicative. We also learned that the Actions of Luck have a Function that is binary—it can only be a one or a zero—and thus these Principles effectively enable the Formula to have its value realized (multiplied by one) or nullified (multiplied by zero). Actions of Luck are conscious and purposeful undertakings; they're what we do with awareness and intention.

THE LUCK MINDSET

FFL PRINCIPLE	MINDSET	OPERATOR	FUNCTION
CURIOSITY	Habit	Additive	Infinite
PASSION	Habit	Additive	Infinite
CONNECTIV-ITY	Habit	Additive	Infinite
POSITIVITY	Habit	Additive	Infinite
EMPATHY	Habit	Additive	Infinite
ADAPTABILITY	Behavior	Multiplicative	Finite
SITUATIONAL AWARENESS	Behavior	Multiplicative	Finite
SERENDIPITY	Behavior	Multiplicative	Finite
CHOICE	Action	Multiplicative	Binary
FAIL FORWARD	Action	Multiplicative	Binary

BRIDGING PRINCIPLES

My intention in offering these broader categorizations is not to be rigid in my determination. Instead, I offer these categories to help you think about how (and when) the Principles are likely to come to bear throughout a life spent developing them. The Habits of Luck, for example, may also cross over into the more situationally dependent Behaviors of Luck on a regular basis. Bringing them to bear in unique situations can amplify or accelerate our luck, but they are always also habits that can be practiced every single day, no matter the presence of special opportunities for utilizing them.

Empathy and Connectivity, in particular, often find in-the-moment applications that create positive, luck-generating outcomes. We can work on cultivating and applying Empathy every day, but we sometimes have opportunities to apply it in situations that call for it. Think back to the story of showing consideration to the family at the airport and the airline desk agent. On the one hand, I was inclined to do the right thing; on the other hand, the situation seemed to demand it. Similarly, building a network of connections to others is first and foremost a habit, and that network is something we cultivate and trim as time goes on. But there are moments when situations call for us to activate or leverage the networks we've made it a habit to develop in order to take advantage of an opportunity, pay forward a good, maintain flow, or simply be a rainmaker for others by helping them connect with key people on their paths to luck.

LEVER AND AMPLIFY

There is a virtuous cycle embedded in the Luck Mindset. When you experience the value that comes from cultivating the Principles, you have the ability and the privilege to share that value.

That brings us to what is perhaps the most important point of this book: the Luck Mindset is only as effective as your ability to create outcomes that amplify the amount of luck in the world. I want you to think about how you can lever and amplify the abilities that you're developing in conjunction with the Principles. One easy way to do that is to become a pivot point or fulcrum for your family, your business, and your community, to pay forward the benefits of the Luck Mindset, to advocate for and facilitate its development in others.

> The Luck Mindset is only as effective as your ability to create outcomes that amplify the amount of luck in the world.

Maybe you start simply, by sharing on social media some of the cool things you've learned along with their value or benefit. Maybe you take up a role in your community, whether it's using your Empathy to increase the circle of people for whom you care or using your Passion to motivate and inspire others. Perhaps you share one of the exercises in this book with your family or team at work. If you're a lifelong learner and constantly curious, you'll likely be a mentor to someone else. Maybe your Positivity or Passion is effusive, and others are easily empowered by it. The important thing is to move beyond considering your own personal luck to find ways of increasing luck all around you.

My point is a simple one: cultivation of each of the Principles isn't just good for you; it's good because when they are applied masterfully and at scale, they're ultimately good for the system overall. You'll contribute to a massive virtuous cycle, a win-win-win for everyone, when you put talents like positive energy, passion, and empathy into the world. Any practitioner of these skills will immediately attest to the reciprocal benefits: the return of energy from an appreciative audience, an enlightened mentee, an engaged team of employees, an inspired family member, or simply a random third-party beneficiary is a feedback loop that fuels even more goodwill and value all around. This self-reinforcing feedback loop is often referred to as a *flow state*, and any of you who have surfed in one long enough will know the adrenaline high that it offers.

Consider those models who epitomized the very best of impact leadership: icons such as the Dalai Lama, Reverend Martin Luther King Jr., Nelson Mandela, Bishop Tutu, or Ruth Bader Ginsburg. Their abilities to be empathetic—to listen, to care, and to be passionate about the needs of others—are the hallmarks of the world's next great leaders and companies, where social responsibility, social impact, and care are fast becoming the next big differentiators of success. Or think of other iconic company leaders—Branson, Winfrey, Musk, Jobs, or Gates—who model the ability to act decisively, to place themselves at the epicenter of the next big move, to be insatiably curious about how to perfect their offerings, to take bold and big risks and trust their instincts. These people also show us that the more the Principles overlap, the more opportunities for greater effects in the world.

THE FORMULA FOR LUCK

At the very start of this book, I offered a review of the commonplace ways we approach the topic of luck. There, I began with the idea that luck was traditionally viewed as half genetics, half true chance, the idea either that "I'm born with it" (like Olympic swimmer Michael Phelps's size-17 feet) or "something lucky happens to me" (like finding a twenty-dollar bill on the street). As a society, we shifted from those early ideas to the notion that there might be three factors instead of two: genetics, chance, and *talent development*. The central idea was that while genetics and chance have a significant role to play in luck, they amount in total to about half the influence; the other half is left up to us insofar as we are responsible for developing our skills and gifts. You'll recall that I happily acknowledged talent development as part of the luck puzzle, especially because it's a tribute to the power of our own actions (or lack thereof) when it comes to developing luck. Genetics and chance are not up to us, but talent development more certainly is. Remember the graphic illustrating the view that talent development is 50 percent of the puzzle with the balance split equally between perceived chance and genetics.

PERCEIVED PERSONAL GROWTH
AND SUCCESS INFLUENCES 2

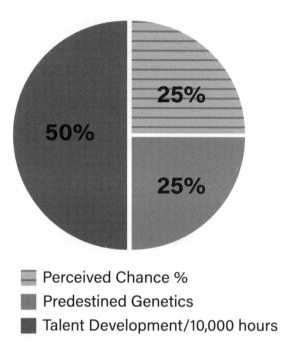

- Perceived Chance %
- Predestined Genetics
- Talent Development/10,000 hours

Still finding that idea insufficient to account for how our thinking so strongly influences what we do, I introduced my contention that the biggest influence on luck is actually our mindset—how we think about ourselves, our experiences, and our world. I also argued that true chance is but the smallest component of luck at only one percent, suggesting that 99 percent of all our luck and outcomes was not true-chance related. If my contention holds, and two-thirds or fully 66 percent of what influences luck belongs to our mindset, that would mean that talent development is halved to 25 percent, and the remaining 8 percent is now allocated to our genetics. The updated graphic with which we began our dive into the Ten Principles was as follows:

ACTUAL PERSONAL GROWTH AND SUCCESS INFLUENCES

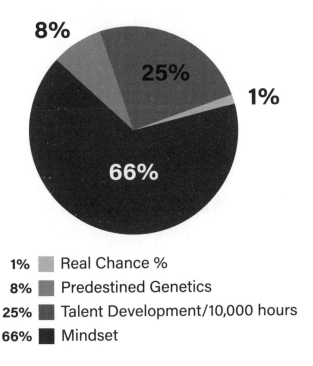

1% Real Chance %
8% Predestined Genetics
25% Talent Development/10,000 hours
66% Mindset

Proving that claim was the impetus for the central ten chapters of this book—each tracing one of the Ten Principles that together comprise the Luck Mindset. We summarized above that these Ten Principles can be categorized into habits, behaviors, and actions, each of which operates somewhat differently and under varying conditions. From the graphic on the cover of this book and throughout its pages, you will have glimpsed mathematical notions that were suggestive of how we might finally combine these Principles into an actual Formula for Luck. Some we contended were additive and infinite (habits), other ones were multiplicative and finite (behaviors), and two were multiplicative and binary (actions). These categorizations and their individual characteristics and effects upon each other ultimately help us combine the Ten Principles into a formula.

Let's build the formula in steps. First, if true chance is only 1 percent, then we are solving for the 99 percent. If we follow the age-old adage that luck is what happens when preparation meets opportunity, we would write that as follows:

$$(\text{Preparation}) + (\text{Opportunity}) = 99\% \text{ of Luck}$$

I have argued that genetics (8 percent) and talent development (25 percent) equal only one-third of this value, or 33 percent. Both can be categorized under the label of preparation (one is *prepared for you* and the other *you prepare*). I then suggested that the Luck Mindset comprises the other two-thirds or 66 percent.

$$(\text{True Chance}) + (\text{Genetics}) + (\text{Talent Development}) + (\text{Mindset}) = \text{Luck}$$

$$1\% + 8\% + 25\% + 66\% = 100\%$$

Finally, the Luck Mindset is comprised of the Habits of Luck, Behaviors of Luck, and Actions of Luck, and we know that they are incredible multipliers when combined:

$$(\text{Mindset}) = (\text{HoL}) \times (\text{BoL}) \times (\text{AoL}) = 66\% \text{ of your Luck}$$

The last thing we need is a formulaic expression for how these three components of the Luck Mindset interact, and then we can solve for Luck.

HoL is comprised of five Principles that are *infinite* (we can develop them without limit) and *additive* and can be expressed as:

HoL = (Curiosity + Passion + Connectivity + Positivity + Empathy)

BoL is comprised of three Principles that are *multiplicative* and *conditional.* (Conditional, from a mathematical perspective, also means they are nonzero numbers. As such, if they are present, they act on the Formula, and if they are not present, they maintain a value of one, neither amplifying nor negating the Formula.)

BoL = (Situational Awareness) × (Adaptability) × (Serendipity)

AoL is comprised of two multiplicative Principles that are *opportunity based* and *binary.* (Binary indicates that if they are present, they affect the Formula, and if they are not, they have the value of zero and thereby negate the Formula). This reminds us that our choices and our attempts, including our choice to act or not act, are the most powerful Principles in terms of their effects on Luck outcomes.

AoL = (Choice) × (Fail Forward)

Therefore, we can now build the following Formula for Luck:

(HoL) × (BoL) × (AoL) = 66% of your Luck

In its detail, that also looks like this:

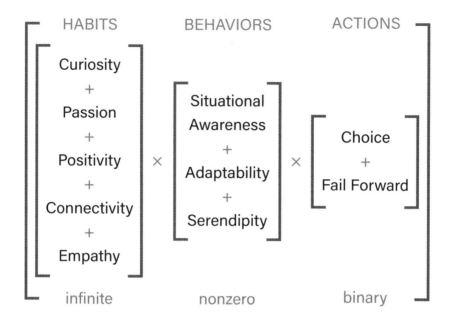

Let me give you a quick explanation of why I've set it up this way.

You already know from reading this chapter why the vertical stacks are grouped as they are. But what yet needs explanation is the Operators connecting them to one another. Habits of Luck are *multiplied* by Behaviors and Actions of Luck for the following reason: the absence of opportunities or circumstances that call for activation of any of the Principles does not render the formula ineffective.

Say you recognize a serendipitous moment that calls for the activation of one of the three BoLs you've been practicing. In this situation, that Principle suddenly gets massively, exponentially amplified. Or say you have been developing the habits over time, and an opportunity calls for action, but there is no immediate behavioral component at stake, just a simple action (pitch one VC to invest in your company) or repeat actions (pitch dozens regularly, as most will say no). This essentially reminds us of how critical action is: in order for the five Habits of Luck to continually work for you, you will always still need to base actions on them. In effect the HoL Principles will always incrementally increase your luck as long as you act on them, but massive gains in luck will almost always require some of the BoL to be present and some macrolevel AoL to occur.

In other words, the BoL and AoL Principles are best thought of as accelerants to the incremental luck already being created from developing good habits regarding the five HoL Principles that comprise the first part of the Formula.

The Formula for Luck that I offer here is a more thorough account—the whole story, we might say—of the well-known formula we referenced at the start: Preparation + Opportunity = Luck. We might merge the two formulas as follows: Preparation encompasses genetics, talent development, and the Habits of Luck. Opportunity encompasses the Behaviors of Luck and the Actions of Luck.

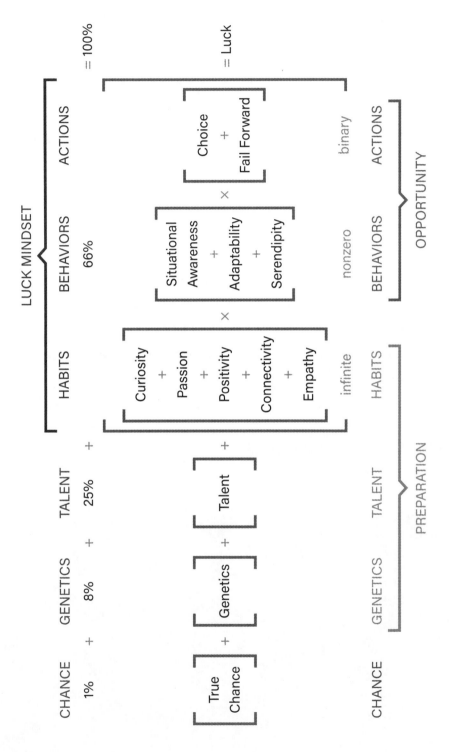

THREE CASE STUDIES

I stand behind my claim that enhancing your capacity for any one of the Ten Principles is a step toward increasing your luck. That said, I'll focus here on the overlap among Principles as a way of showing off their ability to work in combination with one another toward enhanced results. You're likely to discover more points of conjunction or dovetailing among the Principles the more you work on consciously implementing them in your life. Here are just three cases to get you thinking about potential combinations.

Case Study #1: The Unplanned Interview

We first referenced Hafþór Björnsson (the Mountain) back in chapter 1, when I introduced him to help us think through the meaning and value of Malcolm Gladwell's postulate that it takes a minimum of ten thousand hours for mastery of any activity. Björnsson's story of investing almost forty thousand hours helped demonstrate that ten thousand hours is truly a minimum when it comes to determining sufficient "preparation" for luck. Now that you've read through the Ten Principles, I want to focus on the story of how I came to have a serendipitous conversation with Björnsson that led to the inclusion of his insights in this book.

It was Monday, January 14, 2020, and I was sitting at a Boston Logan airport restaurant when I noticed an absolutely unmissable figure sitting next to me. He was being so kind and polite as wave after wave of people interrupted him while he was video chatting with his wife and daughter. Every time a fan came by, he paused, got up, participated in their selfies, high-fived fans, gave his signature, and genuinely thanked them. Curiosity led me to research who he might be and then further to research his real name (as opposed to the name Gregor Clegane of his *Game of Thrones* character) and the story behind the man. That led to more investigating to get an understanding of the World's Strongest Man competition and the art and practice of building one's strength year after year for decades.

If I was going to approach him and truly have a proper conversation, I wanted to do so by appreciating more about him than just his role on a recent television series. I also tuned in to my Empathy, as I thought about how often he is distracted away from his personal life with his family. Given that I wanted to be thoughtful and considerate, I chose *not* to try to speak with him when I recognized him in the restaurant. In fact, I left the restaurant and walked to the boarding gate because my gut told me the timing for introducing myself just didn't seem right.

What happened next, as I sat down at the boarding gate, was truly serendipitous. Björnsson walked up and took the seat right across from me. My spider sense screamed, "You need to talk to him!" All my preparation and forethought became relevant in that moment. I knew I needed to engage with him, and I knew that doing so demanded from me that I be compassionate and sensitive to who he was, rather than just what he'd accomplished.

Situational Awareness played into my assessment of the scene. And the Empathy I'd felt before about respecting his time with family came to bear as a specific behavior. I waited until he was done with a phone call, walked the five feet across the aisle, and sat next to him, and the following conversation ensued:

SL: "I hope I am not bothering you, I just wanted to let you know I noticed you were having a chat with your family, and I wanted to wait until you were done before I spoke to you."

HB: "Oh, thank you, that's very kind."

SL: "Do you mind if I ask you a question about your success as a businessman?"

He put his phone down and looked directly at me.

HB: "No one ever asks me about my business."

SL: "Well, I'm sure, you must get tired of all the people taking photos. I can understand they're your fans, and I can see that you want to do the right thing. I don't want a photo; I just want to chat with you about your secrets to success."

At that point, he turned his entire body toward me, opening up to our conversation and turning away from the action around us. We were going to have a proper conversation. And then, utilizing Empathy again, I started chatting with him about what it was like to dedicate his life to such a demanding competition.

I then listened carefully to a story about the challenges to his family life, the hardships of travel when he's required to eat twenty thousand calories a day, and the loneliness of being away so much. I offered to share with him a book I had read about how to better connect with loved ones when you travel a lot. He really appreciated that gesture, and then we ended up laughing and chatting for almost forty-five minutes!

I had learned earlier from my research while sitting at the restaurant that Björnsson had come in second or third six times in a row in the World's Strongest Man competition before he finally won it in 2018.

SL: "I have learned that people sometimes are happier earning third place rather than second. When they are third, they are happy at least to have medaled, but when they are second, all they can do is think about how they missed gold."

HB: "That's amazing. I now look back, and I was always happier third than second. I'd never thought about that before. It makes so much sense to me now."

We both had a good laugh after I shared my own experience earning fourth place in the Olympic sailing trials, because fourth is definitely worse than third! I then mentioned to him that I was writing this book, and I inquired about the possibility of asking him a few questions for it.

HB: "I'd love to. Please, please go ahead."

I'll briefly summarize here his most compelling comments to me:

- "You must dream big. Only big dreams can give you the life fulfillment that you really want."

- "Dedication is all about goal setting." (Björnsson does this annually and always writes them down.)

- "It takes tremendous mental strength to keep on pushing. Best example is still working out when you are tired and hurting. If you don't have the mental strength, everything falls apart."

- "Sometimes you don't know where your challenges will come from." (In *Game of Thrones*, although he had no speaking parts, Björnsson still had large scripts to read and understand. One of his toughest jobs was learning English in order to be able to take the role.)

- "Energy and strength come from many sources." (One source of Björnsson's energy is helping kids. At Christmas, he made a deal with a department store that it would give away all the toys for kids that he could carry out of the store.)

And that is how I got to interview Hafþór Björnsson and share his insights with you here. My Curiosity and Empathy guided me. The opportunity to have that conversation was serendipitous, and it was Situational Awareness that helped me through the awkward business of introducing myself to him. Without Choice, of course, none of that would have happened. Those several Principles taken together led to a forty-five-minute conversation about a number of different topics—including kids and traveling. Talking with him also reinforced for me the idea that momentous progress can sometimes happen in short and furious spurts, as it had for him when he was cast for *Game of Thrones*.

In this instance, application of the formula looked like this:

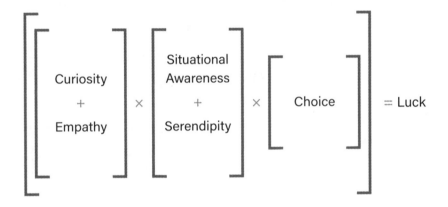

$$\left[\left[\begin{array}{c} Curiosity \\ + \\ Empathy \end{array} \right] \times \left[\begin{array}{c} Situational \\ Awareness \\ + \\ Serendipity \end{array} \right] \times \left[Choice \right] \right] = Luck$$

Case Study #2: The Family Response Plan

As a regional chair for the Young Presidents' Organization (YPO), my responsibility from 2019 through 2021 was to lead a group of about 1,500 CEOs located all along the East Coast of the United States. As you might imagine, during COVID-19 no one was spared the challenges of business closures and other stressors. The group worried about the future of their companies as well as about spending more time around their families than they had in years.

Anyone who has experienced the stresses surrounding confinement as a result of COVID-19 knows that there's a massive amount of pressure put on semifunctioning and even high-functioning relationships as a result of constant close proximity and everyone's need for privacy.

In YPO, we've focused on how to help members and their families through this tough time. Curiosity played a big role, as we needed to research best practices, call on experts, and invent creative approaches to things like working out at home and arranging for everyone to have appropriate space for work and school.

One of our members, Paul Lightfoot of BrightFarms, sat down with his family, and together they wrote up a plan for what success would look like for a family like theirs living under COVID. The plan entailed practices like getting outside for some sunshine and engaging each morning in gratitude and meditation exercises as a family. The plan even included more planning, with the family making decisions together about what would happen each day. They worked as a family to determine criteria for success and discussed different mechanisms they could put in place to help one another through rough patches. When Paul showed his family plan to a couple of people, they immediately asked to use it. Before long, we were able to share Paul's plan with the entire YPO region and eventually with all YPO members as a touchstone for their own thinking about restructuring the everyday lives of their families in positive ways.

The network effect brought to bear the value that Paul and his family had developed. His learnings were shared not just among us but also with our extended families and communities. And the positivity that he shared helped his colleagues choose to make lemonade from lemons, so to speak—to take advantage of the opportunity to be the best possible versions of themselves rather than approach sheltering in place as an excuse for cocooning mentally and emotionally. That took a strong sense of Empathy as well, caring for and appreciating the needs of all of the family members as they approached these new circumstances.

What was also clearly at play here was the call for Adaptability—both for individuals and their family units. Approaching a time of crisis with the positive attitude that thriving was possible under COVID meant that families were actively seeking solutions to stressors, building resilience against the effects of confinement on their relationships, and developing new activities and habits that would render them less fragile going forward.

Not only is the element of Choice reflected in Paul's or any of our decisions to try using a family plan during COVID, but I am sure many families may also have felt inclined to abandon it after meeting with resistance or a lack of immediate results. However, for those that kept at it and became really successful with it, their secret was how they worked through issues, treating failures as opportunities to improve, customizing the plan by adjusting, tweaking, and fixing any issues, and attempting over and over again until they got the desired outcome.

In this instance, application of the formula looked like this:

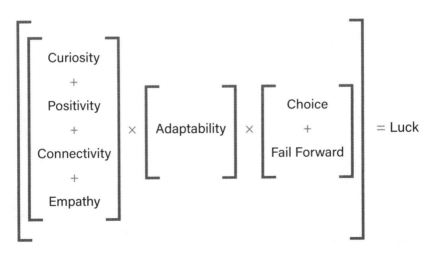

Case Study #3: The Company Pit Stop

I've included this example specifically to show how the five Habits of Luck—Curiosity, Passion, Positivity, Connectivity, and Empathy—bring luck even when the more opportunity-centric accelerants are absent.

You'll remember from chapter 7 my story about the Formula 1 racer who suggested that the pit stop model might work against infections during surgery. As someone who's always been a fan of racing, I decided to incorporate the idea of the pit stop into my company.

I didn't want our strategic planning events to be "retreats," given that their purpose was to energize, to move the company and its people forward, hopefully by leaps and bounds. So I turned to the model of Formula 1 cars that are racing full speed around the track, every once in a while screeching to a halt for all different experts to jump to work making the car ready to go right back into the race. I instilled an annual requirement that our entire company momentarily pause and bring together in one place every specialist that is involved with the health and value of our enterprise.

Now, the pit stop is not just about working on the machine; it's also about building the team: its leadership, learning, engagement, mentoring, and support systems. It's about having fun doing things that give meaning, purpose, and value to the company. So as part of our annual pit stops, I always gave three of my then-favorite books to every team member. That was the result of my general Curiosity at play, both in the book selection and in the eagerness for conversation among the group. Empathy guided what I did with those books: I wrote a personal message in each for every member of the company saying why the book was important to me for them specifically.

We made sure during each pit stop to revisit our values and ensure that they were aligned to whatever actions we took. We aimed for meaningful labor and the achievement of meaningful progress. We also picked group exercises that reflected team members' passions. Once, we made pasta from scratch; another time, we all learned how to DJ. In this and other ways, Passion was a big driver of engagement and team unity. The same rang true for Positivity, insofar as we worked on developing and sustaining a "yes" culture through open and supportive frameworks for team members to bring their ideas to bear in solving pressing issues.

At every pit stop, we featured speakers and artists, drawing from the company's and my extensive network. And we practiced active listening at every session so that Empathy would become a key driver for success. We know that the best leaders in the world are not IQ driven; they're EQ driven, and so we host both team and one-on-one coaching sessions for leaders to improve their skills. That emphasis on Empathy wasn't just a part of the work we did together; it was also part of the way we set up the event so that all would feel welcome and comfortable. For example, at a recent pit stop, we arranged for several team members to be housed at the event location; for the others who wanted to travel back to their homes at the end of each day, we covered all Uber expenses so that they would feel safe and secure whenever they had to travel. In this way and others, we were careful to consider and remove any obstacles that might complicate people's lives and distract their focus.

Those pit stops have created unbelievable outcomes for the team, and thereby for the company; they've generated incredible amounts of luck. And our processes for evaluating and improving the event as we repeat it help us each time to make better and better choices about how to proceed.

In this instance, application of the formula looked like this:

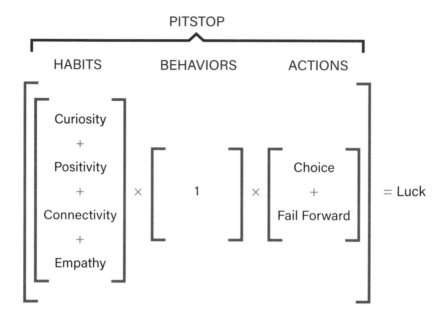

Note that all three of the Behaviors of Luck were absent, but as they are conditional and nonzero, they simply hold the value of one, which neither adds to nor subtracts from the Luck generated from the application of all the of Habits of Luck multiplied by both Actions of Luck.

. . .

My goal in sharing these examples of ways the Ten Principles might work together toward enhanced outcomes is to encourage you to reflect on how you utilize the Principles in your own experience. The more aware we are of what we are capable of doing and where we may need more practice, the better our chances of being our best possible selves, able and ready to make the most of our lives —whether that's in day-to-day happenings or in extraordinary circumstances. As the saying goes, opportunity doesn't happen to you; *you* happen to opportunity.

$$-x \cdot y^2 = 2 \qquad y = \sqrt[2]{3+1}$$

$$1 \cdot \varepsilon = c005 \qquad SO_4$$

$$\left(\frac{2}{3}\right) = x_7 \qquad y = \sqrt[2]{3+1}$$

$$\frac{a}{\ln} \qquad 1 \cdot \varepsilon = c005$$

$$1 \cdot \varepsilon = 0.005 \qquad 1 \cdot \varepsilon = c005$$

$$x_7 = \left(\frac{2}{3} \times 2x\right) a^2 = b^2 + c^2$$

$$N^2 \times H^3 \qquad \frac{a}{9\ln d} = \frac{b}{9\ln d}$$

$$f(3) = 2^{-3}$$

$$NH_3 \qquad y$$

$$-2x \left(\frac{2}{3} \times 2x\right) \quad SO_4$$

$$\frac{a}{9\ln d} = \frac{b}{9\ln d} \quad f(3) = 2^{-3} + 1 \cdot \varepsilon = c005$$

$$(2 \times a^2 = b^2) \qquad x_7 = \left(\frac{2}{3} \times 2x\right) a^2 = b^2 + c$$

$$b^2 + c^2 = bc \qquad 9 + x_7 \qquad \frac{a}{9\ln d} = \frac{}{9\ln d}$$

$$\frac{a}{9\ln} = \frac{b}{9\ln} \qquad NH_3$$

CHAPTER 16

THE LUCK MINDSET

So far, we've discussed possibilities for increasing one's luck by focusing on our mindset. But there's an additional contributing factor that still needs our attention. If the Luck Mindset relies upon our personal habits and abilities, then it's imperative to keep ourselves healthy and high functioning in order to increase our capacity for luck.

How do we do that?

Just as nourishing foods promote our physical well-being, we need to nourish our brains to be of sound mind and well primed for learning and growth. We do that by ensuring that the components of our neurological systems are well fed.

It's true that even the healthiest of brains still experiences times of anxiety or fatigue, or feelings of disappointment and depression. Negative states such as these can occur as part of normal functioning even when we are feeding our brains properly. What's important is that we develop and sustain positive habits of fueling and exercising our brains and minimizing those negative conditions that diminish our cognitive and creative abilities.

DANGER, WILL ROBINSON!

It's critical to acknowledge the capacity of modern-day distractions to reduce our cognitive control. Most of us always have a device at hand and because of this have nearly eradicated boredom, which is widely recognized as an incubator for innovation. When we are bored, we are alone with our thoughts. If we turn off the phone, close the iPad or laptop, and simply stop looking outside of ourselves, we increase our chances of becoming more curious. When we're not overloading on information, we may roll an idea or two around in our minds—wondering, testing, exploring, and challenging it. If our idea doesn't hold water, perhaps we try looking at it from another

> It's critical to acknowledge the capacity of modern-day distractions to reduce our cognitive control.

angle. Or maybe we veer off in a whole new direction and become fascinated with something else entirely. Think of how some of the greatest discoveries of all time have happened in the shower—or of serendipitous occurrences often being the product of our ability to be fully present, undistracted, and open minded.

By removing our ability to daydream or to follow out core thought processes and allowing ourselves to be constantly pulled into checking notifications or scrolling through some app or other, we are actually encouraging a significant reduction in our capacities to innovate, learn, and create.

It doesn't help that the very companies offering us opportunities to socialize or access information online are also designed to encourage us to spend more time being distracted or consumed by what they offer. We truly entered the attention economy in the decade starting in 2020. For example, Instagram and Facebook, Snapchat, Twitter, and others employ neuroscientists and psychoanalysts to help them *design into their products* mechanisms that play off our response to feedback loops. They have built their platforms specifically to trigger the release of feel-good neurochemicals, like dopamine, in order to increase the number of opportunities for their users to experience validation. They know that the more validated their users feel by a given site or app, the more time they'll spend on it.

They also know the importance of controlling that validation by extending it over a period of time. If every like is a mini dopamine shot, a platform may not choose to let a user—let's call her Alison— know that the amazing image she posted generated one thousand likes in the first five minutes, after which time a few additional likes trickled in. Instead of providing Alison with the real time feedback (a large dopamine dosage after which she is more likely to lose interest or even leave as she notices the number of likes plummeting), the platform will mete out the pace and frequency of the likes, artificially extending them to arrive distributed over the course of an entire hour or more. In so doing, the platform increases Alison's time spent checking back from ten minutes to sixty minutes; by staying on an extra five times longer, she helps generate up to 500 percent more ad revenue.

In pursuing this profit-driven paradigm, companies have effectively persuaded us to reduce the time we spend alone with our thoughts in that most fertile ground called *boredom*. These platforms are designed in ways that ultimately pursue a company's economic interest and work directly against brain health.

HEALTHY BRAIN = HEALTHY NEURAL PATHWAYS

In researching this chapter, I was fortunate to work closely with a friend of thirty years and one of Canada's leading psychologists, Dr. Diana Garcia (my thanks to her and her team at Capital Psychological for all their incredible support). As we all learn more about the brain, it becomes harder to separate its health from that of the rest of the body. Let's review just a few terms here to help you better understand the relationship between the two and impress your friends while doing so.

- *Neurons* are nerve cells that transmit electrical impulses throughout our nervous system.

- *Neurogenesis* is the ability to generate new neurons.

- *Neuroplasticity* is our neurons' capacity for rewiring and making new and different connections as we learn and adapt to new situations.

In 1962, the neurobiologist Joseph Altman discovered that humans grow new neurons in what's called the *cerebral cortex*, the outer layer of the cerebrum (the part of the brain that's up front, on top, and consists of two hemispheres). Altman's discovery of ongoing neurogenesis was groundbreaking. In the years since, brain scientists have not only confirmed Altman's findings but also determined that neurogenesis can be *enhanced:* we can actually *help* our brains produce new neurons.

There is a foundational activity without which neurogenesis simply cannot occur, and that is *lifelong learning*. In other words, new neurons don't form and grow unless we feed them with new experiences and new knowledge. The same is true for neuroplasticity—it *also* relies on learning new skills, adapting to new experiences and environments, and building memories.[35]

One way to think about how new knowledge contributes to brain health is like this. If you continue to retread the same path when hiking, with time that path will become more worn, clearer, and easier to follow. However, it's also the case that over time, if you're only ever taking this same path, alternate routes will become more difficult to take. As with all things relating to our habits, age, levels of stress, or fatigue, the path of least resistance will become the one most frequently taken (whether purposefully or not) to the point of reinforcing that single path almost to the exclusion of others. The same is true for pathways in the brain. As path options are reduced, so are our capacities for resiliency, versatility, stress management, and growth.

But by thinking in new ways and making a habit of learning new things, path options increase and even travel in new directions; new connections form, enhancing, extending, and weaving together our neural pathways in ways that reinforce and facilitate *further* learning along with more malleability and flexibility.

All that's to say that if you want to get luckier, one of the surest ways to do so is by *increasing your learning*. If you're old enough to struggle with learning new things, take heart! Brain science is finding that contrary to the old saying, you *can* teach an old dog new tricks. Learning is *not limited* by age, nor does age signal a time for brain decline to automatically commence. Our capacity for learning can be continuously improved upon thanks to our ability to generate new neurons and keep making neural connections.

To be clear, when I argue for learning new things, I don't simply mean taking in new information. What I have in mind instead is deep engagement in the *process* by which we learn and practice devel-

---

35 Alvaro Pascual-Leone, Amir Amedi, Felipe Fregni, and Lotfi B. Merabet, "The Plastic Human Brain Cortex," *Annual Review of Neuroscience* 28 (2005): 377–401.

oping an ability or skill—activities like choosing to cross-reference your daily news source with at least two other divergent sources. In today's world of fake, partisan, sensational, and constantly "breaking" news, we simply cannot rely on information from any single source. This is specifically true of the social platforms we spoke of above. Those have become the source of almost 70 percent of US citizens' daily news—and in many cases, the news on these platforms is curated and targeted to reinforce what we and our closest friends already think and believe. These news sources are also typically poorly moderated and certainly not

> If you want to get luckier, one of the surest ways to do so is by *increasing your learning*.

subject to the requirements for careful source checking—which even mainstream media is accused of not doing properly these days.

Engaging in a process of obtaining news from a minimum of three uncorrelated sources (one might be local, another national, and a third a good independent international source) might take a little extra time, but it is one way of opening the mind to broader sources of information and allowing challenges, cross points and counter-arguments to widen our focus and help us be more empathetic to different well-sourced viewpoints.

Developing information literacy is a commitment to doing more than just consuming information. So is avoiding information overload. Did you know that the technical term for information overload is *education incapacity*? To me, that's a perfect way of describing the result of having impaired cognition/insufficient neural pathways. Without constant improvement and expansion of the web of neural pathways in our brains, we become unable, literally, to take in and process new information. Often people resign themselves to this state by saying something like *I'm just getting old and forgetful* or *My brain doesn't work the way it used to* when in fact these are more often than not self-imposed limits that are fully reversible with retraining. A healthy, well-exercised brain actually increases our chances of being able to "chunk" information and to be judicious about how we receive and consume it.

I was fortunate enough to spend time with Dr. Majid Fotuhi (MD, PhD of Johns Hopkins), the noted neuroscientist and global leader in the fight against Alzheimer's. In Singapore in March 2018, Dr. Fotuhi and I sat down together and discussed at length his research into repairing and often reversing the disease without any drug intervention or protocol. Dr. Fotuhi advised, "Diet, exercise, and sleep will do more to combat cognitive decline than any of the major drug companies. Insomnia, sleep apnea, stress, high blood pressure—all these conditions that bridge psychological state and physical condition can lead to changes in the brain that will result in cognitive impairment."

Big Pharma has been consistently unable to identify a blockbuster drug that successfully targets the proteins associated with Alzheimer's. Dr. Jeff Cummings, the director of the Cleveland Clinic Lou Ruvo Center for Brain Health in Las Vegas quantified this in an influential report. He acknowledged that the Alzheimer's drug-failure rate hasn't budged from 99.6 percent in years, and that the almost $300 billion annual costs of Alzheimer's care in the United States alone was projected to grow to over $12 trillion by 2050. It is no surprise, though, that Big Pharma stands to make no money off of Alzheimer's from setting up cognitive therapy or encouraging people to focus simply on their mental and physical health—even as studies today are showing clear evidence that doing so grows back the hippocampus (effectively regrowing the brain).

The crucial point is that a healthy physical and mental lifestyle and ongoing learning feed our brains in ways that generate neurons and expand the web that connects them. To put it another way, our ability to learn is limited primarily by our unwillingness to engage with those things that help grow our brainpower.

THE BIG FIVE

The primary difference between humans and the rest of the animal world lies in what are called our *executive functions* (EFs). Our frontal cortex is the seat of these cognitive processes, which are necessary for working memory, flexible thinking, and controlling our behavior.

Executive functions include activities like

- paying attention and staying focused;

- planning, organizing, and keeping track of what we're doing; and

- managing our emotions.

EFs allow us to select and to effectively monitor behaviors that permit us to achieve our goals. They are what ultimately *drive and motivate* us, yet most humans do not make maximum use of EFs. In fact, research shows that we use a mere *10 percent* of them![36] But like any other ability, if we don't use and develop our EFs, we can't leverage them to our advantage.

To be sure, the ability to use EFs is limited in some. People with ADHD, for example, tend to struggle a bit, as do others who learn

---

36 A. Diamond, "Want to Optimize Executive Functions and Academic Outcomes? Simple, Just Nourish the Human Spirit," *Minnesota Symposia on Child Psychology (Series)*, 37 (2014): 205–232, https://www.ncbi.nlm.nih.gov/pmc/articles/PMC4210770/.

differently. This far from prevents them from learning to leverage their EFs; they'll simply learn to leverage their EFs differently as well.

A relatively new field, executive coaching, was designed to give an edge to people by helping them learn how to better use and consistently apply their EF. A roomful of CEOs is arguably one full of people who have pretty much mastered EFs. But the key phrase here is *pretty much*. Even those who understand and apply their EFs on a regular basis can get even *better* at doing so.

As it turns out, there are five lifestyle factors that significantly contribute to better EFs and that are instrumental in our overall mental and physical well-being. I call these the Big Five, and they are comprised of proper levels of

- sleep (sufficient and sound);

- nutrition (adequate and varied);

- physical activity (frequent and intense);

- interpersonal relationships (fewer and more meaningful); and

- stress (minimized and managed).

Together, these not only support hearty EFs; they support something else: overall happiness!

Fortunately, entire bookstores are filled with advice and guidance on all these factors, so I will not attend to them in any detail here. What's important here is that no matter who you are, if you don't attend to these five factors, you will not be cognitively efficient, and if you do attend to them, you'll have the capacity and opportunity to expand your luck and gain cognitive control over your life.

As you might expect, cognitive control is measured on a *sliding* scale based on your real time awareness and experience of the five factors. Let's say you've got a big presentation coming up, one that, delivered successfully, could pave the way to long-term success. It doesn't matter if you've invested weeks, months, or years of preparation—if you go out the night before, have a bender, and turn up for the presentation hungover, you likely will not have the cognitive functionality to do much of anything, let alone wow anyone.

The result might be the same if you stayed up all night, not drinking but attending to a sick three-year-old. Not smelling like a distillery for the presentation would certainly be a plus, but lack of sleep, regardless of the reason—and just as with other factors like poor nutrition, a sedentary lifestyle, insufficient personal connection, or just being stressed—your balance can be upset significantly enough to actually reduce your cognitive control dramatically.

Even little things can sometimes have dramatic negative effects. For this reason, we have to develop long-term habits that support the Big Five factors. Then, even when we have limited control over a given situation, we may yet be able to shift our thinking and our general well-being for the better.

In an earlier chapter, I mentioned Dan Harris's book *10% Happier,* in which he talks about our approach to what we can and can't control. Harris encourages development of our ability to take a "Picture in Picture" approach where we permit ourselves to momentarily suspend and step out of our current context and look upon ourselves and "the story we are telling ourselves" about what is happening. This shift in perspective empowers us to ask ourselves whether the story we are telling ourselves is accurate and useful in that moment. Even in situations where there are many factors we cannot control, we can still, at least, decide *how* we'll let that situation or event land on us.

Ultimately, having control over our responses to the things we can't control is a significant part of exercising our EFs. Taking care of the organ responsible for our attitudes and reactions is tremendously important to our ability to be happy and lucky, to live our lives to maximum capacity.

STUART'S SECRETS

A significant amount of research has led to a great number of recommendations for self-care and wellness practices tied to sustaining and enhancing our neurological functions. Many of you likely already engage in mindfulness techniques, practice gratitude, and have identified habits that boost your body's natural chemicals like endorphins and oxytocin to improve social interaction and alleviate pain, stress, anxiety, and depression. I'll share just a few practices here that have stood out to me as among those most easy to implement when it comes to making positive daily changes that can affect our overall well-being.

- Break down big goals into smaller, realistically achievable chunks. This allows our brains to celebrate when we hit multiple small finish lines. Chunking also echoes some of our learnings from chapter 13 on Choice—we can make better decisions by reallocating our resources only to those decisions that really require attention and letting those that don't really matter in the grand scheme of things take a back seat.

- When meeting or speaking with someone, try to use their name three times in that discussion. World-class memory coach Jim Kwik taught me this technique in a class I attended on memory hacking in Vancouver in 2017. Why? Well, (a) people like to hear their own name and appreciate you for saying it; (b) it wires your own brain to more easily remember their names, and (c) practicing saying other people's names keeps you actively listening, meaning you learn more and recall more from the time you spend with them.

- Laugh often and deeply. Even anticipation of laughter is helpful, so plan to attend a comedy show, forward funny memes to your friends, or check out your favorite late-night television host's monologues. Finding the humor in a situation can also enable many of us to cope with negative emotions and retain our focus and energy on the tasks that matter most.

- Try the Square Technique: Inhale for four seconds, hold that in-breath for another four, exhale for four seconds, and then hold that out-breath for another four. Repeat. According to studies from the Mayo Clinic, deep breathing can help regulate our temperature and blood pressure and calm our overall mood.

- Make it a practice every day to tell the people close to you something you appreciate about them.

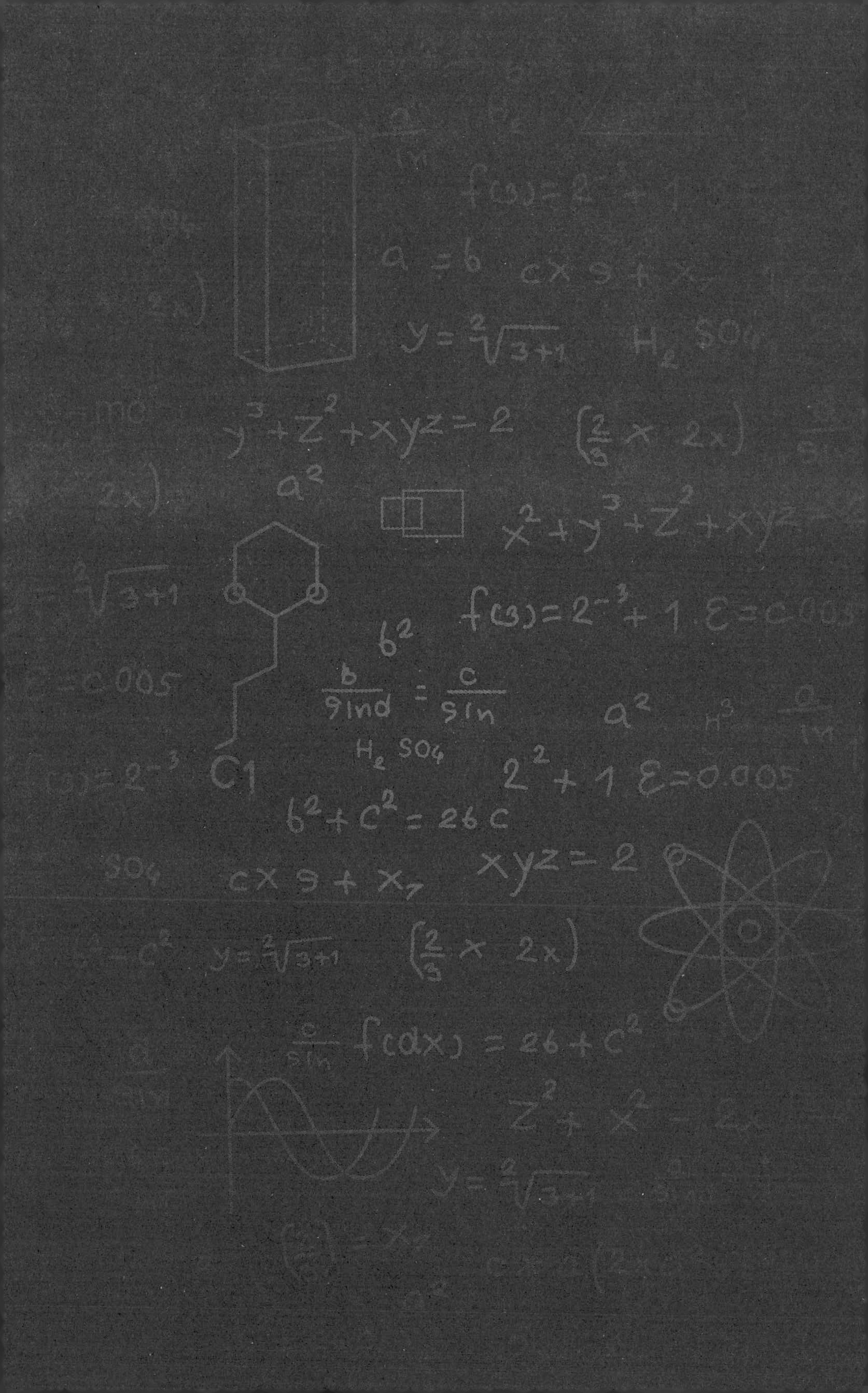
a = b
y³ + z² + xyz = 2
a²
x² + y³ + z² + xyz
f(3) = 2⁻³ + 1
b²
b/sind = c/sin
a²
H₂ SO₄
C1
2² + 1 ε = 0.005
b² + c² = 26 c
xyz = 2
cx 9 + x₇
(2/3 x 2x)
f(dx) = 26 + c²
z² + x² - 2x

CONCLUSION

At the very start of this book, I shared with you some details of my personal history, especially my development from being an awkward young boy who found himself asking *why me* to becoming a more mature adult who is comfortable asserting *This is me.*

My first taste of "success" was marked by a young person's desire for outward-facing displays of having made it: the fancy car, the beach house, the jet-setting lifestyle. It was likely no surprise to you that I got out over my ski tips, only to lose everything and find myself starting out all over again in 1998 at the age of twenty-six. But it may have been something of a surprise when, later in life after having learned this lesson and surpassed many of these earlier goals once again (but this time without fanfare and in a state that many would call *happiness*), in 2011 I actually *chose* to rebase myself voluntarily and start a completely new journey of impact. Now, nine years later, it is clear to me that the meaning of a life well lived has once again evolved for me, and I am about to start another journey (more on this in a minute).

I trust that this book has given you a sense of where my years of research and self-experimentation have brought me to date. I'm absolutely certain there's much more for me to learn about luck, and I even have some plans already in the works for doing just that—including collaborating with several research colleagues to determine quantifiable measures of luck. I am also hopeful that many of you will join me on this journey by sending me your feedback, your progress, and your questions on my website (www.formulaforluck.com), where I will be sharing all my ongoing research, exercises, blogs, and learnings with you. Truly, the more data sets we can share in and learn from, the better the ability for these materials to have lasting and significant impact on all our lives.

It is my hope that I've left you with a strong sense of the ways that you can take action and make impactful progress once you've read through the materials gathered here and written down your plan to utilize them. My personal hope for you is that this book becomes a springboard for your own continued development and the refinement of your skills in implementing the Ten Principles. I want to be able to support you on your journey and to learn from your experience.

If you've finished reading to this point and want a quick guide to getting the most from what you've just reviewed, let me suggest a couple of things you can do right now to keep up the momentum of your engagement with luck.

First, be sure to update your Luck Assessment at www.formulaforluck.com, where an enhanced and interactive Luck Assessment enables you to consider eight key questions for each Principle and then present the outcome on the Wheel of Luck™—a tool for shaping progress and prioritization.

Next, if you haven't already, go ahead and download the *Founda-*

tions of Luck Workbook and commit to using it and following it. In the workbook, you'll have opportunities for defining and confirming your visions and values, as well as for prioritizing which of the Ten Principles deserve your immediate and greatest ongoing focus. The workbook concludes with you committing to a plan to focus on and develop one Principle per month over the next ten months.

I also invite you to share with me—at any time—any of your learnings or your stories about opportunities for implementing the Principles that you find worthy of discussion.

Let's work together and help one another amplify the effects of luck in the world.

. . .

Of the fifteen or so books I read every year, the one that landed best with me in 2019 was David Brooks's *The Second Mountain*, the story of which focuses on people whose lives have a "more-than-one-mountain" shape. They leave school and start climbing the mountain they believe they're expected to climb—achieving all the culturally sanctioned goals like becoming successful and making a mark in their field. The first mountain tends to include goals like fame and fortune, formal education, finding a life partner, and establishing financial security. Then, from the peak of that mountain, people often experience a kind of dissatisfaction that can at times manifest the way a midlife crisis might. This is often heightened by the view of yet other mountains and the promise of new journeys. According to Brooks, that second mountain typically involves people in a shift of perspective: from sanctioned achievements and a focus on personal goals to attempting things that they find more valuable and meaningful and focusing on their interdependence and commitment to others.

I think about Brooks's insights in terms of my own life trajectory. Once I saw past that first mountain to another, more interesting one, I started on a decade-long trek that was focused on impact and service. That led to founding Trunomi and to spending about a third of my time in the Young Presidents' Organization in service of its member CEOs, families, and businesses to help them get the most out of their life experiences. I'm still journeying up that mountain, but I'm starting to feel enough altitude that my third mountain is coming into view. I anticipate this third mountain will be an entirely new journey—one of self-actualization, of self-acceptance, and one in which I will no longer be chasing validation. Simply put, I will be seeking the approval of myself. I will spend more time listening and thinking. My hopes are that on this journey, I can set my intentions to the pursuit of enduring joy—where the outcomes will be peace and contentment.

Ultimately, work-life balance is one of the toughest things for CEOs and other leaders to achieve. For me, climbing my first two mountains felt like the best use of my time and attention, but it's also taken me away from my wife and two boys, and away from mental and physical health and inner peace. I feel fortunate not to have lost sight of that third mountain while attempting to summit the second, and perhaps that is one of the blessings of 2020. I was forced to stop traveling two to three times every month and to shelter in place in Bermuda, which has proved to be one of the safest countries in the world to manage and minimize the effects of COVID and one with an equally incredible quality of life under lockdown. Being here also allowed me to focus all my energies and resources on my family, and to invest time in mindfulness and mental and physical wellness with my full attention and intention.

I want to be present for firsthand experiences of the joys and strains of family life. I want to keep working to discover my truest self. And I want to honor the communities of people who have helped me become capable of making these treks. This community now includes you, and in thanks I offer myself as your partner, guide, and cheerleader on your journey.

Whatever mountain you're on, and at whatever stage of your climb, I want to be able to support your journey to the summit. To do that, I'll also leave you with a reminder about the climb—an insight I take from Guest Star David Breashears: that success on a mountain requires that we recognize and lift up the team of people trekking along with us. And doing that hinges on shared values like selflessness, kindness, and generosity.

Onward and Upward,
Stuart

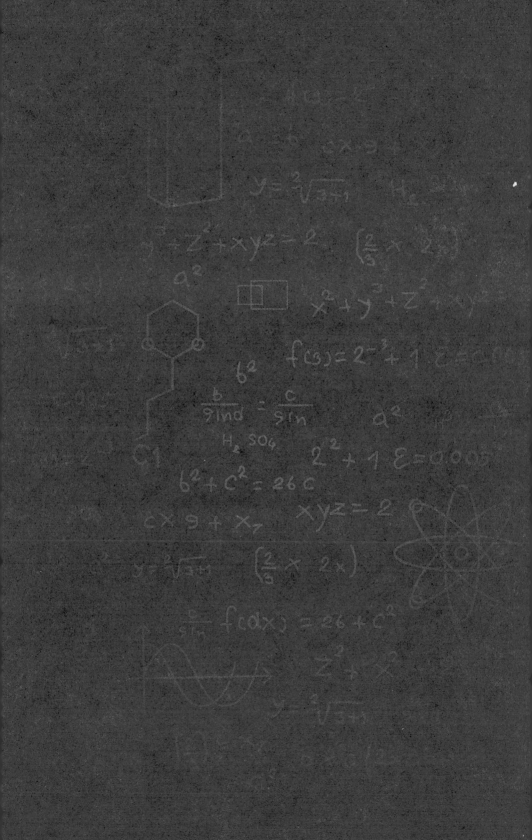

THE FUTURE OF LUCK

At the start of this book, we considered some commonplace ideas about luck, all of them guided by the age-old belief that luck is out of our hands in the sense that it defies human logic, human learning, and the development of our most human capacities.

Instead of thinking of luck as a resource in short supply and arbitrarily doled out by some powerful force that we could only hope to sway by charms and ritual incantations, it's been my contention in this book that luck is both infinite and very much up to us. We are capable of manifesting luck more frequently and continuously the more savvy we become at developing our Luck Mindset, and we can further accentuate the powerful outcomes associated with this mindset by taking care of our physical and mental health. We can manifest luck through developing our Habits of Luck, the associated Behaviors of Luck needed when opportunity strikes, and the critical Actions of Luck that we can take to maximize any opportunity to our benefit. Through stories, statistics, case studies, and interviews, we have evidence that putting effort into the Ten Principles invites luck into our lives.

Many of you may have seen me take the stage as a futurist, so I hope you'll indulge me as I devote some space in this book to thinking ahead about the effect and implications on the Principles in the Formula for Luck as we cast our eyes toward the future. Specifically, I'd like us to consider ways that the most-dominant technologies and current advances in science can either be utilized to enhance our human capacity for luck or detract from it. If you've read books like *Abundance* by Peter Diamandis or *Factfulness* by Hans Rosling, you know that the data show we are clearly on a positive trajectory as a species. Modernity and progress have brought with them incredible technologies that have advanced food production, cured diseases, opened markets, and democratized learning and access to the benefit of all.

The modern world does, however, have its shortfalls, the majority of which are attributable to the tragedy of the commons and the overriding belief, as I once witnessed Clem Sunter share from a stage in Cape Town, South Africa, that "the fundamental failing of our species lay in the two great lies we have continued to tell ourselves: (1) that we can continue to take whatever we want from this planet without consequence, and (2) we can continue to put back all of the byproducts and trash from this same behavior without consequence." This same point was passionately argued by then-sixteen-year-old Greta Thunberg at the 2019 United Nations climate change conference, where she criticized world leaders for their failure to take sufficient action to address the climate crisis.

Interestingly enough, humankind's propensity to "take without consequence" was paused during the 2020 COVID-19 crisis when many of the world's people found themselves sheltering at home and increasingly connected digitally. To the extent that their consumption and carbon footprints plummeted, the planet was allowed to heal a little. Citizens of Venice saw their canals run with clear water for the first time in many of their lives, and millions in the state of Punjab in India, after only three weeks in lockdown, managed to see the Himalayan mountains two hundred kilometers to their north for the first time in thirty years.

That said, temporary pauses in our regular habits brought on by global crises bring to the fore only some of the issues that we must consider and address. Let's carefully review the elements of the Formula for Luck to consider how each might affect and be affected by the overall trajectory of scientific, technological, and human development in the twenty-first century.

PREPARATION

Genetics and Talent Development

If we imagine the technological advances that would allow for customizing our genes, there is a possibility that future generations might be able to enhance the genetic components of their luck. The ten thousand hours of time needed for talent development might become susceptible to advancements in science and technology that push frontiers when it comes to those Olympic values Citius, Altius, Fortius, or "faster, higher, stronger." Will it be possible to influence human genetics such that we can guarantee swimmers with size twenty feet? Or high jumpers guaranteed to be nine feet tall? To be fair this is not only a consideration of science but also one of morality; and too, it is far enough down the timeline as to not yet make the top-ten list of things for us to focus on.

For the purposes of the Formula for Luck, I thereby contend

that in the future, genetics will remain at less than 10 percent, and talent development will remain roughly at 25 percent. In sum, these two preparation-based components of the Formula for Luck will continue to leave the Habits of Luck as the primary foundation upon which we rely.

Habits of Luck (HoL)

There are certainly some Principles that I think will remain much the same in light of technological advances or even be positively enhanced by them. Of the five foundational HoL, there are four— Curiosity, Passion, Positivity, and Connectivity—that I believe we can continue to commit to openly and just keep on building and growing. One—Empathy—warrants some additional exploration.

It is a fair assertion that the focus of millennials and Gen Z on finding passion and meaningful progress in their careers, along with a growing focus on mindfulness and gratitude in general, tends toward an expansion of Empathy. However, we run into some roadblocks as we start to project the effects of technology on this particular Principle.

In an episode of the popular television series *The Big Bang Theory*, the lead character, Sheldon Cooper, comes across a machine that helps him read people's emotions and become more empathetic. Can computers really get so intelligent that they could actually do this?

At the 2020 CES convention (an annual trade show organized by the Consumer Technology Association), Samsung STAR Labs unveiled NEON, a virtual being that looks and behaves like a real human, effectively showing both emotions and intelligence. In late 2019, Humana Pharmacy introduced an AI system called Cogito, and the Israeli firm INFI claims its similar new EmpathAI can effectively predict traits, feelings, and internal motivations.

With loneliness and depression steadily rising, empathetic AIs could provide much-needed companionship. There have been digital pets for at least two decades, and the movie *Her* suggests that a person could even fall in love with an operating system that speaks to its owner like a companion. As if to make good on that suggestion, Gatebox has developed a digital assistant called Hikari, the world's first "virtual wife," a doll-sized hologram in a glass tube. Similar AIs could also become tremendously valuable as companions for the elderly and the dying.

If technology is encroaching into the space of Empathy, how will Empathy be transformed in the future?

Psychology reminds us that there are three aspects of empathy: cognitive—our ability to *understand* feelings; affective—our ability to *respond* appropriately to those feelings; and somatic—the *physical reaction* associated with the experience of feelings. A computer can become more humane, but failing the proper combination of cognitive and affective aspects of empathy and at least some layer of somatic empathy, an AI is perhaps nothing more than a psychopath—knowing what an emotion is, not necessarily knowing how to act on information it receives, and potentially making decisions without any comprehension or felt sense of human good.

As a result, even with efforts at empathic AI, for now the threats appear far greater than the potential benefits of any applications. After all, it's those three aspects of empathy—the cognitive, affective, and somatic, taken together—that become critical to distinguishing ourselves from machines and thereby to preserving our unique ability to make decisions based on fundamental categories such as right and wrong.

Unlike with Curiosity, Passion, Positivity, and Connectivity, for Empathy, I suggest a *cautious* optimism, so long as we are mindful of what is at stake in our willingness to use and rely on certain technological innovations.

OPPORTUNITY

Let's turn now to those components of the formula for which the story is quite different.

As I have shared often from the stage in futurism and thought leadership keynote addresses, I am concerned that the explosion of data and the application of key technologies are as much of a liability as they are an asset. Our increased reliance on AI—including machine learning and neurolinguistic programming—will bring harm as much as it brings benefits. I am of the opinion that AI will increasingly threaten many of the remaining Principles of Luck.

I believe those Principles that are behavioral and situational are under serious assault, in large part as a result of all the data collection about us and our activities along with the personalization engines deciding for us based on our past behaviors and choices. To the extent that we rely more frequently on these technologies, I think we also remove Serendipity, override Situational Awareness, reduce our Adaptability, and arguably impugn our abilities to choose and act.

Let me elaborate.

Based on the aforementioned learnings from thought leaders such as Diamandis and Rosling, we know it's not technological developments themselves that threaten human well-being; instead, it's how those developments and advances are put to use by us. Now consider that luck is a valuable resource. It's got economic worth, and it's a form of power. As such, some big corporations and wealthy individuals, insofar as they want to possess luck, have essentially built into their goals the aim of robbing us of ways to produce it.

That's one big reason why we need to be careful, thoughtful, and disciplined about the extent to which we allow ourselves to be influenced by large decision, matrix-based personalization mechanisms. What we risk is nothing less than surrendering ourselves and our uniqueness by abdicating sources of our luck.

Many of the insights I'll share here come from learnings I've developed primarily over the last decade at the intersection between human lives and data, data rights, AI, and smart/advanced computing. Those

> It's not technological developments themselves that threaten human well-being; instead, it's how those developments and advances are put to use by us.

learnings got underway for me one evening back in 2012 during a dinner table conversation with my niece, Francesca.

Those were the early days of Snapchat—the disappearing-messages app—when Snapchat was stating publicly that it deleted everything that passed through the app, that the messages, in other words, *really did* disappear. Francesca and I got into a friendly debate as she took pictures of our meal and my son Ethan and posted them to Snapchat. Francesca argued that the app deleted all the data, so it did not really matter that she was posting and sharing photos of young Ethan. "Francesca," I said to her, "I don't believe they delete the messages." And then I blurted out another thought, "That's their entire business model, and that data is very valuable," followed by this simple and powerful truth: "I believe you own all the data you create." When Francesca left that night, I couldn't go to sleep. I couldn't stop thinking about how the largest asset class in the world is personal data. I was inspired to rethink the ownership of data and do something to return the sovereignty, dignity, and value of that data to people.

From there, I self-founded what would later be known as the company Trunomi. Every year thereafter, I extended this trajectory: writing in 2013 the foundations for the invention of data sovereignty, filing thirteen patents by 2014, and taking the TEDx stage in 2015 on "The Future of Your Personal Data." I was focused on consent in the early days of the landmark EU regulation called *GDPR* (General Data Protection Regulation), which later gave rise to dozens of new global laws including the CPPA (California Privacy Protection Act); and in 2017 and 2018, I was invited to deliver many global keynotes about the growing Pandora's box around trust as it related to existing data empires and to personal data becoming more of a liability than an asset.

These events led me to have a singular view on how data is being used and what that means for how the changes in data and computing will fundamentally affect our lives and our futures.

In all, I'd say that what's happening with data is nothing short of the world's second big bang. Following Moore's law, the universe of data doubles every two years, and trillions of bytes are generated every single day. The function of networks such as 5G are further accelerating the importance of computer power in relation to the data deluge. With increased usage of smartphones and the Internet of Things, another law—Metcalfe's law—has also come into play; that law states that these networks increase in value as they grow in size.

We can express the overall impact of all these changes as having led to the valuation of three *V*'s: volume, variety, and velocity. *More* data (i.e., *volume*) is considered better. *Variety* of data allows us to make better inferences and predictions. And *velocity* allows for close-to-real-time decision-making. Unfortunately, most of the algorithms that make possible quick inferences and predictions are targeted at recommendation engines, ad tech networks, and personalization for the sake of profit rather than truly making our lives any better.

There are ways in which these advances are being used to magnify the interpretation of data in order to effectively make decisions on our behalf—in the practice of customized medicine, for one. This is one

> What's happening with data is nothing short of the world's second big bang.

exciting domain where data might well be used for good, although the track record of pharma has not been good at all. (Recall Martin Shkreli [the Pharma Bro] who as CEO of Turing Pharmaceuticals jacked up the cost of antiparasitic drug Daraprim by over 5,000 percent overnight and was later convicted of securities fraud in 2017. Note that the price of Daraprim went from $13.50 to over $650 per tablet, and the price remained there until March 2020 when it finally qualified for generic replacement).[37] Equally, our trust in next-gen biotechnology companies has been undermined. (Take the example of genetics testing company 23andMe that was banned by the FDA in 2013, or blood-testing unicorn Theranos, run by twenty-something Elizabeth Holmes, which went from a valuation peak of over $10 billion in 2014 to a complete dissolution in 2018 after Holmes was arrested for fraud showing that the entire business was effectually a scam.)[38]

---

37 "Martin Shkreli," Wikipedia Foundation, last modified November 29, 2020, 02:04, https://en.wikipedia.org/wiki/Martin_Shkreli.

38 "FDA Bans 23andme Personal Genetic Tests," BBCNews.com, November 26, 2013, https://www.bbc.com/news/technology-25100878; "Theranos," Wikipedia

The very real other concern, however, is how the continued development of artificial intelligence will result in privacy discrimination. We've already seen some of the dangers of machine learning, as in the well-known story of how Amazon experimented with a hiring algorithm to assist in recruiting its company staff and disproportionately hired male workers as a result.[39] So, to evaluate the effects of these changes on luck, at a minimum we need to understand whether there should be some form of use restriction or other regulation as that relates to ethics, accountability, and the protection of civil rights.

What makes these issues even more pressing is that the use of AI has generated a new frame of understanding, something called *superintelligence*. Superintelligence is the use of AI not just in a single domain but across all domains, effectively creating a system that's smarter than any human in science, engineering, law, economics, and the like—*combined*. The capacity to generalize across all fields raises questions about power—about who or what is in control.

One example of the way that this technology is being put to use is the work being done by Google DeepMind using AI neural networks to advance scientific discovery and problem-solving. The real question is whether such a powerful network should be the domain of a company like Google, Facebook, or Apple or whether it should be open source (i.e., available to everyone to freely use through the principles of decentralization, distribution, and democratization). To what extent are the companies developing and making use of this technology prepared or able to guide or control the super-intelligences they create?

Foundation, last modified November 28, 2020, 07:06, https://en.wikipedia.org/wiki/Theranos.

39 Jeffery Dastin, "Amazon Scraps Secret AI Recruiting Tool that Showed Bias Against Women," Reuters.com, October 10, 2018, https://www.reuters.com/article/us-amazon-com-jobs-automation-insight-idUSKCN1MK08G.

Quite simply, in order for artificial intelligence to work, it's the data that is key. And it's *data generated by human beings* that ultimately is the most valuable. I believe the point attributed to Stephen Hawking is abundantly true—that it's the particular composition of human-generated data and *the way in which we process and think* that is the key store of value.

There are four ways that humans learn, only three of which computers can figure out. We humans learn by *experience*, which computers also do—by getting more data. Secondly, we humans are *reasoners*. We use logical rules, which computers do well, as this is the basis of most programming languages. Third, we are *linguists*—we use and analyze languages and the inferences therefrom, abilities that computers also possess through NLP and machine learning.

Where we differ as humans is that we are also divergent thinkers; we innovate, and we are creative, imaginative beings who intervene in the world in surprising and unpredictable ways. Much as computers are able to solve real problems by collecting and analyzing huge amounts of data, visionary thinking is yet one area where computing power is woefully short. If we want to protect this most human of our capacities—and appreciate its import as a significant differentiator—then we need to work on developing our abilities when it comes to the five Principles that compose the Behaviors and Actions of Luck.

> Much as computers are able to solve real problems by collecting and analyzing huge amounts of data, visionary thinking is yet one area where computing power is woefully short.

BEHAVIORS OF LUCK (BOL)

Adaptability

Think of how you feel if you've left the house without your phone; then imagine if instead of minutes, you had to function without it for hours, days, or even months. And where do we stand if the power or network goes out? Our reliance on technology has made our lives significantly easier, but having choices made on our behalf or reasoning processes completed for us is reducing our ability to manage change or to function in the absence of the technologies on which we basically now codepend. Reliance on our gadgets and the services they provide cuts against our capacity for Adaptability. How often do today's children use trial and error or research something by trying to design it on paper or build it with blocks? Most just google whatever their questions are and rely on Wikipedia and other popular internet sources to answer them.

Nassim Taleb was kind enough to address the YPO in the midst of the COVID-19 crisis and focused his commentary on how to adapt quickly enough to conditions under COVID to become more anti-fragile—especially in our business practices. Independent thought, creativity, human instinct, and our ability to innovate under duress were all identified by Taleb as key traits during crises. Following established rules during a crisis often only creates mayhem. Reliance on programmatic trading and market algorithms, for example, can result in such massive downward swings that global stock markets have had to build in circuit breakers to slow down the cascade of market sell-offs when the programs all self-trigger.

We often feel as if there's no way to develop Adaptability before actually facing a challenge. But I'd like to encourage you to think otherwise. In my coaching business, I actively work with CEOs, thought leaders, and even a US congresswoman on improving skills in public speaking. I often work with them to prepare and imagine those situations in which they might need to face adversity. Doing so can help you prepare for, and master, those situations simply on the basis that at some point they are likely to occur. Let's take the example of someone preparing to give a large public address. Proper preparation can help that otherwise-stressful situation go more smoothly—can reduce, in other words, the amount of adversity with which we are unprepared to deal.

Situational Awareness

Think about our general dependence on Google Maps or other direction apps that load balance driving routes in real time. These can be very helpful in certain circumstances but are also quite capable (as many of us likely know already) of directing us poorly: down a one-way street in the wrong direction or through an unsafe area regardless of inclement weather or urban hazards. The app may have reasoned that the route was a shorter distance between two points, but it was not also calculating carefully enough whether traveling that same route would be without hazard or any safer. Situational Awareness demands of us that we don't blindly follow machines, and yet we hand our attention and our short-term destiny over to them in small and large ways every day.

Now imagine the power of computer viruses, hackers, or attacks on power grids alongside increased velocity in computer power and speed. The growth of 5G networks suggests that malicious code and intentional errors could propagate across the globe in a matter of microseconds rather than a matter of days or weeks. Does anyone remember watching Matthew Broderick in the 1983 science fiction film *War Games*, not to mention *Skynet* and the Terminator series? The real threat of situations like this requires an increase in critical thinking, prediction and scenario analysis, and deduction, all of which are critical for individuals to nurture in themselves and not just leave for machines to address. Our ability to opt out of something because it "feels wrong" is something we should never want to lose the ability to do. No police officer I have ever met would choose to trust a computer program rather than follow a hunch.

With an increase in terrorism, advanced weapons of war, and other modern mechanisms for harming large numbers of people at once, congregating in groups has never borne as much risk as it does today. Our awareness of things like the sound of automatic gunfire, the location and proximity of exits, or the ability to identify leftover luggage and bags—these are things that cannot be the domains of our Apple Watch, smartphone apps, or third-party providers. What we need most is the agility to consider variable outcomes and to engage in real time judgment and decision-making using all of the information available to us.

I was fortunate to spend time in Singapore in 2018 with Annie Sarnblad, one of the world's leading trainers in negotiation and reading microfacial expressions. She taught me to "better understand people's emotions in the exact moment they are feeling them, thus gaining insight into their wants, needs, and priorities." Did you ever wonder why some people stand with one foot aimed in or out (out equals a sign of openness) or why a person might put their hand to their throat/necklace (an old fight-or-flee instinct to protect one's neck) or whether someone is lying to you (read their eye directions and the slant of their smile) or know the difference between dislike and disgust (look to the nose and brows being wrinkled). Any of these can in real time inform you to proceed or retreat, to press on or pass, to open up or close off.

To the extent that we hand over these and other aspects of noticing, we remove a tremendous amount of intuition, gut instinct, and bodily responsiveness that would otherwise play a critical role in some of our most important decisions.

Serendipity

Perhaps more so than any other Behavior of Luck, Serendipity is under direct assault by the personalization engines that increasingly make most of our decisions for us. Our current dependence on technology removes opportunities for experiencing the sheer delight of stumbling upon—or the pride of doing ourselves—something we didn't anticipate or expect. Think of dating apps that use algorithms to match traits for the sake of relationship "success." Those points of overlap and conjunction may be helpful, but most of us know that some of what attracts us to others (and makes us attractive to others) exceeds what can be determined by even the most savvy or thorough of questionnaires.

As we start to become more aware of and understand the drivers behind major tech companies that use our personal data to help "make our lives better," we need to always ask ourselves if this is indeed so. Once we appreciate that many of their algorithms by design exploit variability and differences and then offer programs that reduce that differentiation (stock, bond, and currency traders call this *arbitrage*) we can quickly surmise the outcome. The quicker you exploit the difference, the faster the variability narrows, and opportunity diminishes until such time as parity is established. As we continue to rely more on computer power to make decisions, we reduce both variability and our cognitive ability to capitalize on Serendipity. It is imperative that we maintain enough distance between ourselves and an algorithmic herd mentality; otherwise we will increasingly relive the fabled story of what happens to sheep when they blindly follow the authority of others.

ACTIONS OF LUCK (AOL)

Choice

We know from our earlier discussion that we are in a period of choice overload, which means that to have a predictive system make selections for us can seem like a relief. But of course, limiting our *capacity* for judgment and decision-making is never a good result. Whether that's because decisions are already made for us or because we are being encouraged to choose according to a set of already-limited options, we sacrifice our capacity not just *to choose* but also to engage in the *process* of decision-making itself. Decision-making algorithms were exploited when Cambridge Analytica famously used them to help direct different types of news and advertising to specific Facebook profiles, not just customizing the media flow but allowing fake news to influence individual sentiment and affect voting behaviors during key national elections.

Fail Forward

I won't say much about this Principle except to leave you with the positive thought that it may be enhanced by the advance of technology. Whether simply through basic cut-and-paste efforts, lean thinking, or scenario analysis, it's becoming easier to build outcome-focused models that help speed up our ability to keep trying by testing and retesting at rapid speeds. AIs for rent, which allow you to rapidly validate whether an outcome is possible and if so to what percentage, are readily available today and dramatically reduce the cost, time, and risk of rapid testing and prototyping.

Browning the Rainbow

In an important sense, our growing dependence on machines and software ultimately standardizes and normalizes outcomes, effectively reducing luck by reducing our role in it. Assuming that machine learning will result in an optimum outcome, the optimum outcome is likely also to become the normalized outcome. The sheer fact that an algorithm can rapidly and independently identify an opportunity necessitates that said opportunity will be exploited by that same algorithm and hence cease to be an opportunity. A case in point: Google Maps will divert traffic to a less busy road, reducing the load on the busy one and in turn making the less busy road busier until such time as they are equally busy. I picture this process like the mixing of rainbow-colored paints. Each and every color is distinctively bright, but then mixed altogether, unified, everything just looks brown. If uniformity reigns under artificial intelligence, machine learning, and 5G systems, then the availability of luck will necessarily decrease.

That reduction to algorithmic sameness—the reduction of variability—means that it will become increasingly important to engage in practices invulnerable to algorithmic influence. Those will be the most likely to increase luck.

A FINAL WORD ON VARIATION AND SELF-DIFFERENTIATION

In his book *Homo Deus*, Yuval Noah Harari makes some predictions about the likelihood of changes in human decision-making based on continued technological development. Harari suggests, and I would agree, that the technological future will entail the use of biometric monitoring by corporations and governments in order to access "more complete data about people, about their desires and liabilities, than those people have about themselves." He adds that "a life under such scrutiny will be one long stressing job interview."[40] As I write this, countries are planning to emerge from COVID using contact tracing—a vast array of network intelligence purported to help identify potential exposure to the epidemic. Fraught with privacy risk and increased worries about Big Brother, such levels of monitoring will inform data models that are sure to enable governments and large organizations to further disintermediate our ability for self-determination and agency over our own outcomes and futures.

At the same time that Harari implores us to start a serious conversation about our shared future when it comes to use of these technologies, he also believes that we need to work through the challenges that technological developments ultimately bring. On his reading, companies' approach to complicated issues should ideally resemble "engineers trying to fix bugs rather than that of overlords attempting to control humanity in the longer term."[41]

Whereas Harari worries about the loss of individual autonomy alongside a corresponding rise in digital dictatorships, theorists like Stephen Pinker in *The Better Angels of Our Nature* are more optimistic. Pinker is skeptical about technological change being used against individuals and suggests that humanity is more likely than not to continue along a path of progress with technology as its aide.

I think that the critical difference between their views speaks to

---

40   Ian Parker, "Yuval Noah Harari's History of Everyone, Ever," *New Yorker*, February 17, 2020, https://www.newyorker.com/magazine/2020/02/17/yuval-noah-harari-gives-the-really-big-picture.

41   Ibid.

the real and growing difficulty of addressing challenges to our democratic institutions. In particular, it seems to me that a good amount of controversy is likely to center around valuing efficiency on the one hand, ethics on the other.

Quite honestly, when it comes to technological advances, it's the growing conflict between these two values—efficiency and ethics—that motivates me even more strongly to make the case for the five Habits of Luck I brought into focus at the start of this epilogue. I don't think it is surprising that some of the most-respected statesmen and greatest thinkers of our time have worked to shift the focus onto ethical concerns. Take Pope Francis's "revolution of tenderness"; the learnings of the late Ruth Bader Ginsburg, or of Nelson Mandela and Bishop Desmond Tutu, on equality; the Dalai Lama's teachings on tolerance; and the perspective of business icons like Oprah Winfrey and Bill Gates on compassion and inclusivity. I think enhancing this shift in thinking will be critical to our capacity for self-differentiation as we head into the future.

I've been quite taken by what Jack Ma, CEO of Alibaba, shared in a recent address to Bloomberg Global Business Forum—that "soft skills" will play a critical role in the future of employment as hardware and software start to replace entire workforces. His insight is focused on the importance of roles that only humans can fill. As human beings we have an incredible capacity for care and empathy. We need only look to healthcare workers around the world, classroom teachers, and our first responders for exemplary instances of this ability. Although machines will be faster and stronger than humans, there is no easy way for them to match our hearts and values—*if* we protect and nurture our capacity to share the riches of this world.

So here's the opinion with which I'll leave you for now: our newest technological tools may be amazing in their capacity and easy to implement, but we need to be careful—thoughtful—about the extent to which we apply them across all aspects of our lives. We owe it to ourselves and one another to develop good habits in all the areas of concern we've reviewed in this book. And we need to be sure to leverage technology in ways that reduce risk and opportunity cost without surrendering our individuality.

How we choose to utilize the tools we develop will be what differentiates between luck's abundance and its scarcity.

ACKNOWLEDGMENTS

If the only true currency in the world is gratitude, then at the time of starting this acknowledgment I am Jeff Bezos, and by the time I will have finished it, I will be Oliver Twist.

Here is what I learned on this journey, and these are the people, in appreciation, to whom I am indebted:

1. *Two "I do"s make a "we do."* Attempting this would have been impossible without the constant flow of support, care, encouragement, understanding, and belief from my amazing wife Lisa. For all the nights her gentle, loving voice asked "Can I get you something?" or "Do you know what time it is?" so I could take a break and sit down to family dinner; for the countless times I said "almost there" or "publishing soon" and was greeted with nothing but support and room to continue creating—Lisa, your incredible loyalty, patience, and untethered love and support *complete me* and are what made this book and my journey possible.

2. *Play often, always be grateful, and hug a lot.* Ethan and Max—my two coconspirators in all things fun, creative, experiential, and wonderful—through your eyes I see the world as I wish it to be, and because of your pride, I am hell bent on making sure that as your father, I never let you down. I learn more every day from you two, and it's a privilege also to be your buddy. ☺

3. *When explaining the time-space continuum in* Back to the Future, *Doc Brown said it perfectly: "Great Scott!"* Revisiting my youth was both traumatic and a revelation. As I traveled back to recount my foundational moments and stories, I realized how little I understood their value at the time, and I reconciled the gifts I had been given with what is now a full appreciation of how lucky I was to have had the upbringing I did. I cannot fully thank my mum for all her love, encouragement, and interest, nor Mario and his entire family for giving her and our Lacey clan a bridge, a port, and wide-open arms.

4. *Sister Sledge knows a lot about my family too.* When music executive Jerry Greenberg pitched the group to Atlantic Records, he said, "Whenever they come to the label, everybody thinks that they're wonderful girls, and they stick together like birds of a feather, and they're really like family to us." Not only did this become the base for their epic song—but it foretold just how I feel about my incredible extended family "sisters": Kristy, Gemma, Francesca, Jeanne, and Marlene—all of whom have given me "love in a family dose." Simply put, "We are family. Get up everybody and sing."

5. *Everyone needs a tribe of brothers and sisters.* These are people as close as family and who are always there for me as my sounding board, my editorial team, my cheerleaders, and my toughest critics. This tribe is the Zermatters: James, Ross, and Robbie and team PMF: Tim, Alex, Phil, Kathleen, Douglas, and Cara. There also a few who have been with me since I was in college and who have shaped and influenced my journey for over thirty years: to my brother Neil—my mentor, there for me in every way imaginable—and my sister Diana—my inspirator and the wind beneath my wings—thank you.

6. *Authors actually* do *need a hut in the woods.* When setting out to attempt something of this scale, having the right environment to focus, ideate, create, and research is critical. To Don, my partner, cofounder, and first investor in so many of my ventures, thank you for all your support and advice and especially for the gift of the amazing hut at NVH.

7. *Writing a book is like building a house.* It takes a lot of people, ideas, time, treasure, and way too many changes along the way, but it also is never really finished. Our innate need to always make them better is why they end up costing twice as much and taking twice as long. ☺ However, at some point, you just have to say "good enough" and start enjoying it. To the architects, builders, and designers of this house of luck: Elaine, Laura, Patti, Adam, Bree, David, and team Advantage—this was impossible without you.

8. There is a reason we sing in the shower. It's because our "voice" always sounds better when we are unencumbered by process and are free to ideate, create, and flow outside tra-

ditional bounds. My hands can never type quickly enough to keep up with my thoughts, and I have always been more creative in talking things out aloud with others than plotting away by myself. This is especially true when talking with a conversation partner who is a great listener and who asks all the right questions at exactly the right times. Jen, you were and are such a total rock star for being there with me every word of the way.

9. *When running an Olympic Torch Relay, don't drop the torch.* I am not just talking about me running with the Olympic torch in the wee hours of the morning at Château Montebello in December 1997, but about how incredibly lucky I was that my guest stars for each chapter grabbed the baton with authority, ran with it purposefully, and then handed it on with grace. My sincere thanks to my friends and FFL All-Stars: James, Jacqueline, Jared, Chris, Travis, Bobby, David, Kristina, Vandana, McKeel, Barbara, and Hapfor.

10. *Having and pursuing your MTP is a life-changer.* From learning about massive transformational processes (MTP) from Salim (who kindly wrote my foreword) to learning from all those who provided me with the guidance, support, and critical oversight over the past eight years from founding Trunomi to it growing up, this book would never have happened had you not all given me the stars to dream of and the rope to be tethered by. To my start-up dynamos: Kartik, Naresh, Douglas, Chia, Brian, Sally-Anne, and Dion, and my outstanding board and advisors: Don, James, Aaron, Bill, Kim, Adrian, Casey, Alex, Marcelo, Celso (RIP), and Andrew—and to the rock-star additions Alexa and Jacques,

led by our fearless skipper Shawn—all of you enabled me to bring this book to life.

11. *Don Julio and Juan Valdez are long lost cousins.* Don sent me off on too many adventures with a smile on my face and a zest for discovery, and Juan has helped me recover in the aftermath and push through in the face of tiredness. Ying and Yang, Vice and Virtue, in moderation and not—life has been more interesting because of you. You bring together new and old friends, console us in times of difficulty, and always remind us to put on our dancing shoes and put our feet up. Cheers! ☺

$f(3) = 2^{-3} + 1 \cdot \mathcal{E} = c\,005$

$cx\,3 + x_7 \quad 1\,\mathcal{E} = c\,005$

$y = \sqrt[2]{3+1} \qquad H_2\,SO_4 \qquad 2x \cdot a^2 = 6^a$

$+xyz = 2 \qquad \left(\frac{2}{3} \times 2x\right) \qquad \frac{a}{9m} = \frac{b}{9m}$

$x^2 + y^3 + Z^2 + xyz = 2 \qquad y = \sqrt[2]{3}$

$6^2 \qquad f(3) = 2^{-3} + 1 \cdot \mathcal{E} = c\,005 \qquad SO_4$

$\frac{b}{9md} = \frac{c}{9m} \qquad \left(\frac{2}{3}\right) = x_7$

$H_2\,SO_4 \qquad a^2 \qquad H^3 \qquad \frac{a}{m} \qquad 1 \cdot \mathcal{E} = c\,005$

$2^2 + 1\,\mathcal{E} = 0.005$

$+C^2 = 26\,c \qquad x_7 = \left(\frac{2}{3} \times 2x\right)$

$xyz = 2$

$x_7 \qquad N^2 \times H^3$

$\left(\frac{2}{3} \times 2x\right) \qquad O \qquad f(3) =$

$(dx) = 26 + C^2 \qquad NH_3$

$Z^2 + x^2 - 2x \left(\frac{2}{3} \times 2x\right)$

$y = \sqrt[2]{3+1} \qquad \frac{a}{9md} = \frac{b}{9md} \qquad f(3) =$